Ty Cobb

His Tumultuous Life and Times

Ty Cobb

His Tumultuous Life and Times

Richard Bak

Foreword by Ernie Harwell

Taylor Publishing Company
Dallas, Texas

page ii: Ty Cobb, circa 1915
page vi: Cobb, Yankee Stadium, circa 1923
page viii: Babe Ruth and Cobb, 1920s
page 184: Studio portrait, 1920s

Front jacket background photo hand-tinted by Transcendental Graphics.
Inset photo hand-tinted by Meisel Photographic.

Published by Taylor Publishing Company
1550 West Mockingbird Lane
Dallas, Texas 75235

Designed by: Hespenheide Design

Bak, Richard, 1954–
    Ty Cobb: his tumultuous life and times / Richard Bak.
        p.   cm.
    ISBN 0-87833-870-5
    1. Cobb, Ty, 1886–1961.   2. Baseball players—United States—Biography.   I. Title.
    GV865.C6B35   1994
    796.357'092—dc20   93-39530
    [B]   CIP

Printed in the United States of America
10   9   8   7   6   5   4   3   2   1

For my parents, Edward and Lillian Bak
Thanks for the encyclopedias

CONTENTS

ix   Foreword by Ernie Harwell

1   **Chapter 1**   Somewhere in Georgia

19   **Chapter 2**   A Fresh Peach

33   **Chapter 3**   The World's Greatest Ballplayer

61   **Chapter 4**   You Auto Be in Detroit

79   **Chapter 5**   Glory Days and Others

103   **Chapter 6**   Damned Yankee

141   **Chapter 7**   Philadelphia Story

159   **Chapter 8**   The Long Way Home

183   Ty Cobb's Playing Record

185   Bibliography

189   Acknowledgments

191   Index

194   Photo Credits

Foreword

By Ernie Harwell

Anyone familiar with the movie *Field of Dreams* remembers the scene where an Iowa farmer named Ray Kinsella (played by Kevin Costner) introduces novelist Terence Mann (James Earl Jones) to Shoeless Joe Jackson (Ray Liotta) and several ethereal teammates on a diamond carved out of a cornfield.

"You wouldn't believe how many guys wanted to come play here," says Shoeless Joe. "I had to beat them off with a stick."

"Hey, that's Smokey Joe Wood!" says Ray, surveying the field in astonishment. "And Mel Ott . . . and Gil Hodges. . . ."

"And Ty Cobb wanted to play," interrupts Shoeless Joe. "None of us could stand the son of a bitch when we were alive, so we told him to stick it!"

While pure fantasy, the dialogue in this Capraesque baseball film is instructive: more than three decades after he passed away in his native Georgia, Tyrus Raymond Cobb is still sorely in need of a press agent.

As history would have us believe, the Georgia Peach was baseball's last angry man, a wholly unredemptive crank who, when he wasn't busy intentionally spiking infielders, probably pulled the wings off flies for amusement. Sporting razor-sharp spikes, he'd slice a player from chin to shin just to swipe a base or score a run. His rotten disposition didn't change off the field, either. He was rude, abusive, selfish, vindictive, and utterly lacking in any virtues. In the end he finally died as he had lived—bitter and friendless.

At least that is what we've all heard and read for years. But is this a complete and fair portrait?

No, argues author Richard Bak, who has given us a welcomed, balanced look at the life of the man who has fascinated so many of us through the years. Combining page after page of rare photographs with an engaging writing style, Richard has helped us all with his sharp insight into Cobb, his times, and the forces that helped shape his character on and off the diamond.

Cobb produced numbers with which we've all become familiar: 4,191 base hits, a dozen batting titles, 892 stolen bases, a .367 batting average over 24 big-league seasons. However, his "vying nature," as he once described it, wasn't the kind that could be turned on and off like a spigot. It won games, but it also alienated many around him.

However, without this temperament Cobb never could have been the player he was, sportswriter Harry Salsinger once observed: "The trouble with most ballplayers is that they are too phlegmatic, taking matters as they come. Cobb never did. He created his own situations. Cobb had his faults as all mortals have, but he had virtues as well. Physical courage was one of them. His enemies were many and bitter, but nobody ever called him a coward."

Richard, like Salsinger before him, makes a case for compassion and understanding. For while all of us can claim to have at least some of Cobb's imperfections, few can also boast his tremendous gifts of drive, intelligence, dedication, and courage. For all his bad points— and there were many—there still is much to admire about Cobb, whose good points are frequently buried beneath the weight of his reputation and apocrypha. How many people, for instance, know of the hospital he built in his native Georgia, still going strong after more than four decades? Or of the educational foundation he established for disadvantaged youths? If this biography seems at times unusually sympathetic, it's because it was written with the notion that no person passing through this world even approaches perfection, so that those of us in glass houses had better be careful where we pitch our baseballs.

All of us have our impressions of Cobb—from reading about him, hearing firsthand stories about him, or perhaps from actually having met him. I crossed paths with Ty several times, and I have to admit that I still have difficulty trying to figure out this complex man.

My first meeting with the Great One came in 1941. I had just started my job as sports director for radio station WSB in Atlanta. Word came that Ty was visiting his hometown of Royston, Georgia, so I suggested that the station send me there to interview him.

"He's a mean old man and he won't even talk to you," was the response. "But go anyway and do the best you can."

Foreword

I made the journey. Ty met me at the door with a hearty welcome. I had no trouble at all with the interview. He talked for the entire 15-minute show and was both gracious and entertaining. The visit proved to me that every man has to judge for himself.

Looking back, I can see where Ty had varying degrees of influence on several memorable occasions in my life. In fact, I hold him at least partially responsible for the first severe spanking of my life. Let me explain.

When I was growing up in Washington, Georgia, swatting at sawdust baseballs and doing tongue-tied imitations of my favorite announcers, the name Ty Cobb was burned deep into my psyche. Not only did we schoolboys and our fathers consider the Georgia Peach the greatest ballplayer of all—greater than even Babe Ruth—he was one of our state's most famous native sons. Doc Green, the local druggist, had once played semipro ball with Cobb and would not let me or anyone else forget it.

It was after my family moved to Atlanta that I first got the chance to see this living, breathing legend in action. Cobb was scheduled to play in an exhibition game against the Georgia Tech team, and my buddies persuaded me to go with them and to sneak into the game without paying.

Now, my dad didn't object to me going to the game. He loved baseball. But he didn't approve of me sneaking into the game—Ty Cobb or no Ty Cobb. When I came home that night he gave me the whipping of my life.

Ty also had an influence on my so-called literary career. One year I covered the Masters golf tournament for WSB. Cobb, a good friend of golfer Bobby Jones, was a Masters regular. One day I sat around and listened as he and some golfers exchanged stories.

Grantland Rice, the granddaddy of all sportswriters, was in the group. Cobb turned to Rice and said, "Granny, you won't remember this. But when you were sports editor of the *Atlanta Journal* in 1904, you got a lot of letters from around Anniston, Alabama, telling you how great I was while I was playing there.

"You finally came down to Anniston, saw me in action, and wrote a glowing story which helped me on my way. I never admitted it until now, Granny, but I was the guy who sent all those telegrams."

I wrote down this surprising story and submitted it to the *Saturday Evening Post*, which snapped it up. That marked my first sale to a major national publication.

I had occasion to meet Ty several more times in the last few years of his life. He was always a gentleman. As sick old men are wont to do, he slowed down considerably toward the end, the effects of a long, losing bout with cancer and other ailments. But by then it was already too late to salvage a lifetime of wrecked relationships or his reputation. When he died on July 17, 1961, I was in my second season of broadcasting in Detroit. The club asked me to write a tribute to be read over the public address system that night, which I gladly did. Here is what I wrote:

> *Baseball's greatest player—Tyrus Raymond Cobb—died today in his native Georgia.*
>
> *Cobb was a genius in spikes. His mind was the keenest ever to solve the strategy of the diamond. He was fiery and dazzling on the base paths. For 24 years of high-tensioned baseball action, his name led all the rest. He was the best—in hitting, base-stealing, run-making—in everything.*
>
> *Cobb's rise to fame in the early 1900s kept step with the progress of baseball as a national spectacle. His dynamic spirit was a symbol for the ever-growing industrial community he represented: Detroit, Michigan.*
>
> *And now, here in a baseball stadium where the cheers were the loudest and longest for this greatest of all Tigers, let us stand and pay final tribute to him in a moment of respectful silence.*

On that long-ago summer night, I pronounced Ty Cobb the greatest of them all. No one has come along since to make me change my mind, although several of his important records have been broken since his death. The very next year, 1962, Maury Wills stole 104 bases for the Los Angeles Dodgers, breaking Ty's single-season mark of 96. Another of his stolen-base records was eclipsed in 1977, when Lou Brock of the St. Louis Cardinals registered career steal number 893.

Eight years later, amid great hoopla, another mark was shattered. At precisely 8:01 P.M. on September 11, 1985, Pete Rose of the Cincinnati Reds slapped a 2–1 pitch from San Diego's Eric Show into left field for career hit 4,192. The confetti-filled storm of applause from the sellout crowd of 47,237 at Cincinnati's Riverfront Stadium delayed play for seven minutes. It was 57 years to the day that Cobb had played his last major-league game.

Despite his distaste for the modern game, I think Ty would have approved of Rose, a throwback to baseball's earlier days who had earned his nickname "Charlie Hustle" through an aggressive, unrelenting style of play. (Although Ty, remembering "the teach" Kid Elberfeld applied on him as a rookie, would have frowned on Rose's trademark head-first slides.)

To his credit, the new base-hit king acknowledged that the crown as baseball's greatest hitter still belonged to the ghost that he had chased since entering the major leagues in 1963. "At no time did I say I'm a better hitter than Cobb," said Rose, who would retire in 1986 with 4,256 base hits, but with a career batting average far below

Cobb's. "He was the greatest hitter in history. Nobody will ever hit .367 again."

Rose was an astute student of the game's history and its immortals, even naming a son born during the chase after Ty. In the final days before his historic hit, a reporter melodramatically asked him if he thought Cobb was following the proceedings from his box seat in heaven.

"From what I've heard," replied Rose, "that's not where he's at."

Over the last couple of decades, the study of sports in society has taken on a greater importance. The result has been a series of books that have broken out of the Frank Merriweather-style ones I read as a boy. These unvarnished studies portray athletes as human beings with faults, instead of infallible, milk-drinking gods. As a result, their subjects come across as more sympathetic and genuine, and thus more heroic.

In constructing America's pantheon of sports heroes, it's problematical whether Tyrus Raymond Cobb is spending eternity inside a skybox or, as Pete Rose implied, inside the furnace room. What is certain is that we will never see his like on a baseball diamond again—to which those old ballplayers stepping out of Ray Kinsella's cornfield would surely add, "Thank God!"

A wide-eyed Tyrus Raymond Cobb photographed early in 1887, not long after his birth in the small Georgia farming community known as The Narrows.

CHAPTER ONE

Somewhere in Georgia

Good speed to your faithful valor, boy!
So shall you scale the stars!
　　　　　　　　—Virgil, Aeneid.

One temptation facing biographers is to write that so-and-so put such-and-such a place "on the map." In the case of Tyrus Raymond Cobb, born December 18, 1886, in The Narrows in Banks County, Georgia, such a cliché would be more than a literary misdemeanor, it would be geographically incorrect.

The Narrows, then and now, is more a state of mind than an actual dot on the Rand McNally. The name refers to a community of scattered farms in the Appalachian foothills of northeast Georgia. Like the two historical markers that today line Georgia Highway 105, it honors a Confederate victory at the Battle of the Narrows, which was fought in a gap in the nearby mountains in the fall of 1864.

No markers honor Cobb's birthplace. The house where he was born—a thirteen-room white frame dwelling with carpentered gingerbread that belonged to his maternal grandfather, Caleb Chitwood—burned down years ago. A small frame house has since been built on the site; at last report, a Southern Baptist minister and his wife were living there. Sprinkled about the property are a few outbuildings from the original homestead: a well shelter, a corn crib, and the old cotton house. Not that these traces of Cobbiana engender much excitement among the locals.

In fact, a few years ago, when Pete Rose was getting ready to overtake Cobb as baseball's base-hit champion, an out-of-town writer visited The Narrows to ask about the community's

Ty's demanding and distant father, William Herschel Cobb, was born in 1863 in Cherokee County, North Carolina. He left home in a covered wagon to attend school in Hayesville, then graduated with first honors from the North Georgia Military College at Dahlonega and became an itinerant rural schoolteacher. After settling in Royston in about 1892 as principal of the one-room schoolhouse, he established a newspaper, bought a farm, and started a career in politics. Ty would spend a lifetime trying to live up to William's standards.

most famous native. Those who knew who Ty Cobb was were generally of the opinion that records are made to be broken. The lack of passion about the subject disappointed the writer, though the indifference was perhaps understandable in the light of a recent event. Area residents were still buzzing about the poultry farmer who had buried a large number of dead chickens in a shallow grave. The built-up gases had exploded, showering feathers and chicken parts all over the old Chitwood place.

Presumably no ghosts complained. Explosions, after all, were old hat to Caleb Chitwood, an infantry officer in the Army of Tennessee who had survived the six-week siege and fall of Vicksburg. Paroled on July 8, 1863, along with 20,000 other Confederates, Chitwood broke his vow not to take up arms against the union and was captured a second time in Raleigh, North Carolina, near the close of the war. Such tenacity served Captain Chitwood well when he returned to Banks County after the war. He was able to scratch out a decent living growing cotton, eventually employing several tenants on his 200 or so acres of land. In the summer of 1883 the mildly prosperous farmer reluctantly allowed his 12-year-old daughter, Amanda, to be married at the Chitwood "plantation." The groom was a 20-year-old schoolteacher, William Herschel Cobb.

William, born and raised across the state line in North Carolina, had recently graduated with first honors from North Georgia Military College in Dahlonega. Eager to raise their social standing, the North Carolina Cobbs always insisted they were related to the more distinguished Georgia Cobbs, a family that included several prominent men of the Old South. Despite the tenuous lineage, the tall, dignified William was always careful to emphasize the family's bloodlines to his three children.

The first was Tyrus Raymond, born when Amanda was fifteen. William, who read widely, had always admired the story of the ancient Phoenician city of Tyre, which in 332 B.C. had put up a gallant but doomed resistance to the legions of Alexander the Great. Hence his first-born's unique name. By the time Ty was six, he was sharing his parents' attention with a brother and a sister. John Paul was born in 1888, followed by Florence Leslie in 1892.

As a rural schoolteacher, William was always captive to the whims of the community he served. One-room schoolhouses survived only in areas where families could afford a schoolmaster's pay—and spare their children's participation in the crushing load of everyday chores. Consequently, for the first few years of his marriage William moved his family throughout northeast Georgia. One of Ty's earliest memories was "of a buggy, bumping along a red clay road" as his father traveled to yet another village and another teaching position. "I seem to recall that I was barefoot and wore a hickory shirt under a pair of bib overalls," Ty said in his autobiography. "With my legs dangling over the tailgate, I was busy winding yarn around a small core ball. It was slow work."

So was setting down roots. There were stops in Commerce, Lavonia, Carnesville, Hickory Grove, and other farm communities. Finally, sometime in the early 1890s, when Ty was six or seven, the peripatetic teacher was offered a position in Royston, Georgia. The town of 500 or so people was located in Franklin County, about seventy-five miles northeast of Atlanta.

At the time America was still a constellation of small towns. In many ways, turn-of-the-century Royston resembled those drowsy "little white towns in the hills" Thornton Wilder paid homage to in his play, *Our Town*. There was a compact commercial area, its wide, dusty streets flanked by sleeping dogs and pimpled with horse apples. Awnings shaded the plank sidewalks in front of the post office, bank, pool hall, saloon, blacksmith, barber shop, feed store, and other businesses common to Main Streets everywhere. The surrounding countryside was a quilt of cleared fields and rolling hills, intersected by narrow packed-dirt roads and topped by the occasional farmhouse. The soil was rich here, enabling cotton, corn, and wheat farmers to prosper and local commerce to thrive. Royston had the money to support a good school and to pay the new schoolmaster a living wage. William Cobb was able to buy a comfortable two-story house in town and, a few years later, a 100-acre farm on which he raised cotton and other crops to supplement his teaching salary.

In his old age, Ty would reminisce often about the small-town sensations of his youth. The sound of croaking frogs near a favorite swimming hole. The sight of rockers and flower boxes on a wide veranda. The smell of red clay as it baked and shimmered in the hot August sun.

Ty's fondest childhood memories centered around summer trips to his paternal grandparents' house in the Smoky Mountains near Murphy, North Carolina, about 100 miles from Royston. William's father, "Granddad Johnny," was an avid outdoorsman and raconteur who could get his grandson's heart pumping with a vigorous day-long tramp through the woods, or stop it completely with stories of tracking bears with only his musket and his wits.

"There he was, glaring at me red-eyed," the lean, bearded old man would say, packing his pipe with tobacco as he settled into another story. "A slavering monster, twelve feet tall, with fangs as long as a

3

Church Street, Looking South, Royston, Ga.

A view of Royston at century's turn. The town of 500 or so people was indistinguishable from the thousands of others that characterized America then. All featured a wide, dusty Main Street, flanked by sleeping dogs and pimpled with horse apples.

The Cobb family tree boasted several notable Southerners, including Howell Cobb, born in 1815 in Franklin County, Georgia. Cobb was speaker of the U.S. House of Representatives, governor of Georgia, and secretary of the treasury in the years before secession. He presided over the convention that organized the Confederacy, then raised and commanded a regiment of volunteers. He was promoted to major general and commanded the District of Georgia for most of the war.

corncob and claws on him the size of a scythe. Looked like a fieldpiece couldn't bring him down . . . and me with just a long-rifle."

"What happened?" Ty would gasp.

Granddad Johnny would take his time lighting his pipe.

"Tyrus," he'd finally say with a solemn expression, "if I'd missed, you wouldn't be here today."

Granddad Johnny "couldn't talk without being dramatic," Ty later admitted. But Ty dearly loved his father's parents. Simple, dignified, and wise in the ways of the natural world, they instilled in him a lifelong passion for the outdoors.

Like most rural youths, Ty grew up around guns, knives, and fishing rods. He took his dogs, including a favorite hound named Old Bob, into the fields, hills, and streams to hunt deer, raccoons, opossums, and fowl. (He also once sneaked Old Bob onto the train up to Granddad Johnny's place.) As a hunter, Ty displayed the same lightning reflexes and superb hand-eye coordination that would make him a great hitter; hunting partners would always remember Ty as a crack shot. This easy familiarity with guns, taken for granted in his time and place, would later get him in trouble in the urbanized North.

Even a shooting accident when Ty was about fourteen didn't diminish his enthusiasm for firearms. On one occasion he propped a loaded .22 rifle against a fence while slaughtering hogs. The rifle discharged, hitting him in the left shoulder. Doctors, unable to find the bullet, sewed up the wound and pronounced him fit. Ty wasn't as sure, but he didn't complain. For the rest of his life he walked around with the slug imbedded near his left clavicle.

For all the bucolic charms of growing up in Royston, there were disadvantages as well: gossip, bigotry, narrowmindedness, limited opportunities, and a suffocating sameness to life. In addition to these problems, other factors viewed as traditionally Southern helped shape Ty's character.

When Ty was young, keepers of the Confederate faith still numbered in the millions. Although the Confederacy had been defeated three decades earlier, misty-eyed memories of the Old South were kept alive through monuments, books, pamphlets, sermons, lectures, memorial addresses, and various veterans' organizations. According to historian Charles Reagan Wilson, the movement was in effect "a functioning civil religion," its expressions of faith ranging from the lithograph of Gen. Robert E. Lee on the parlor wall to the ubiquitous rebel yell at communal gatherings.

Ty's grandfathers, both of whom had fought for the Confederacy, undoubtedly told him stories of the war and of its "sacred causes." (Although Granddad Johnny, true to his iconoclastic nature, had been an anti-slavery Republican.) Certainly Ty's father, mindful as he was of the family's famous name, mentioned the wartime

The house in which Ty was born in Banks County, Georgia, on December 18, 1886.

exploits of a pair of Cobbs: Howell Cobb, secretary of the Confederate treasury, and T. R. R. Cobb, a brigadier general who had died at Fredericksburg.

Also plenty of surviving Georgians had experienced Gen. William T. Sherman's infamous campaign to "make Georgia howl" in the closing months of the war. Stories of atrocities later dramatized in *Gone With the Wind*—the burning of Atlanta (the Confederate army actually set the city on fire before fleeing), the wanton destruction of the Georgia countryside, the plundering and the rape—were destined to be handed down from generation to generation. It's even possible that the bitter legacy of Sherman's march played a part in William Cobb's naming of Tyrus, because after the war Atlanta often was referred to as "the Tyre of the South," calling to mind the fate of that other unlucky city. Some mused that when Cobb broke into the major leagues as one of the game's few Southern players, he in a sense brought the flames of the Confederacy's funeral pyre with him. This overdrawn but convenient explanation was an attempt to understand his complex, combustible personality.

"He came up for the South, you know, and he was still fighting the Civil War," teammate Sam Crawford later said. "As far as he was concerned, we were all damn Yankees before he even met us." Today, Cobb's home state and three others—Alabama, Mississippi, and South Carolina—still display the Confederate stars and bars on their state flags, proof of the former Confederacy's enduring fascination with "the lost cause."

As a boy, Ty was slim as a reed and had a temperament as flammable as his red hair. Intelligent and sensitive, he wore his combative, competitive nature like a sandwich board, for all to see.

5

Gen. Thomas Reade Rootes Cobb, born in 1823, was Howell Cobb's younger brother. He was widely known for his published defenses of slavery, including the famous Cobb On Slavery, and helped create the Confederate constitution. A brigadier general in command of Cobb's Legion during the Civil War, he bled to death during the Battle of Fredericksburg after his femoral artery was severed by an explosion.

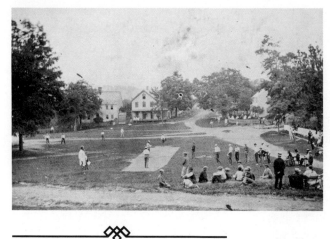

Baseball was a national obsession in the decades following the Civil War. Every city and hamlet in America had a team. "There is no healthier amusement in vogue," went a typical editorial of the period, "and the time spent in its practice is so much taken from pursuits that may be far less moral in their tendencies."

"You saw it the moment you set eyes on him," recalled schoolmate Joe Cunningham, whose father ran a furniture store in town. "He just seemed to think quicker and run faster. He was always driving and pushing, even in grade school."

"I was a boy with a vying nature," is how Ty once described himself. "I saw no point in losing, if I could win." In fifth grade he once pummeled a classmate for misspelling a word that allowed the girls' team to win a spelling bee.

Ty won Cunningham's respect early, standing up to the larger boy in a schoolyard fight. They quickly became best friends. Whether it was accepting a dare to cross a tightrope strung across a downtown street or playing ball against the older boys, Ty felt compelled to measure himself against those bigger and older than he was.

In Cobb's South, such displays of primal honor were part of an entire cultural pattern. Ty would rather be cut to pieces than surrender an inch, an attitude that drew admiration in the South but played to mixed reviews up North. When Ty was beaten to a pulp by a bigger and stronger Charlie Schmidt shortly after joining the Tigers, for example, his teammates viewed his refusal to quit earlier than he did as foolishness, not courage, just one more "lost cause" engaged in by the hot-headed Georgian.

Honor preoccupied Ty and was at the root of many of his endless altercations as an adult. On one infamous occasion in Detroit, Ty took umbrage at the way a fish merchant spoke to his wife on the telephone. Leaving his dinner guests behind, Ty rushed to address the insult. He stormed into the fish store and, at gunpoint, extracted an apology. Despite the irrationality of his actions, Ty's heritage would be taken into account often when assigning blame. In 1907, when he got into a fight with a Black groundskeeper and his wife during spring training, the *Augusta Herald* ran a headline: "Georgia Peach Defends the Honor of the Southland." Five years later, Ty climbed into the stands in New York to beat senseless a foul-mouthed fan. "The fan yelled an epithet," sportswriter Fred Lieb later recalled, "one that any Southerner would well resent. . . ." That particular fan had called Ty a "half-nigger." In his world, those were more than just fighting words—they were grounds for justifiable homicide.

Ty was an unrepentant bigot, although such an attitude in postbellum America was hardly remarkable. In fact, due to a tangle of Jim Crow laws and customs, racism was firmly woven into the fabric of everyday life throughout America. As with all social prejudices, Ty's racial attitudes were the result of conditioning, not genetics. As a child, he worked or played often alongside Blacks, who comprised about one-quarter of the population of Franklin County. In later years he would recall how he had learned to swim by repeatedly clinging to the neck of a young Black man who would swim to the middle of a stream and then release him, forcing Ty to reach shore on his own. Despite the occasional warm memory of contact with Blacks, as an adult Ty was guilty of outrageous conduct toward Black waiters, maids, clerks, groundskeepers, and any other non-whites who didn't exhibit the automatic deference white Southerners had been raised to expect.

There's no excusing Ty's bigotry; the best one can do is to try to understand it. Like many farmers, Ty's father regularly employed Black "freedmen" in his fields—as free, that is, as uneducated former slaves and their offspring could be in a climate of suspicion, hostility, and almost insurmountable social barriers. Despite emancipation, Blacks were not allowed to vote, hold office, or attend school with whites. Such restrictions helped reinforce the superiority whites on both sides of the Mason-Dixon line felt in the decades following the Civil War. They also were a manifestation of the fear that the country's growing number of Blacks might somehow shed their traditional role of subservience. Although based on pseudoscience or anecdote, the conventional wisdom in turn-of-the-century America was that the Black race was genetically inferior.

Negrophobia was especially pronounced in Georgia, which during Cobb's lifetime recorded more lynchings than any state except Mississippi. Royston and the rest of northern Georgia exercised a semblance of tolerance, but God still help the Black man who "forgot his place" in mixed society. Hoke Smith's influential *Atlanta Journal* daily "played up and headlined current stories of Negro crime, charges of rape and attempted rape, and alleged instances of arrogance, impertinence, surly manners, or lack of prompt and proper servility in conduct," wrote C. Vann Woodward in his landmark study of American race relations. Ty and his father both read the *Journal* religiously during its race-baiting heyday. It would be surprising if their racial attitudes were not partially shaped, or at least confirmed, by the paper's sensationalistic and inflammatory rhetoric.

At the turn of the century, North and South were bound together by more than institutional racism. From Texas sandlots to Wisconsin schoolyards, from Kansas pastures to New York alleys, the favorite pastime by far was baseball. Sundays especially were filled with adults and older boys who, free for an afternoon from the chains of factory, field, or office, taxed their muscles socking and chasing a lopsided ball around some communal ground. Idle youths, assuming they had completed (or ignored) their chores or schoolwork, had it even better, playing throughout the week. It's hard to overestimate the grip baseball had on the country's affections at the time. In absence of

Ty (left) at age twelve with his sister Florence, seven, and brother John Paul, ten.

7

The North Carolina Peach? Cherokee County has a partial claim on Ty Cobb because he spent summer vacations as a boy at his paternal grandparents' house near Murphy, North Carolina. This is Murphy, with the Smoky Mountains in the background, as Ty remembered it. "I felt secure and, like small boys, I harbored big dreams," he later said of this idyllic period.

Granddad Johnny's house, which he constructed in 1863 following his discharge from the Confederate army for an undisclosed injury, still stands about eight miles outside Murphy. Ty's father probably was born here shortly after it was built.

the professional sports and entertainment options later generations of Americans would take for granted, baseball was usually the only game in town. In fact, it was more than a game. It was a national obsession.

"Every town had its own town team in those days," said Sam Crawford, who recalled the glorious summer of 1898 when he and several other teenaged boys representing Wahoo, Nebraska, struck out for the open road in a horse-drawn grain wagon. "One of the boys was a cornet player, and when we'd come to a town he'd whip out that cornet and sound off. People would all come out to see what was going on, and we'd announce that we were the Wahoo team and were ready for a ball game. Every little town out there on the prairie had its own ball team and ball grounds, and we challenged them all. We didn't have any uniforms or anything, just baseball shoes maybe, but we had a manager. . . .

"We were gone three or four weeks. Lived on bread and beefsteak the whole time. We'd take up a collection at the games—pass the hat, you know—and that paid our expenses. Or some of them anyway. One of the boys was the cook, but all he could cook was round steak. We'd get twelve pounds for a dollar and have a feast. We'd drive along the country roads, and if we came to a stream, we'd go swimming; if we came to an apple orchard, we'd fill up on apples. We'd sleep anywhere. Sometimes in a tent, lots of times on the ground, out in the open. If we were near some fairgrounds, we'd slip in there. If we were near a barn, well. . . ."

While "Wahoo Sam" was touring Nebraska in a wagon (and then quickly moving into the professional ranks with the Cincinnati Reds), his future teammate was testing himself in town ball competition as a member of the Royston Rompers, a team comprised of 12- to 14-year-old boys. Even during vacations at Granddad Johnny's, Ty would hunt down a game in the mountain villages of Murphy and Andrews. No matter where the pasture or sandlot, opponents saw an earnest competitor awkwardly growing into a young man's body. In the outfield, he galloped like a puppy among the cow pies and wildflowers; in the infield, he choked back the instinct to turn his face at wickedly hit ground balls. Out of necessity, he held his heavy homemade bats with hands wide apart on the handle. That grip, the only way the youngster could get around on the ball, would become his trademark through his professional career.

"It wasn't that I gave baseball a second thought as a career—skinny ninety-pounder that I was," Ty later reflected. "My overwhelming need was to prove myself a real man. In the classroom, I was merely adequate—except for a flair for oratory, which brought me a few prizes. I couldn't hope to match my celebrated father for brains. In town ball—pitted against older boys and men at the age of fourteen—was the chance to become more than another schoolboy and the son of Professor Cobb."

Ty's feelings for his father were a deep blend of love, awe, and respect. "Professor" Cobb's lofty title had more to do with his exalted standing in the community than actual university credentials, but the townspeople's admiration was no less deserved for that. In addition to being a schoolmaster, landowner, and successful farmer, by his late thirties William had created a weekly newspaper, the *Royston Record* (which he wrote and edited), and been elected mayor and then state senator. As a legislator he was instrumental in reforming Georgia's public school system. He once delivered an address peppered with citations from history that showed education to be the foundation of democracy. Naturally, the voters of Franklin County elected him their first school commissioner. What spare time remained in William Cobb's busy life was spent reading mathematics, science, and classical literature.

Granddad Johnny had managed to provide his six children with at least partial college educations, and William expected to achieve no less for his own offspring, starting with the oldest. But Ty had the same jumbled feelings regarding the future that all youths have. His father thought Ty might enjoy a career in law or medicine, once going so far as to have Ty apprenticed to the local doctor. The sight of blood didn't affect Ty at all; one memorable evening he even assisted the operation on a youngster who had been shot in the stomach. At other times William thought his son might be right for a career in the military and spoke openly of securing for him an appointment to West Point or Annapolis.

Although Ty wasn't sure what he wanted to be when he grew up, he knew what he *didn't* want to be: a farmer. Ty considered himself a "townie." In fact, he was so embarrassed at being seen working his father's crops in dirty overalls that he would hide in the lower end of the field rather than let a girl he was sweet on catch him plowing like an ordinary clodhopper. He also showed little inclination to study harder than needed to pass a grade. To William's horror, it soon became obvious that what Ty *really* enjoyed more than anything else was playing ball. By 1901, when he was fourteen years old, Ty had earned a spot as the starting shortstop (and occasional outfielder) on the local men's team, the Royston Reds.

"Ty was still a little, skinny, spare-built fellow," recalled Reds manager Bob McCreary, who clerked in the local bank. "But I thought at the time that he was about the best natural ballplayer I had ever seen."

A skinny but determined Ty (front row, left) poses with his older, bigger Royston teammates sometime around 1900. Notice the gloves which are only slightly larger than today's garden gloves (with the exception of the catcher's mitt).

10

One spring day in 1902, 15-year-old Ty talked his father into letting him take a train to Atlanta, where Cleveland was training. Sneaking into Piedmont Park with his box camera, Ty saw his first major leaguer. His biggest thrill was striking up a conversation with veteran third baseman Bill Bradley, who posed for some snapshots. "After that, Bill Bradley was a hero of mine," said Ty. "I kept those pictures until they turned to dust."

William Cobb, who appears to have had little need (or time) for recreation, hardly knew a baseball from a boll weevil. But his stiff and formidable manner disguised a real love for his children. Rather than force his intentions on Ty, he decided eventually that the best strategy was to surrender to his son's fancy, with the expectation that he would eventually come around to more serious pursuits. Once before, when Ty had tried to swap some of his father's law books for a new fielder's glove, William had punished him so severely Ty refused to discuss the particulars even in his autobiography. But now there was a subtle softening in William's objections. Assured by Bob McCreary that he would guarantee Ty's well-being, William allowed his son to accompany the team on a trip to the neighboring town of Elberton. Hitting left-handed, Ty responded by stroking 3 hits, including the game-winner in the eighth inning.

The heroics continued later that season against Harmony Grove. This time playing center field, Ty made a circus catch of a fly ball to save the game. The hometown crowd showered the young star with cheers, applause, and about eleven dollars in change. Moments like this, Cobb later admitted, were his epiphany. "Once an athlete feels the peculiar thrill that goes with victory," he said, "he's bewitched. He can never get away from it."

The catch was the talk of the town for days. With his son elevated into the unaccustomed role of local hero, a chagrined William proudly devoted space in the *Royston Record*, which normally shunned sports, to an account of the game.

At the same time, William continued his campaign to find more practical applications for his baseball-loving son's energy. In the spring of 1903, when Ty was sixteen and in his junior year of high school, William assigned him a section of the family farm to put in the season's cotton crop. Wrestling with a hoe or a mule, sweating alongside Black field hands like "Uncle Ezra," normally held no appeal for Ty. But this time it was different. William made him in effect the sole proprietor of this patch of land, trusting him to make all the decisions regarding purchasing and equipment. The responsibility of keeping the books, supervising the crop, and ensuring a decent return on investment produced a remarkable change in Ty. Watching his long hours of seeding and plowing slowly blossom into ten acres of whitish-gray cash crop, he felt the first stirrings of the visceral reward of farming. He also enjoyed speculating on what his labor would yield at harvest time and in the marketplace. In the process he felt closer to his father, whose own estimation of Ty began to swell.

"It was the sweetest thing in the world to be fully accepted by my father," admitted Ty. "All at once, he was willing to hear my ideas, discuss them, and even exchange opinions. We'd talk about crop production, English import of cotton which competed with our Georgia output, and I never felt closer to him than when he said, 'Do you think we should sell now, or hold on for a better price?'" Demonstrating a new enthusiasm for agribusiness, Ty took a job with a local cotton factory and learned all about ginning, baling, grading, and moving the crop to market.

More than cotton had been planted. The seeds of Ty's fabled business acumen (as well as his equally storied stinginess) also were sowed that spring. "That was the most valuable lesson I ever received," he said twenty years later, by which time he had become a millionaire through shrewd stock investments. "I learned to produce. I learned that money had to be earned. I learned the value of a dollar, the joy of earning it. I could not have learned it in any better way."

But always there was baseball to dash William's hopes. That year Ty pocketed a few dollars playing ball in South Carolina. This could have destroyed his amateur eligibility when he went on to college—which, of course, is what was fully expected. In the spring of 1904, however, as the weeks to graduation were winding down, Ty secretly wrote letters to the six clubs then forming the brand new South Atlantic (Sally) League. The only reply came from the Augusta club. Manager and part-owner Con Strouthers invited Ty for a tryout at his expense. If he made the team, he would be paid fifty dollars a month. Ty eagerly signed the enclosed contract and sent it back.

"If that one team hadn't answered," Ty reflected in his autobiography, "I wonder if I'd ever have made baseball a career, for my ambition hung by a tenuous thread . . . suspended between my duty to my father, and my own desire."

Ty confided in his mother, who reluctantly gave her blessing. But he waited until the night before he was to leave to approach his father for his permission—and, just as important, for expense money. Instead of blowing up, the senior Cobb patiently tried to explain why it was imperative that Ty develop his mind, not his muscles. He also had considerable influence, he explained, which could help smooth a career path into law, medicine, or the military.

"You are seventeen and this is the decisive moment for you," he lectured, pacing back and forth, hands clasped behind his back. "In baseball, you can't help but fall into the company of a riffraffish type of men who drink and carouse and lead a pointless life."

"I just have to go," Ty protested over and over.

The discussion went on until three in the morning, when William finally capitulated.

"Well, son, you've chosen," he said wearily. "So be it. Go get it out of your system, and let us hear from you once in a while." With that he sat down at his desk and wrote six fifteen-dollar checks to

Grantland Rice and Cobb remained close friends until the sportswriter's death in 1954, although Ty waited until both were old men before confessing that he had written Rice the letters and postcards praising his play in the outlaw league in Alabama. "Why did you do it?" Rice asked. Replied Cobb: "I was in a hurry."

11

cover Ty's expenses. Although he wouldn't be around to fully appreciate it, in terms of return on investment it was the soundest business decision William Cobb ever made.

The following morning Ty traveled the eighty miles by train to join the Augusta Tourists. He was not an immediate hit. Eager to impress, he instead angered the older players by cutting in front of them on fly balls and grounders. He alternately dismayed and amused Con Strouthers by running the bases like an empty-headed fool. As a result, Ty sat on the bench throughout the exhibition season.

On opening day against the Columbia (South Carolina) team, however, Strouthers unexpectedly penciled Cobb's name into the lineup. Augusta's first baseman was holding out in a contract dispute, so the starting center fielder was moved to first and Ty took over in center. In his first professional game, Ty batted 7th and whacked out a single and a double in 4 at-bats against George Engel. Columbia won, 8–7.

Had William Cobb been sitting in Warren Park that afternoon, the classics scholar might have reminded his son of an old Latin

---

William Herschel Cobb represented the 31st District in the Georgia State Senate from 1900 until his tragic death in 1905. His legislative duties in Atlanta often required him to spend several days at a time away from home.

"BE GOOD"

Fifteen-year-old Ty was spending his winter school break at his grandparents' house in North Carolina when he received the following letter from his father. Like many educated men of the Victorian age, William Cobb's overblown prose contrasted sharply with his stiff and formal manner. But the professor's rhapsodic correspondence reveals an affection that he had difficulty expressing to his son in person. That may be the reason, years later, Ty kept the letter tucked into his wallet or suit pocket and eventually had copies printed.

Royston, Ga., January 5th, 1902

Tyrus, Dear Boy—The first snow of the year of account is down today. It is two inches I reckon. It is all of a round fine hail not a single feathery flake, some lodge on the limbs of the trees. Our wheat and oats have stood the winter all right, wheat is up nicely. We are all snowed in today principally on account of the cold weather. Hardly a sound has been heard today. It is nearly six o'clock. I knew the past cold weather would furnish you with some fine scenery up there and I am glad you have been receptive of its austere beauty and solemn grandeur, as to color, sound, and picturesque contour or outline. That is a picturesque and romantic country with solitude enough to give nature a chance to be heard in the soul. The presence of man and the jargon of artificiality and show do not crowd out the grand aspect of God's handiwork among those everlasting hills covered with its primeval forest, nor hush the grand oratorios of the winds, nor check the rush of her living leaping waters.

To be educated is not only to be master of the printed page but be able to catch the messages of star, rock, flower, bird, painting and symphony. To have eyes that really see, ears that really hear and imagination that can construct the perfect from a fragment. It is truly great to have a mind that will respond to and open the door of the soul to all the legions of thoughts and symbols of knowledge and emotions that the whole universe around brings to us.

Be good and dutiful, conquer your anger and wild passions that would degrade your dignity and belittle your manhood. Cherish all the good that springs up in you. Be under the perpetual guidance of the better angel of your nature. Starve out and drive out the demon that lurks in all human blood and ready and anxious and restless to arise and reign.

Be good.

Yours affectionately,

W. H. COBB

proverb: *Sic transit gloria mundi* (or, fame is fleeting). Because the following day Ty went hitless and was cut. Strouthers explained that his first baseman had signed and Ty's services would no longer be needed. Cobb was convinced that Strouthers just didn't like him.

Dazed, Ty fell in at his hotel with Thad Hayes, a pitcher who also had been cut. Hayes knew of a team organizing in Anniston, Alabama, that they might be able to catch on with. Ty dreaded calling his father to explain his release and to ask his permission to head for Anniston, a sooty mill town halfway between Atlanta and Birmingham. Instead of saying "I told you so" and demanding his return, William Cobb gave his son the greatest surprise of his young life.

"Go after it," said William. "And I want to tell you one other thing: *Don't come home a failure.*"

Anniston was one of eight charter members of the Tennessee-Alabama League. The "outlaw" league (which meant that it operated outside of the jurisdiction of organized baseball) had just been created with three teams in Tennessee and five in Alabama. The caliber of play was somewhere between that of a good semipro league and a Class D circuit (the lowest of the organized leagues), which undoubtedly contributed to its quick demise. When Anniston disbanded on July 11, Cobb had played in all 45 games, hit .336, and stole 10 bases in the games for which statistics are available.

Ty's three-month stint with the Anniston Noblemen is the most under-reported part of his professional career, but it may have been the most valuable; it gave a youngster with only two games of professional experience a chance to sharpen his raw talent and boost his self-confidence against inferior competition. It also gave him a prolonged taste of the baseball life, which he discovered he enjoyed. Ty admitted he "managed to look like the berries" in this group, although little mention of his exploits made the *Atlanta Journal* and other major dailies. When a brief blurb did appear, he often was referred to as "Cyrus" Cobb.

Before long, however, the *Journal's* up-and-coming sports editor, Grantland Rice, started receiving a stream of letters and postcards from fans named Jackson, Smith, and Kelly. One signed by a "Mr. Jones" informed Rice that "Tyrus Raymond Cobb, the dashing young star with Anniston, Ala., is going great guns. He is as fast as a deer and undoubtedly a phenom." It wasn't until years later that Cobb confessed to Rice that he, eager to get back into organized ball, had written the letters himself.

The ruse worked, to the extent that Rice wrote in his column that "rumors had reached Atlanta from numerous sources that over in Alabama there's a young fellow named Cobb who seems to be showing an unusual lot of talent." Rice even traveled to Anniston to see for

14

Augusta's reputation as a resort town, established in the years before highways and air conditioning made Florida more accessible to vacationers, inspired the nickname of its Class C ball club, the Tourists. Ty started his professional career in Augusta in 1904, but his affiliation with the charming city didn't end after he entered the majors the following summer. He would train in Augusta for several springs with the Detroit Tigers, marry the daughter of a prominent local businessman, and make the city his off-season home.

Augusta B.B. Club. 1905 South Atlantick

Ty (top row, third from right) and the 1905 Augusta Tourists. Within a ten-day span that August the team's star 18-year-old outfielder would receive two pieces of news that would rock his world: his father had been killed, and he was being called up to the big leagues.

15

himself. Faced with this kind of evidence from "interested fans" and a popular sportswriter, Augusta had a change of heart. At the same time that the Anniston Noblemen were disbanding, Con Strouthers was saying good-bye to Augusta. The Tourists' new management welcomed the "dashing young star" back into the fold, with Ty rejoining the lineup on August 9 in a game against Columbia.

Although he only hit an aggregate .237 during his two stints with Augusta, Ty returned to Royston that fall as a minor celebrity. Far from succumbing to the evils of dissipation, he had even managed to save $200 during the season. Although William Cobb continued to be spare in his praise, during the season he had carried around a clipping of Grantland Rice's column to show his legislative friends. Tragically for Ty, who over the winter signed a new contract with Augusta for ninety dollars a month, he wouldn't discover this small but meaningful item about his father until after he had been snatched away from him.

Like many preoccupied men, William Cobb often was blind to events unfolding in front of his eyes. A staple of gossip around Royston during the summer of 1905 (by which time Ty was playing left field and batting leadoff for Augusta) was that Amanda Cobb, who at thirty-three was still young and attractive, had a lover. (Although the paramour, if indeed he did exist, has never been identified.) One day William stood around downtown arguing with several men about closing a local brothel.

"Why don't you take care of your own house first?" one irritated citizen finally suggested.

That William apparently did not challenge the man suggests that he was already aware of Amanda's infidelity, or at least the rumors of it.

Game played at *Anniston* on *May 16* 1904

Anniston	1	2	3	4	5	6	7	8	9	10	11	AB	R	IB	SH	PO	A	E
Lane ss												3	1	0	1	2	4	2
Young 2b												4	0	1	0	3	3	1
Buhe cf												4	0	1	0	0	0	0
deVaune c												4	1	0	0	9	1	0
Cobb lf												4	1	1	0	2	0	1
Emme 1b												4	0	2	0	9	1	1
Sorrell 3b												4	0	0	0	0	3	0
Grover p												4	0	0	0	1	0	0
Horn p												4	1	0	0	1	9	0
Runs	3	0	0	0	1	0	0	0	0			35	4	5	1	27	21	5

Umpire McB: C. Smith.

Earned Runs 2   2 Base Hits 3   3 Base Hits 0   Home Runs 0   Passed Balls 1   Wild Pitches 3
Bases on Balls 0   Bases on Hit by Pitched Balls 0   Struck Out 7   Left on Bases 4   Double Plays 1   Time 2:12

A page from the past. This scoresheet of a game played at Anniston on May 16, 1904—reportedly Cobb's first game for Anniston—shows him playing left field and batting fifth. Ty has often been identified as the Tennessee-Alabama League's top hitter, but surviving scoresheets revealed he finished seventh with a .313 average. However, he did lead the circuit with 8 triples. Ultimately, the numbers meant little: by the middle of July the Noblemen would be history and Ty would be on his way back to Augusta.

But being acknowledged publicly as a cuckolded husband undoubtedly stung William, as it would most men. He decided to take action.

Early in the evening of August 8, 1905, William left the house for the family farm. He probably would be there a couple of days, he told Amanda. Later that night, with Ty in Augusta and the other two children staying with friends, Amanda locked the windows and went to bed.

Unbeknown to Amanda, after night fell William had doubled back to town. With a pistol in his coat pocket, he quietly climbed up a ladder to the second-story landing outside their bedroom. As Amanda later testified, she was awakened about midnight by a shadowy figure trying to lift one of the windows to her bedroom. Scrambling for the loaded double-barreled shotgun that was always on hand, she pointed it at the intruder and pulled one of the triggers. A short while later, she pulled the other trigger.

The explosions rocked the muggy night air. First on the scene was Ty's friend and next-door neighbor, Joe Cunningham, who was sickened by what he later described as "the worst thing I ever saw."

The Anniston Noblemen, a charter member of the short-lived Tennessee-Alabama League, was the first professional baseball team to represent the smoky mill town. Ty played in all 45 games of Anniston's abbreviated 1904 season, during which the Noblemen were 17–28, placing them sixth in the eight-team circuit.

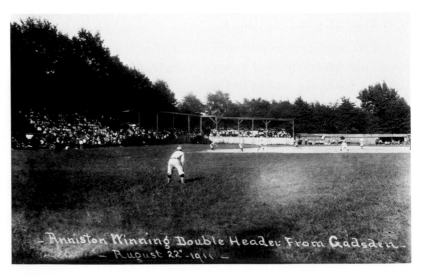

William Herschel Cobb lay, barely breathing, in a pool of blood, brains, and viscera. The blasts had ripped out his stomach and blew off part of his head. Cunningham ran to find H. F. McCreary, a doctor and the father of Ty's old manager on the Royston Reds. The doctor pronounced William dead at 1:30 A.M.

Amanda Cobb was arrested on a charge of involuntary manslaughter, posted bond, and was tried the following spring. She hired five defense attorneys. The prosecution, unwilling to ask the hard, indelicate questions about her alleged infidelity, failed to make its case. The all-male jury needed just one hour to return a verdict of not guilty.

The yellow frame house where Ty Cobb's father died no longer stands. The site is now the parking lot of a funeral home. All of the principals involved in the case are long gone. The shooting will probably never by resolved. Yet, after all these years, it is still a topic of speculation around Royston, fueled by key unanswered questions that have been handed down from generation to generation like grandma's treasured quilts. Why were the windows closed on such a hot, stuffy summer night? Was it to guard against intruders or to provide privacy for a clandestine coupling? And why the long delay between shots? Joe Cunningham, whose father built the coffin that William was buried in two days later, always maintained that Amanda didn't pull the trigger. Others in town whispered that they knew exactly who else was in the room at the time, although no one ever revealed his name. Still others insisted that it truly was a case of mistaken identity. As proof of Amanda's fidelity, they pointed out that she never remarried.

One of the few certainties about William Cobb's death is that it devastated Ty, who learned of the tragedy by telegram the following morning. He described it as "the blackest of days," but for the rest of his life he rarely spoke of it, and even in his autobiography he dismissed the episode in one sentence as "a gun accident." Although he was never close to his mother, he remained convinced outwardly of her virtue. "This isn't the kind of people Cobbs are," he insisted after hurrying home from Augusta.

The extent of the damage to Ty's psyche can only be guessed at. Today emotionally traumatized youths are surrounded by a phalanx of social workers, child psychologists, and assorted other "grief counselors." None was available in the summer of 1905. All 18-year-old Ty Cobb could do was wrap up as many loose ends as possible and return to the profession his father had opposed. Only now the full and unequivocal approval Ty so desperately sought from his father would be withheld forever.

Amanda Chitwood Cobb, who probably met William when she was a schoolgirl and he was a teacher, was eight years younger than her husband. They were married in 1883, when she was just twelve. Despite the scandalous rumors surrounding her husband's death, infidelity was not an issue during her trial in the spring of 1906.

17

A sight that would become familiar around the American League for the next quarter-century:
Ty Cobb, hands held wide apart, ready to smack the ball to any part of the field.

CHAPTER TWO

A Fresh Peach

He wasn't like this when he came up, you know. He was only eighteen, and as scared as they all are. But he had all that talent, and so the veterans went after him more mercilessly than I had ever seen in all my years in the game. They ridiculed him, and splintered his bats, even intercepted his mail from home. And I don't think Mister Cobb has ever really trusted anyone but himself since then.

—Harry Stein, Hoopla.

19

Ty rejoined the Augusta Tourists on August 16, 1905, just a week after his father's fatal shooting. Three days later, club president Charles D. Carr sold him to the Detroit Tigers.

It had already been a strange and tragic summer for Ty, one in which events were moving almost too fast. Just four months earlier he had startled the same Tiger ball club with his wild base-running and fielding antics during spring training exhibitions between Augusta and Detroit. "He's the craziest ballplayer I ever saw," remarked the Tigers' resident loon, Germany Schaefer. At the time of his sale to Detroit, Augusta, a team that featured several future major leaguers including infielder Clyde Engle and pitchers Eddie Cicotte and Nap Rucker, had fallen into a funk that left the team floundering near the bottom of the standings and its talented but immature left fielder counting the days until the end of the season. Ty became so nonchalant that during one game he missed a fly ball because he was munching on a bag of popcorn in the outfield.

This was when one other major influence in Ty's life stepped forward. George Leidy, a career minor leaguer whose diamond smarts outweighed his skills, had been the Tourists' sore-armed outfielder and team captain when he was promoted to manager in midseason. Leidy, whom Cobb described as "the type who tore into every play with all he had—a team man to the bone," had spent the best years of his life trying to make it to the majors. That Ty seemed intent on throwing away his own chance upset him deeply.

COBB EXPECTED TO MAKE HIS LOCAL DEBUT TODAY

Georgian in Town Anxious to Start Work in Tiger Outfield.

Detroit probably will present a new face in the outfield this afternoon. Tyrus Cobb, the speedy youngster from the Augusta South Atlantic league club, having arrived in the city last evening, ready to go in as soon as called on. Cooley is out of the game for a time, and Bob Lowe is willing to surrender an outfield job to anybody that wishes it. Accordingly, it is likely that Tyrus will get his chance in a hurry. The Georgian was a little fatigued last evening, having been on the way since Saturday. Ordinarily the trip is one of about thirty hours, but missed connections at Atlanta and Cincinnati set back the tourist. He thought, however, that one night's rest would put him on his feet.

Cobb played on Thursday and Friday with Augusta, and in those two games hit a batting clip that regained for him the leadership of his league, which he had lost for a time to Sentell, of the Macon club. He quit the South Atlantic with a hitting batting average of .328. He won't pile up anything like that in this league, and he doesn't expect to. If he gets away

TYRUS COBB.

with a .275 mark he will be satisfying everybody.

The local players had opportunity to watch Cobb last spring, when training in Augusta, and were impressed with his speed. Bill Byron, who umpired in the South Atlantic, says the youngster is one of the fastest men getting away he has ever seen.

The Detroit Free Press announced Cobb's arrival in town in its August 30, 1905, *edition. The writer of this unsigned article predicted that the Sally League batting champ with the .328 average "won't pile up anything like that in this league."*

"The Tabasco Kid," Norman Arthur Elberfeld. The tough-as-nails Highlander shortstop knew all the tricks of his trade—as Ty would discover painfully on his first big-league steal attempt.

"The reason I made good in the majors was Leidy," Cobb acknowledged years later. Leidy took Ty aside and through lecture and instruction turned his baseball career around. In the mornings before games Leidy taught him the mechanics of the hit-and-run, the drag bunt, the double steal, and the squeeze play. They worked on drawing the third baseman in on a fake bunt, then slapping the ball past him. Leidy had Ty bunt into a sweater placed strategically on the diamond, in spots where an infielder had little or no chance of making a play. "I bunted until I was worn out," recalled Ty. But the grueling hours of self-improvement paid off in the afternoon, as Ty tore loose at bat and on the bases, using what he had just learned to upset and out-think opponents. And over evening meals and during post-game strolls through the muggy Southern towns, Leidy counseled his young pupil on the rewards and recognition that came with being a big leaguer.

Then came the painful events of early August—his father's shooting, his mother's indictment for murder, and the rumors about her infidelity. His sudden promotion to the major leagues evoked only one thought he later admitted: "Father won't know it."

Cobb's final game for Augusta was on August 25. Play was stopped so fans could present him with a floral bouquet and a gold watch. Ty said thanks, shook hands, waved to the Warren Park crowd—and then struck out. "Let Detroit have him!" someone in the stands bellowed. Two subsequent singles produced Ty's final batting mark of .326, which would prove good enough to lead the Sally League.

As Ty would learn quickly, the American League was far removed from the Sally League, in skill level and culture—and distance. That he was making the 700-mile train trip at all was not entirely due to his talent but owed more to economics—and possibly a social disease.

That April the cash-strapped Tigers had left behind a promising pitching prospect, Eddie Cicotte, in lieu of the $500 the club owed Augusta for spring training expenses. However, Augusta agreed that the Tigers could later claim any player off its roster for the same amount. The Tigers, looking for a cheap replacement for its injury-depleted outfield, decided against buying an experienced (but more expensive) player from the higher classifications. Reviewing the Augusta roster, club officials seriously considered Clyde Engle. But largely on the advice of Detroit scout Heinie Youngman and pitcher Bill Donovan, as well as Sally League umpire Bill Byron (a native Detroiter), Tiger manager Bill Armour and club secretary Frank Navin settled on Cobb.

A Fresh Peach

Years later, Ty confided that Engle wasn't selected because he was suffering from a venereal disease (an occupational hazard of professional ballplayers during this period) that had affected his play. Whatever the reason, Tyrus (or was it Cyrus?) Cobb headed north to finish out the year with the Tigers. Because he joined Detroit before the end of the Tourists' season, Augusta received an additional $200 for his contract. Total purchase price: $700.

Ty broke into the Detroit lineup on August 30 in a Wednesday afternoon game against the New York Highlanders at Bennett Park. In the top of the first inning, an estimated 1,200 "bugs" (as fans were then known) watched with mild curiosity as Cobb nervously trotted out to his position in center field, flanked by Matty McIntyre in left and Sam Crawford in right. In the bottom of the inning, Ty drew several stares and comments as he swung three bats in the on-deck area. No one had ever done that before. Spectators and teammates may have thought the new fellow was showing off, but Ty had been following that ritual for some time. Throwing down the other two bats before entering the batter's box, it made his heavy, thick-handled club feel two-thirds lighter.

Ty, batting fifth, came up with a runner on third and two out. Facing him was Jack Chesbro, a grizzled spitballer who had won 41 games—still the 20th-century high—a year earlier. Ty swung and missed Chesbro's first offering, took a called strike on the second, and then slapped the third pitch into the gap in left-center field for a run-scoring double. It was an auspicious beginning, although Ty went hitless the rest of the game and was thrown out attempting to steal second after reaching base on a walk. Observed the *Detroit Free Press:* "Cobb, the rookie, may consider a double and a walk a much better career-opener than usually comes a young ballplayer's way."

The following afternoon Ty contributed a pair of singles as the Tigers beat the Highlanders for the second straight game. The rookie's most memorable moment came on a stolen base attempt after his first hit. Waiting for him at second base was Norman "Kid" Elberfeld, a scrappy, sawed-off shortstop who had played several years for Detroit. As Cobb dove head first into the bag—a bush-league slide in 1905—Elberfeld put the "teach" on him, sticking his knee into Ty's neck and rubbing his nose into the dirt. Cobb got up sputtering and red-faced, as the crowd and veterans on both teams hooted and laughed. From that point on Ty rarely slid head first into a base.

Ty's first major-league at-bat was against spitballer Jack Chesbro, the Highlanders' veteran 41-game winner of a year before. "Happy Jack" won 199 games, posted a career 2.68 ERA, and was elected to the Hall of Fame in 1946. Cobb touched him for a .426 average in 54 career at-bats.

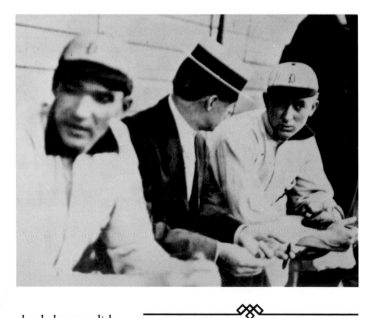

Sporting a straw boater and with cigar in hand, manager Bill Armour takes time to explain the situation to Ty during the 1905 season. In the foreground is third baseman Bill Coughlin.

Feisty, two-fisted Edward Grant Barrow was Bill Armour's predecessor as Tiger manager. After quitting Detroit in August 1904, Barrow managed Indianapolis in the American Association. Early in the 1905 season, Augusta offered him a chance to buy either Cobb or Clyde Engle off its roster for $500, or both for $800. "Thinking Cobb the less desirable of the two, I offered $300, which Augusta turned down," Barrow later recalled. "So I lost this great player for $200."

Fleet-footed Davy Jones joined the Tigers' outfield in 1906 and stayed 7 seasons. Jones once described playing alongside Cobb and Crawford as "being a member of the chorus in a grand opera where there are two prima donnas."

With regular Jimmy Barrett sidelined with a bad leg, Ty started each of the Tigers' final 41 games. He wound up batting .240, with 2 stolen bases and a home run, as the Tigers roared home a surprising third. Ty, whose play was occasionally brilliant but often unpredictable, deserved little of the credit, but everyone around the circuit recognized him as a raw talent—"an infant prodigy," as *Sporting Life* called him.

The Tigers thought enough of him to raise his annual salary from $1,200 to $1,500 for 1906—an important consideration, as he was now expected to provide for his widowed mother and sister. However, no amount of money could compensate Cobb for what happened in the spring of 1906, a period he later called "the most miserable and humiliating experience I've ever been through."

Specifically, Ty became the target of a relentless hazing campaign aimed he thought at driving him off the team. Starting in spring training and continuing through the season, a core group of veterans made life practically unbearable for him. They shoved him aside at the batting cage and turned away when he spoke to them. In the clubhouse they tied his clothes in knots. Back in the hotel after practice, they kept the grime-streaked youngster waiting in the hallway for hours as they took their time soaking in the communal bathtub. Perhaps the lowest moment was when Ty discovered his homemade bats had been destroyed.

His teammates' unexpected behavior shocked, angered, and ultimately inspired Ty. He had made it through his abbreviated 1905 stay in time-honored rookie fashion, keeping to himself while the veterans ignored him. But in the spring of 1906, last year's late-season substitute suddenly was a threat to someone else's full-time employment. With Sam Crawford a fixture in right field and newly acquired veteran Davy Jones conceded center field, Ty figured to compete with Matty McIntyre for the final outfield spot. This made him wide open to abuse by the popular McIntyre and his circle of friends.

To his teammates, Ty was as much a foreigner as the millions of immigrants then flooding America's shores. At century's turn, the overwhelming majority of big leaguers were Irish or German Catholics who hailed from the North. When Ty spoke, his thick drawl—which transformed the name of his home state into something approximating "Jo-ja"—immediately marked him an outsider, as did his youth, inexperience, and Baptist upbringing. Unlike most veteran ballplayers, Ty neither smoked, drank, cussed, nor frequented brothels. He also had the appearance of a Southern rube. Although he would later fill out to an imposing six-foot-one and 190 pounds, at the time he was about three inches and thirty-five pounds smaller. His wispy, reddish-blond hair and wide blue eyes added to his vulnerable look. In Ty's mind, this treatment helped account for his legendary ferocity. "Those old-timers made a snarling wildcat out of me," is how he often put it.

From university dorms and infantry barracks to baseball clubhouses, hazing was a staple of American life, although it often crossed the line from innocent high jinks to meanspiritedness and maliciousness. The following spring, for instance, Detroit veterans drove an unfortunate rube who had committed the gaffe of labeling his luggage "Jameson Harper, Ballplayer" out of camp and nearly out of his mind with a series of heckles, pranks, and cold shoulders. And in 1908, Philadelphia rookie "Shoeless Joe" Jackson, an ignorant mill hand from South Carolina, was so thoroughly humiliated by his teammates he quit the club several times, forcing an exasperated Connie Mack to finally sell him to Cleveland.

In Ty's case, veterans encountered a high-strung, serious-minded, and stubbornly proud teenager who wouldn't retreat. Cobb made no apologies for his defiance. "If I'd been meek and submissive and hadn't fought back," he later explained, "the world never would have heard of Ty Cobb."

It appears that Ty's principal antagonists were McIntyre and his roommate, pitcher Ed Killian. Cobb's future Hall of Fame outfield mate, Sam Crawford, didn't like the newcomer, either, but he apparently did little more than agitate in the background. Six years older

The Detroit Tigers gather inside Warren Park in Augusta for a team photo during spring training in 1906. Top row, from left: pitchers Bill Donovan and George Disch, first baseman Pinky Lindsay, catcher Tom Doran, outfielder Matty McIntyre, and pitchers John Eubank and George Mullin. Second row: outfielder Bobby Lowe, catcher Lew Drill, pitcher Ed Killian, outfielder Sam Crawford, manager Bill Armour, pitcher Jimmy Wiggs, Cobb, outfielder Jimmy Barrett, shortstop Charlie O'Leary. Bottom row: pitcher Frank Kitson, catcher Jack Warner, third baseman Bill Coughlin, second baseman Germany Schaefer.

23

Ty had this studio shot taken of him during the 1906 season.

24

It's still spring training, 1906, but this time several Tigers are relaxing out of uniform. Seated from left are Eddie Summers, George Mullin, Cobb, and Germany Schaefer. Standing in the doorway is trainer Harry Tuthill.

than Cobb, Wahoo Sam was already a star with the Cincinnati Reds when Ty was still fielding grounders with the Royston Reds. The left-handed hitting Crawford was probably the top slugger of the dead-ball era (the years before 1920). His 312 lifetime triples and 56 inside-the-park home runs—both major-league records—are as much a testimony to his power and surprising speed as they are to the cavernous ballparks of the period.

Crawford, the acknowledged star of the team since joining the Tigers in 1903, was a proud man with a high opinion of himself. Like Cobb, Crawford could be petulant, calculating, and vindictive. The thought of someone stealing his thunder accounted in large part for Crawford's attitude toward Ty. Although the two played 13 seasons together, they only barely tolerated each other. So tense was their relationship that Crawford would occasionally foul off a pitch on purpose if it looked as if Ty had a base stolen.

Late in life, Crawford gave his side of the story. "We weren't cannibals or heathens," he explained to Lawrence Ritter. "We were all ballplayers together, trying to get along. Every rookie gets a little hazing, but most of them just take it and laugh. Cobb took it the wrong way. He came up with an antagonistic attitude, which in his mind turned any little razzing into a life-or-death struggle. He always figured everybody was ganging up against him."

Ty never had much of a sense of humor, added Davy Jones, who did his best to befriend him. "Especially, he could never laugh at himself. Consequently, he took a lot of things the wrong way. What would usually be an innocent-enough wisecrack would become cause for a fist fight if Ty was involved." It's impossible today to apportion blame for what happened in Cobb's early years. But if it's true that Ty suffered from a persecution complex, then it's equally true that wiser or more charitable teammates would have realized it and eased off.

That spring, Joe S. Jackson of the *Detroit Free Press* coined Ty's soon-to-be-famous nickname, "the Georgia Peach," although no one called him that in everyday conversation. To those few who did speak to him, Ty was simply "Ty" or "Cobb" or, especially in the early years, "Tyrus." In time, however, as his moniker gained universal currency (thanks to nationally syndicated writers like Grantland Rice), some people in and out of baseball came to call Ty "Peach."

A Fresh Peach

At that, the name proved wonderfully descriptive. Ty Cobb *was* a peach of a player, as he proved when given the chance. Coming out of spring training, the Tigers' outfield consisted of Crawford in right, Jones in center, and McIntyre in left. However, when Crawford injured his leg on April 21 against Chicago, Ty entered the starting lineup and, despite uneven play, stayed there. When Crawford was ready to come back, Armour benched Jones and installed Cobb in center.

Despite his starting status, Ty remained shut off from most of the team. He ate alone, roomed alone, and continued to endure random acts of mayhem. On train trips he would be smacked in the back of the head by soggy wads of newspaper. Grabbing his hat after a meal, he would find that its crown had been crushed. He was never able to identify his attackers though. "Who did this?" he would yell, his hands balled into fists. No one ever stepped forward. Although some players, such as Bill Donovan, Germany Schaefer, and Davy Jones, were friendly toward him, Ty had no close companions. During his free time he would wander alone to a vaudeville show or take in a classical performance at the Detroit Opera House. Or he would stroll down to lush Belle Isle Park in the Detroit River, always a popular destination on summer Sundays (especially since baseball was still prohibited on the Sabbath). Edgar Willet, a rookie pitcher from Virginia, moved into Ty's cramped downtown hotel room for a time. More important than sharing expenses was the opportunity for companionship with a fellow Southerner. But a short while later the anti-Cobb faction convinced Willet that it was in his best interest to move out. After that, Ty's closest companion was the pistol he started carrying.

Beyond the physical isolation, his agile mind truly set Ty apart from everyone else. He was intelligent and creative and a fast learner. In fact, the ostracism hastened Ty's development. Time that otherwise might have been spent inside pool halls and saloons was used to better advantage, as Ty stared at his hotel room ceiling and dreamed up ways of foiling the opposition. When Ty broke in, he ran the bases "like a fool" and "couldn't hit a left-hander very good," an admiring Ring Lardner once recalled. "That was when he first come up here. But Ty ain't the guy that's goin' to stay fooled all the time. When he wises up that somebody's got somethin' on him, he don't sleep nor do nothin' till he figures out a way to get even. . . . He seen he couldn't hit the curve when it was breakin', so he stood way back in the box and waited till it'd broke. Then he nailed it. . . ." Three months into the season, Ty was nailing it often enough to be challenging for the batting title.

In mid-July, Ty left the team in Boston and was missing from the Tigers' lineup for several weeks. The newspapers didn't explain or make much fuss over his absence, other than to report that he had

Edgar Willett, a strong, handsome rookie pitcher from Virginia, was Ty's roommate until players unfriendly to Cobb convinced Willett that it was in his best interests to move out.

The leader of the anti-Cobb faction was Matty McIntyre, a popular veteran whose dislike of the rookie was based almost evenly on the fear of losing his outfield job and a personality conflict. A .269 lifetime hitter and better-than-average fielder, McIntyre was out of the big leagues by the time he was thirty-two; he died seven years later in Detroit without once shaking Cobb's hand.

Sam Crawford of Wahoo, Nebraska, at the wheel of his 1907 Cadillac. The 6-foot, 190-pounder probably was the top slugger of the dead-ball era. In 4 seasons with Cincinnati and 15 more with Detroit, "Wahoo Sam" banged out 2,964 hits, including a record 312 triples. In 1901 he led the National League with 16 home runs; in 1907 he topped the American League with 7. A durable player with deceptive speed, he also stole 366 bases during his career.

been sent back to Detroit because of "stomach trouble." One biographer has speculated that the reason for Ty's "rest" was to remove an ulcer, but there's no conclusive proof of that. (Although if Cobb *had* undergone such an operation, he would never have admitted it.) Ulcer or not, Ty's illness undoubtedly was a case of physical and emotional exhaustion, brought on by his rugged playing style and compounded by the pressures of dealing with his teammates and his mother's recently concluded trial.

His collapse also may have owed something to the butchery he had endured several weeks earlier in Toledo. Coming north from spring training, Ty developed an agonizing case of tonsillitis. Fearful of losing his spot on the roster, he kept the condition to himself, until a high fever and swollen glands finally forced him to visit the hotel physician. Over three bloody sessions, each of which left Ty dazed from hemorrhaging and pain, the doctor went at his tonsils with more enthusiasm than surgical skill.

"He sat me in a chair, tipped it back and went to work, without anesthetic," remembered Cobb. "My tonsils were in such a condition that they had to be removed in sections. Each time a piece of them came out, blood surged into my mouth, choking me, and I had to demand a rest period. Putting a stranglehold on my neck, the doc would probe and cut for ten or fifteen minutes before letting me collapse on a sofa." Germany Schaefer, who had come along for moral support, wound up half-carrying his teammate back to his room after each gory episode. Ty later would discover that the man who had happily hacked away at his tonsils had been committed to an insane asylum.

In his autobiography Ty makes no mention of a mid-season operation, instead pointing out that during 1906 he was "invalided" at a Fort Street hospital to drain and heal his raw and infected left hip, which had been rubbed into hamburger by repeated slides on Bennett Park's concrete-like infield. The Tigers' home field had been built in 1896 on the site of an old hay market, and a decade later cobblestones still regularly emerged through the thin layer of topsoil. Pitcher Bill Donovan, whose own base-running style had earned him the sobriquet "Wild Bill," said of Cobb during this period: "Every time he slides he loses a pint of blood." Also, management may have wanted to get their young firebrand away from his antagonistic teammates for a while, hoping that time would mend any hard feelings.

A Fresh Peach

Whatever the truth behind his absence, Ty was soon playing himself back into shape with the Detroit Athletic Club, for years one of the area's top amateur nines. The D.A.C., breeding ground for several major leaguers, including Christy Mathewson's batterymate on the New York Giants, Frank Bowerman, played its games behind a handsome brick clubhouse on Woodward Avenue, about two miles north of downtown. "I can still see Ty getting the opposition up in the air," team captain George McClure remembered years later, "placing one over third, then over first, and then crossing 'em up by bunting. He was just a boy then. But we knew he had the stuff." According to McClure, Ty played some 40 games in the outfield for the D.A.C. that summer and the team won them all.

Competing among mature older men and apple-cheeked sandlotters, Ty found the environment friendly and mercifully free of the petty jealousies that had characterized his brief time in the majors. The newcomer made several valuable and lifelong contacts, including men involved with the fledgling auto industry. One was Ben Guiney, a former National Leaguer and a starter on the D.A.C.'s two national amateur championship teams of the early 1890s. At forty-eight, Guiney was a successful executive of the Kelsey Wheel Company, which provided automakers with wheels and brake systems. In his spare time he still enjoyed playing and coaching the game at the amateur level. It was Guiney—not Ty, as is commonly supposed—who originated an offensive maneuver that became famous as a textbook example of Cobbian baseball.

The tactic was devastatingly simple. Having reached first base, Cobb would flash the "bunt" sign to the batter. Then, as the pitcher went into his wind-up, Ty would dart for second and—instead of staying there as the ball was bunted toward third base—roar around the bag as the third baseman temporarily abandoned his station to field

Ben Guiney was born in Detroit in 1858 and remained active in baseball around the city for most of his life. After Guiney died in 1930, John C. Lodge, a teammate on the Detroit Athletic Club's national amateur championship teams of the 1890s, ridiculed the notion that Cobb had originated the strategy of a runner going from first to third on a bunt. "When Cobb was in swaddling clothes Ben Guiney thought out that play," said Lodge, "and always insisted that the fast men on our team make the attempt, and often they succeeded."

The Detroit Athletic Club on Woodward Avenue, north of downtown. It was on the diamond behind this fieldhouse that Ty played himself back into shape following his illness in 1906.

As Ring Lardner once observed, Ty "don't stay fooled long." After left-hander Guy "Doc" White struck him out 3 times in a Memorial Day game in 1906, prompting the manager to insert a pinch-hitter for him, Cobb experimented with moving to the back line of the batter's box and shortening his stance and swing. This allowed him to wait until the last moment to judge the break of the ball. Then, quick as a lizard's tongue, he would flick his bat at the ball and punch it to the opposite field.

Joe. S. Jackson of the Detroit Free Press was a free-spirited journalist who knew the best flesh spots and watering holes in every city in the American League. It was Jackson—not Grantland Rice, as is supposed—who first called Ty "the Georgia Peach" (in the spring of 1906). Invention, it seems, was Jackson's bailiwick. Two years later he founded the Baseball Writers Association of America in Detroit, the result of complaints over poor press facilities during that year's World Series between the Tigers and Cubs.

the ball. Usually Cobb was able to slide safely into third before the fielder could complete his throw to first and hustle back and receive the return throw. The tactic, which required a skilled sacrifice bunter to work, wasn't used fully by the Tigers until the following season, when Ty teamed with long-armed first baseman Claude Rossman to execute the play to perfection.

Ty returned to the Tigers' lineup on September 3 to find that he was still not free of what was *really* ailing him. If anything, opposition to him had solidified during his seven-week absence. With McIntyre in left field and Ty back in center, sparks flew when they converged on a fly ball or otherwise crossed each other's path. The smoldering animosity finally burst into flames on the next-to-last day of the season, in St. Louis, when George Stone of the Browns slapped an Ed Siever pitch into left-center field. As everyone in the park watched in amazement, what should have been a humble single rolled past Cobb and McIntyre to the flagpole while the two enemies stood planted in the grass yelling at the other one to retrieve it. Stone, on his way to edging Nap Lajoie for the batting championship, gratefully circled the bases for an inside-the-park home run.

The exasperated Siever almost came to blows with Ty in the dugout between innings and again in the clubhouse after the game. Finally, that evening in the hotel lobby, Siever confronted him at the cigar counter. Before anything could happen, Bill Donovan—regarded as the best boxer in the American League—stepped between them. "Let's not have any trouble, boys," he said.

But a short while later, as Ty tried eavesdropping on the murmurings of Siever and a group of his friends, Siever suddenly hurled a curse and a left hook at Ty. Cobb deftly blocked it and returned a right to Siever's jaw. Then, as the pitcher scrambled to get off the floor, Ty punched and kicked him several more times in the face and head until teammates broke up the fight. The ferocity of Ty's counterattack did more than serve notice to the anti-Cobb group to keep their distance. It also underscored an elemental cruel streak in Cobb's nature, a flaw that would create countless unflattering headlines over the coming years.

When Ty arrived in camp the following March, it was not as a high-strung

JOE. S. JACKSON
DETROIT FREE PRESS

FRANK B. HUTCHINSON JR.
ASSOCIATED PRESS

rookie eager to make an impression but as an established, slightly swell-headed big leaguer. His .320 mark had not only placed him fifth on the American League batting list, it was 35 points higher than the next nearest Tiger, Sam Crawford, had hit. And although Ty had played in only 98 games, he had still managed to swipe 23 bases and compile the majors' longest hitting streak—25 games—since his idol, Bill Bradley (a potent hitter for the Cleveland Indians), had hit safely in 29 straight four years earlier. To top it off, Ty was given a raise to $2,400, making him one of Detroit's better-paid players. (Crawford ended a short holdout that spring by signing for $3,000.) Whatever else his teammates thought of him in the spring of 1907, they had to concede him his obvious talent and his growing popularity with Detroit fans. Although McIntyre and company continued to simmer with hate and jealousy, the hazing gradually disappeared.

Part of the reason was a change of managers. Dissension, injuries, and Bill Armour's lackluster bench leadership had led to the Tigers' 6th-place finish in 1906. Armour was replaced by Hughie Jennings, a generously freckled, live-wired disciple of John McGraw's storied Baltimore Orioles of the 1890s. The 37-year-old ex-shortstop was one of the most colorful men ever to don flannel, with a large share of his legend revolving around his periodic brushes with calamity and his everyday antics in the coaching box. As Detroit players would learn over the next 14 seasons, during which Jennings would

29

PINCH-HITTING FOR THE PEACH

In 1906, Cobb's first full season in the majors, he was still enough of an unproven batter for manager Bill Armour to occasionally send up a pinch hitter. Although Ty undoubtedly disagreed with the strategy, he could hardly argue with the results. That season Ty was pinch-hit for 3 times, and each time the substitute batter delivered a base hit. The only other occasion was in 1922 when Cobb, now managing the club, ordered Bob Fothergill up to the plate for himself.

Pinch-Hitter	Date	Opponent	Result
Sam Crawford	April 24, 1906	St. Louis	Singled
Fred Payne	May 30, 1906	Chicago	Singled
George Mullin	September 18, 1906	Boston	Tripled
Bob Fothergill	May 5, 1922	St. Louis	Flied out

Second baseman Herman "Germany" Schaefer, a zany, ruddy-faced alcoholic and one of the few players to unconditionally accept Ty as a teammate. Many of Schaefer's antics have become part of baseball lore, including stealing first base and wearing a rain slicker out to his position during a drizzle in Cleveland. Once, when asked what he intended to do when he retired from baseball, Schaefer thoughtfully replied that he was going to buy a little corner saloon: "Not a big gaudy place, but a cozy spot where my friends can enjoy a glass of beer and a sociable evening. And along about ten o'clock every evening I want one of my pals to say to the bartender on duty, 'Where's old Schaef tonight?' And I want my bartender to be able to say, 'He's upstairs, drunk.'" Schaefer was traded to Washington in 1909 and died in a New York sanitarium ten years later.

George Stone's innocent ground ball on the next-to-last day of the 1906 season helped cap a miserable year for Ty and the Tigers. The gift inside-the-park home run helped the St. Louis Browns outfielder cop his only batting championship with a .358 mark, 57 points above his lifetime average. In his first full American League campaign, Ty finished fifth at .320. Stone would be the last man until Tris Speaker in 1916 to beat Cobb out of a batting title.

30

In the spring of 1907, Cleveland turned down an offer from Detroit manager Hughie Jennings to swap his troublesome outfielder for 30-year-old Elmer Flick, the league's top hitter in 1905. It turned out to be a terrible decision for Cleveland, because injuries soon ended Flick's Hall of Fame career.

guide them to 3 pennants and a couple of near-misses, their noisy manager was a warm but firm boss—firm, that is, except when it came to his star. Jennings recognized Ty as a special talent, someone who exhibited the same fire, grit, and desire that he had when he was helping the Orioles hip-check, belt-hold, and base-cut their way to 3 straight National League pennants a decade earlier. Although they often would feud over the years, a mutual respect grew between these two red-haired, blue-eyed competitors. Jennings decided from the start to allow his young star to do what he wanted on the diamond. There was little, he conceded, that he could teach him about the game. Ty's off-field deportment, however, resisted instruction. Just four days after the pair met at spring training and went over ground rules for their relationship, Ty chalked up the first in a long line of controversial and embarrassing incidents under Jennings' tenure.

It was nearly his last. This time Ty's bigotry, the ugliest part of his personality, rose to bite him in the ankle. Perhaps he felt emboldened by the race riot in Atlanta a few months earlier, when white Georgians had rampaged through the streets, killing several Blacks. The turn-of-the-century South clearly was no place for a Black person to challenge a white, which is what happened the afternoon of March 16, when the Tigers arrived at Augusta's Warren Park for practice. The park's groundskeeper, a tipsy Black man named "Bungy," weaved toward Cobb with an extended hand.

"Hello, you Georgia Peach," said Bungy. Ty, who had known the old man since breaking into pro ball with the Tourists, tried shooing him away. When Bungy persisted, he slapped him and then chased him toward the clubhouse. There Ty ran up against Bungy's large, buxom wife, who started screaming, "Go 'way, white man! We ain't done nothin' to you!" Cobb, his temper boiling, decided to shut the woman up by choking her.

Ty may have felt he was defending the honor of the South, as at least one local paper later proclaimed, but several witnesses saw it differently: an unprovoked attack on a woman by an out-of-control bully. Charlie Schmidt, a solidly built catcher from Coal Hill, Arkansas, who spent time as a miner and prizefighter, came to her rescue.

"Whoever does a thing like that is a coward," said Schmidt.

"I don't see as it interests you," responded Cobb, who then exchanged some ineffective blows with Schmidt before teammates quickly separated them.

The newspapers played up the feud until Schmidt-Cobb II was a certainty, although the catcher wisely waited until the team had left Georgia before arranging the rematch. It occurred on an off-day at a ballfield in Meridian, Mississippi, and judging by accounts the pre-arranged match must have resembled the beating George Kennedy administered Paul Newman years later in the movie *Cool Hand Luke.* Rubber-legged and arm-weary, Ty refused to stay down until players finally broke up the one-sided fight. Ty returned to his hotel room with a broken nose and a bouquet of purple and blue bruises. After licking his wounds for several days, during which he missed two exhibitions, he finally emerged for a game against a minor-league team in Little Rock. Displaying his usual zest, Ty stole home—with two black eyes.

By then the Detroit management had tried—and failed—to trade him. The morning after the fracas with the groundskeeper, Jennings had offered Cleveland a straight one-for-one swap of malcontents: Cobb for Elmer Flick, a 30-year-old former batting champ who was holding out for more money. But Flick soon signed, killing the deal. Later, Frank Navin received some feelers from the New York Highlanders regarding a part-time outfielder named Frank Delahanty. "Pudgie," one of five Delahanty brothers to play in the majors, had hit .238 in 1906. New York manager Clark Griffith insisted the offer was serious.

Navin and Jennings, who weren't conducting a fire sale, resigned themselves to bringing their raccoon-eyed problem child north. For better or for worse, Ty would remain a Tiger.

Take a close look at the mangled fingers on the throwing hand of Charlie Schmidt, the result of countless foul tips and more than a few bare-knuckled brawls. The scar tissue allowed the Detroit catcher to occasionally amuse teammates by driving nails into boards with his bare hand. To no one's surprise, the ex-coal miner from West Virginia—who had once fought an exhibition match with heavyweight Jack Johnson—made short work of Ty when the two tangled during spring training in 1907.

31

The Georgia Peach, circa 1907.

CHAPTER THREE
The World's Greatest Ballplayer

*With young Cobb in the game, there's never any
telling what might happen: whether he's at bat, on
base, or in the field, the fantastic, impossible twist is
an easy possibility and we sit there like children
wondering what miracle he will perform next. There
is an infectious diabolical humor about his coups.
Cobb, charging home when he was expected to stay
on third, seems to derive much unholy joy at the
havoc he causes.*

*The charm of Cobb lies in his head. His eye and
arm, heaven knows, are such as most; but when in
addition to directing these against the ball, he directs
them against men, then we see more than a game—
we see drama. He is a Br'er Fox of baseball, and
Br'er Fox, wherever we see him, is a never-failing
source of enchantment.*

—New York World, 1907

By the beginning of the 1907 American League season, 20-year-old Ty had
reached his adult size. More aggressive and imaginative than any other player, he exhibited a
lethal combination of speed, size, and muscle—all linked to a mind that moved faster than
one of Thomas Edison's "flickers" and, as Grantland Rice put it, a determination to "hurl red
hell on his way to a score." Cobb rose quickly to the top of his profession and made his name
and deeds a topic of conversation in barber shops, school yards, and parlors throughout
America.

By early July Ty had become the first major leaguer to reach 100 hits. More important,
Hughie Jennings' decision to give Ty free rein on the field helped him become the catalyst of
the Tigers' rise from the second division. Ty's batting genius alone would have been enough to
warrant the league-wide superlatives over his play. That he also was a rolling ball of hell on
the basepaths—"daring to the point of dementia," the *Detroit Free Press* said—added to his
notoriety and effectiveness. "My whole plan on base was to upset batteries and infields," he
explained. "How? By dividing their minds, by upsetting and worrying them until their con-
centration was affected. I was always looking to create a mental hazard—by, as some writer
once put it, the establishment of a threat." That his plays often appeared suicidal or down-
right stupid bothered Ty not in the least. "All I had to do was make the opposition keep on
throwing the ball. Sooner or later, somebody would make a wild throw."

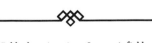

"Wild Bill" Donovan (right) with batterymate Charlie Schmidt. Donovan, who won 186 games during an eighteen-year career, had his finest season in 1907, going 25–4. The genial right-hander was considered the top boxer in the league and had a reputation as a reckless base runner, stealing his way around the bases in one 1906 game against Cleveland. He was one of the few veterans to stand behind Ty when the Georgian came up as a rookie. Guilt may have played a part; Donovan's father was one of General Sherman's "bummers" who had marched through Georgia in 1864.

In September, as the surprising Tigers battled Philadelphia and Chicago down to the wire for the pennant, the New York Highlanders got a taste of the mayhem Cobb regularly created on the field. In the ninth inning of the series' opener, Ty reached base, then promptly stole second. Seeing that the ball had rolled a few feet away from the second baseman, Ty jumped up and dashed for third. He was a sure out—except that Ty contorted his body so while sliding the throw hit him in the back and bounced away. Two outs later, Cobb's repeated dashing up and down the base line caused the pitcher to fumble an easy tap back to the mound. The rattled pitcher finally recovered but not before the batter had beaten the throw to first and Ty had streaked across the plate with the only run in the Tigers' 1–0 victory.

The war of nerves continued the next day. With Claude Rossman at bat, Ty pulled off the bunt-and-run. Hal Chase, perhaps the finest fielding first baseman ever, made the putout at first—then looked up to see Cobb unexpectedly storming toward third. Chase's hurried throw pulled third baseman George Moriarty off the bag. As Moriarty pirouetted, his back to the play, Ty kept coming, sliding home a split second ahead of the catcher's tag.

New York's frustration reached a climax in the third game. The Highlanders, vowing that Cobb would not be allowed to repeat his base-running antics, held him at bay until the seventh inning. But upon reaching first base, he again executed the bunt-and-run with Rossman. This time, as Ty stood on third base patting dust off his knickers, the frustrated Moriarty slammed the ball into the dirt. By the time the bounced ball fell back to earth and Moriarty had thrown it home, Ty had slid across the plate with another run.

The Ty Cobb that American League infielders came to fear and Bennett Park fans loved to cheer: clenched teeth, an explosion of dirt, and more often than not, another creatively crafted run or stolen base. (Opposite page) Philadelphia shortstop Jack Barry is the victim in this 1909 photograph.

This was thinking-man's baseball at its best. Professor Cobb, who had dismissed baseball players as "muscle-workers," would have undoubtedly approved of his son's cerebral style of play. Like a rotating ceiling fan, Ty's mind was constantly humming. With Matty McIntyre sidelined for the year with a broken ankle and the rest of the team channeling its energy into winning instead of bickering, Hughie Jennings' Tigers captured the pennant by 1$^1/_2$ games over Philadelphia.

For all intents and purposes, the race was decided on September 30 with a wild non-decision at Philadelphia, a game that Ty always regarded as the most thrilling of his career. Going into the game, the Tigers and Athletics were locked in a virtual tie for first place. After six innings Philadelphia held what looked to be an insurmountable 7–1 lead. But the Tigers chipped away, finally knotting the game at 8–8 when Ty walloped a 2-run homer in the ninth inning off ace southpaw Rube Waddell. The blast not only silenced the overflow crowd of 30,000 raucous fans at Columbia Park, according to legend it caused the Athletics' normally stoic manager, Connie Mack, to slide off the bench in shock and into a pile of bats.

The home run was another example of Cobb's heady approach to batting. Waddell, an eccentric hard thrower who was on his way to leading the league in strikeouts for the sixth straight season, had fired an inside fastball on his first pitch to Cobb. Ty took it for strike one. Figuring Ty was looking for a certain pitch, Waddell decided to "feed this cuckoo one in the same spot and get him in a hole." Instead, Ty turned on the pitch as if he had been expecting it all along—which he had.

35

DETROIT'S CHAMPIONS OF THE AMERICAN LEAGUE 1907.

EUBANKS	ROSSMAN	CRAWFORD	DONOVAN	MULLIN	WILLITS	PAYNE	KILLIAN
	D. JONES	DOWNS	COBB	COUGHLIN		SCHAEFER	E. JONES
	SEIVER	ARCHER		JENNINGS		SCHMIDT	O'LEARY
	O'BRIEN, Mascot.						

The 1907 American League champs. They would repeat the next two seasons.

Even with an unwieldy box camera in his hands and an unlikely subject in Sam Crawford, Ty was an avid amateur photographer. The pair was never as close as this pose suggests, except in the final batting statistics. During each of their three pennant-winning seasons Cobb and Crawford finished 1–2 in the league in slugging and total bases. Wahoo Sam won the home run title in 1907 and was runner-up to Cobb in RBI the following two seasons.

"I figured if I let the first one pass and make out I don't notice it and am looking for something else, you'll try to cross me up and shoot the next over the same spot," Ty explained to Waddell after the game. "I feel so sure, when the ball leaves your hand I jump back, take a toe-hold and swing."

"Kid," Waddell replied admiringly, "you had me doped a hundred percent right."

In the tenth the Tigers pushed across a run to go ahead, but the Athletics tied the score in their half of the inning. Then, in the bottom of the fourteenth, all hell broke loose. Philadelphia's Harry Davis hit a long fly ball to center. Just as Sam Crawford was getting ready to make the catch in front of the roped-off overflow, a pair of overzealous policemen caused him to drop the ball. The umpire ruled Davis out for interference, igniting a brawl among players, fans, and cops. At one point an officer started to arrest Bill Donovan, but after learning that the Tiger pitcher was a Philadelphia native, he took Claude Rossman into custody instead. Despite the commotion and threats, the umpire's decision stood. After order was restored, the next batter followed with a long base hit that would have scored Davis and won the game for Philadelphia. Instead, the teams battled in the dusk until it was declared a 9–9 draw after seventeen innings. The Tigers left

---

Diminutive Owen "Donie" Bush joined the Tigers in September 1908 and stayed 14 years. The popular switch-hitting shortstop from Indianapolis was an ideal set-up man for Cobb and Crawford, leading the league in walks 5 of his first 6 full seasons and stealing 400 career bases. Only Cobb stole more bases in a Detroit uniform.

37

On August 2, 1907, the Tigers faced Walter Johnson in his major-league debut. They got around on enough fastballs to win, 3–2, with Cobb beating out a bunt his first time up. Imagine how many pennants pitching-poor Detroit might have won during Cobb's prime with "The Big Train" on the mound, a fantasy that almost came true. Before the rawboned rookie signed a contract with Washington, a traveling salesman had written Frank Navin a glowing letter about Johnson's exploits in an Idaho semipro league. But Navin pigeonholed the correspondence in his rolltop desk and Johnson went on to win 416 games in 21 seasons for the Senators.

Frank Navin (sitting alongside Chicago catcher Billy Sullivan in 1908) joined Detroit as its business manager in 1904. Four years later the inveterate gambler reportedly won a coin flip with Bill Yawkey to become owner. Although he became the most influential owner in the American League and one of its wealthiest, his teams would continue to flop in the postseason until Mickey Cochrane and company finally delivered a championship in 1935. Five weeks later Navin died in a horseback-riding accident.

town with a razor-thin lead that they never relinquished, while Connie Mack complained to the end of his days about being gypped out of a pennant.

The Tigers' opponents in only the fourth "World's Series" played between the established National League and the upstart American League were the Chicago Cubs, a powerhouse that had won a still-standing major-league record 116 games in 1906 before unexpectedly succumbing to the crosstown White Sox in the Series. The Cubs had followed up with 107 wins in 1907 and were eager to avenge their embarrassing loss to the junior circuit. The Cubs were led by mounds-men Orvie Overall, Ed Reulbach, Jack Pfiester, and Three-Finger Brown, and an infield immortalized in verse: shortstop Joe Tinker, second baseman Johnny Evers, and first baseman-manager Frank Chance. (Third baseman Harry Steinfeldt, whose nonlyrical name was left out of Franklin P. Adams' famous ode, rounded out the quartet.)

For Tiger fans, all geeked up over the city's first pennant since the National League "Detroits" in 1887, the 1907 Series was a tremendous letdown. The Tigers, who led the majors in runs scored, managed but 6 tallies in 5 games against the Cubs' staff. Half of those came in the first game, when 25-game-winner Bill Donovan let a two-run lead slip away in the bottom of the ninth. The tying run scored when Charlie Schmidt dropped what should have been a game-ending third strike on pinch-hitter Del Howard. The game was called a 3–3 tie after twelve innings because of darkness, but they could have just as well canceled the rest of the Series for lack of interest. The Tigers went on to lose 4 straight to the Cubs, with demoralized Detroit fans staying away from Bennett Park in droves for the final 2 defeats. Cobb hit just .200 with only 1 run scored, no RBI, and no stolen bases. Sam Crawford, who had finished second to Cobb in batting during the regular season, was similarly stifled, hitting just .238. But the goat's horns really belonged to the catching duo of Charlie Schmidt and Fred Payne, who allowed 18 Chicago stolen bases and the momentum-shifting gaffe in game one.

The five-day Series was an abrupt, dismal climax to an otherwise exciting and stellar season for baseball's brightest new star. In 150 games Ty had hit .350 with 212 hits, 116 runs batted in, and 49 stolen bases. All were league highs. He had also signed a contract with Coca-Cola for his first commercial endorsement, a good gauge of his blossoming fame. Had there been a Most Valuable Player award in those days, he would have been the obvious choice. As it was, he was tickled to receive a handsome diamond-studded medal for winning the batting championship—a medal he had coveted since spotting it in a St. Louis jewelry store window at the start of the season. Two months shy of his twenty-first birthday, Ty would remain the youngest man to win a batting title until another Tiger outfielder, Al Kaline, came along a half-century later. Kaline would be exactly one day younger than Cobb when he won the batting championship in 1955.

Sportswriters had described the 1907 American League pennant race as "the greatest struggle in the history of baseball," but they ran out of adjectives the following summer, as both leagues featured suffocating races that weren't decided until the final day of the season. Once again the national spotlight fell on Ty, who—at least in uniform—responded in championship style. In a season dominated by pitchers, he won his second batting title with a .324 average, and became the only American Leaguer to knock in more than 100 runs. He also led in doubles, triples, and hits.

Off the field was another matter. Ty started the season by demanding a three-year contract at $5,000 per year, ending his holdout for a one-year deal at $4,000, plus an $800 bonus if he won the batting championship. In June he managed to get into another racial confrontation, punching a Black laborer named Fred Collins after Collins had yelled at Ty for accidentally stepping into freshly poured

Ty missed four games during the 1908 pennant race to travel back to Georgia to marry Charlotte "Charlie" Lombard, the 17-year-old daughter of a well-to-do Augusta businessman. Like many proper young ladies of the South, Mrs. Cobb was educated in a convent; staying married to Ty for some forty years undoubtedly qualified her for sainthood.

39

The Cobb cut.

The Tigers won the 1908 pennant with a 7–0 victory over the White Sox in Chicago, then returned home to a victory celebration through downtown streets. Players were feted in that new-fangled invention, the automobile.

40

asphalt outside the Pontchartrain Hotel in Detroit. Cobb was found guilty of assault and given a suspended sentence but wound up paying Collins seventy-five dollars to avoid a civil lawsuit. And then in early August, with first-place Detroit clinging to a one-game lead in the standings, he impulsively left the team to get married in Georgia. Who was more surprised was a tossup: his teammates, who were fighting to get back into the World Series, or management, which had not been informed of Ty's plans.

The bride was 17-year-old Charlotte Marion Lombard, the quiet, dark-haired daughter of a prominent Augusta businessman. Educated in a convent, "Charlie" nonetheless enjoyed the outdoors, particularly horseback riding. Ty had known her for at least a couple of years and proposed shortly after the 1907 World Series. The ceremony, performed on the afternoon of August 6, was witnessed by a handful of guests at the Lombard estate. A luncheon and then an evening banquet at the Hotel Genesta followed, after which Ty and his bride boarded a northbound train. Meanwhile, those back in Detroit pondered the unpredictable behavior of a young man who in just two years had changed from an ostracized rookie into the quintessential 800-pound gorilla. As one local writer rhetorically asked: "What can you do about it? The player is there with the goods on the diamond." When Ty rejoined the team a week later, a fine Sunday crowd at Bennett Park greeted the newlyweds with warm applause. Charlie accompanied her husband on the long eastern road trip that followed, during which time Ty was noticeably spaghetti-legged on the basepaths and his average dropped about 20 points.

All the same, Ty had enough vim to push the Tigers over the top. Fortified by the addition of rookies Ed Summers, a strapping right-hander who led the staff with 24 wins, and Donie Bush, a pint-sized shortstop who would be a favorite for the next thirteen summers, Detroit roared into the final weekend with Cleveland and Chicago clutching its tail. On Friday, October 2, Cobb scored the winning run in a 7–6 victory over St. Louis. Meanwhile, in one of the greatest clutch pitching performances ever, Cleveland's Addie Joss pitched a 1–0 perfect game against Chicago, offsetting "Big Ed" Walsh's brilliant 4-hit, 15-strikeout performance. However, Walsh—en route to a 40-win, 464-inning season—returned the next day to beat Cleveland, seriously damaging their chances.

The Tigers then moved into Chicago, losing Sunday to Doc White and Monday to Walsh. Cleveland blew a chance to move into first place when they lost to St. Louis. This set the stage for the final day of the season, with the Tigers up by half a game over Cleveland and Chicago. Because of the uneven number of games the contenders had played—current rules did not require rained-out games to be made up—the winner of the Tigers-White Sox game on Tuesday, October 6, would claim the pennant by a half a game; the loser would finish third behind Cleveland.

Earlier in the season, White Sox fans had awarded Cobb a loving cup for being their favorite opposing ballplayer—an irony that undoubtedly troubled more than one disappointed Chicagoan as the Tigers pounded out a decisive 7–0 victory at South Side Park to grab their second flag in a row. Ty was at his best, banging out a triple and 2 singles, driving in 3 runs, and forcing Walsh into a wild throw that allowed another run to score. Two days later, jubilant Tiger fans greeted their conquering heroes with a motorcade through downtown streets.

That same day, the Chicago Cubs and New York Giants faced off at the Polo Grounds to determine the National League winner. Two weeks earlier, in what remains the biggest goof in baseball history, young Fred Merkle had cost the Giants a victory—and ultimately the pennant—when he failed to touch second base on what should have been a game-winning hit against these very Cubs. In a storm of controversy, the Giants' victory was rescinded and the tie game was rescheduled for the end of the season. In what amounted to a one-game playoff, the opportunistic Cubs then went on to beat Christy Mathewson, 4–2, for their third straight pennant.

41

While still in the minor leagues Ty originated the now-common practice of swinging three bats in the on-deck circle.

"These are the saddest of possible words: Tinker to Evers to Chance." Thus begins newspaperman Franklin P. Adams' enduring bit of double play doggerel, which immortalized three-quarters of the Chicago Cubs' infield. Shortstop Joe Tinker (left) and second baseman Johnny Evers were bound together in verse, but off the field they never spoke to each other. Nonetheless, they were an integral part of the Cubs' success, which included 4 pennants between 1906 and 1910. During this five-year period the Cubs—who relied on tight defense, team speed, and suffocating pitching—averaged 108 wins a season. Managing this mini-dynasty was first baseman Frank ("The Peerless Leader") Chance, who is conferring with Hughie Jennings and umpires before a World Series game at Bennett Park (bottom). The Cubs' 2 Series wins over the Tigers in 1907 and 1908 remain their last national championships.

The World's Greatest Ballplayer

Third-place Pittsburgh finished just one game back. Thus ended the two closest three-team races in big-league history.

Compared to two draining, circus-like races, the World Series between the survivors fizzled instead of sizzled. For the second year in a row it took the Cubs only five days and five games to dispose of the Tigers, although this time Detroit managed a win instead of a tie. That came in the third game, when Ty had his finest postseason game ever: 4 hits in 5 at-bats, including a pair of RBI. In the ninth inning of the Tigers' 8–3 victory, Cobb put on a show for Chicago fans, announcing beforehand that he would steal second and third, which he did. The Cubs finally quieted Cobb when he was gunned down trying to steal home. Ty's silence grew deeper as the Tigers returned home to endure consecutive shutout losses to Three-Finger Brown and Orvie Overall, which closed out another disappointing Series. "Don't feel too badly about it," Hughie Jennings told his disconsolate players afterwards. "We were beaten again by a great team."

Although the Tigers lost their second fall classic in a row, Ty had a better go of it, hitting .368 against the same Cub staff that had handcuffed him a year earlier. The improvement underscored what helped make Ty the hitter he was: the ability to dissect a pitcher's success against him and then, over repeated encounters, to successfully adjust to that pitcher's style. In his first 13 at-bats against Doc White in 1905–06, for example, Ty had gone hitless. But after solving White's curveball, he extracted a .381 average from the Chicago dentist.

Another example is Cobb's success against the Washington Senators' Walter Johnson, the long-armed Kansan who made his major-league debut against the Tigers in 1907. Ty faced Johnson more often that any other pitcher. Although it was occasionally reported that Johnson, arguably the greatest pitcher of all time, more or less "owned" Ty, he in fact hit .366 against Johnson—just one point under his lifetime average. (The rest of the American League hit a combined .226 against Johnson during his remarkable 21-year career.) Few of Ty's hits off "the Big Train" were for extra bases, but that's because Cobb realized even a skilled place hitter like himself had an almost impossible task getting around on Johnson's fabled fastball. Ty decided to cut down on his swing and concentrate on spanking the ball to the opposite field. Doubles and triples are nice, he reasoned, but he could always steal his way around to second or third.

The result was a remarkable consistency. Slumps were infrequent; he rarely went hitless for more than two or three consecutive games. His strategy for ending a dry spell was simple. In batting practice he would concentrate on bunting the ball back to the mound, gradually increasing the arc of his swing until he was whistling hard ground balls and line drives up the middle. "After a few such sessions," he explained, "my timing returned and my slump went away."

On the flip side, Ty compiled the league's longest hitting streak on five occasions, the most by any player: 1906 (25 games), 1911 (40), 1917 (35), 1926 (21), and 1927 (21). For his career Ty batted

As was true with most big-league parks at the turn of the century, the outfield at Bennett Park resembled a cow pasture. Nonetheless, Cobb played his position with skill, using his speed and quickness to good advantage. Until he ruined it by fooling around with pitching, his arm was better than average (he threw out 30 base runners in 1907). His 392 career outfield assists is second only to Tris Speaker. He also committed 271 errors, more than any outfielder in history.

Ty played center field throughout his Tiger career, except for the three pennant-winning seasons when he was stationed in right. The reason, left fielder Matty McIntyre, is pictured in this 1908 photo. Hughie Jennings decided that placing Sam Crawford in center field between the two feuding players would help maintain harmony on the team—and he was right. (Rising behind the outfield fence are "wildcat stands," which enterprising property owners around Bennett Park erected with impunity, charging a nickel or a dime for a seat.)

.370 at home and .363 on the road, and he hit southpaws at a .347 clip. No matter how one twists and folds the numbers, the simple, unavoidable fact that pitchers had to deal with for so many seasons was that Ty could flat out hit—against left-handers, right-handers, speedballers, curveballers, spitballers, at home and on the road.

Hungry to erase their two postseason blemishes, the Tigers roared to an unprecedented third straight pennant in 1909, winning a then league-record 98 games in the process. They ultimately beat out Philadelphia by 3¹/₂ games, thanks to a revamped infield, George Mullin's major-league-leading 29 victories, and Ty's Triple Crown season. Ty hit .377 with 9 home runs and 107 RBI. But, as rattled pitchers, befuddled infielders, and nervous catchers were learning, a base hit usually was just the start of their problems with Cobb. Pitchers couldn't even intentionally walk him, for once Ty had arrived at a base, odds were that he wouldn't stay long. "Infielders didn't know what the hell he'd do next," said Philadelphia catcher Rube Bressler, "and neither did he until the last split second. You couldn't figure Cobb. It was impossible."

That year Ty fully arrived as a base runner and a base stealer, leading the circuit in runs scored and setting a modern individual

Ty was only three when Denton "Cy" Young broke into the major leagues in 1890. The steel-armed pitcher, who won a staggering 511 games (and lost another 313), despised Cobb, which made Ty's success against him (a career .340 average) that much harder to swallow. Their encounters were characterized by a stream of obscenities, challenges, and brush-back pitches. "His trouble is he takes life too seriously," Young complained before retiring to his Ohio farm in 1911. "Cobb is going at it too hard."

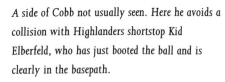

Calamity had a way of finding Hugh Ambrose Jennings, who survived a near-fatal beaning, a head-first dive into an empty swimming pool, and a car accident that killed two others. Nonetheless, the generously freckled Irishman had a "smile that echoed," said umpire Tim Hurst. Although he was licensed to practice law in his home state of Pennsylvania, he preferred the primitive theatrics of the coaching box.

record with 76 stolen bases. All of his home runs were inside-the-parkers, putting his distinctive running style on display for the fifteen or so seconds it took him to circumnavigate the bases. "He ran like a pacer," Ken Smith wrote, "never lifting his knees much, his body weaving from side to side and his hands standing out like fins. He could run like a streak with his head over his shoulder, watching the ball, and he never needed a coach."

Ty's scorched-earth approach to base-running featured an assortment of slides, including his famous "fadeaway." Before Cobb, runners typically had slid straight into a bag. Ty perfected the art of pulling his body away from an infielder's tag and tucking his toe into a distant corner of the base as he slid past. At other times he used the "down-and-up" slide, hitting the dirt and then bounding up, running. He was a wonder to watch, unless you happened to be the poor soul he was bearing down on. "Hold onto your pants," Germany Schaefer would yell out, "or he'll steal those too!"

According to catcher Henry Beckendorf, who joined the Tigers in 1909, his contortionist teammate was "the hardest man in the league to get. He is fast and he can throw his body like an eel. You can't figure on what side he is coming. It seems as though he can throw his body while he is diving at the base. You can make a pass for him on one side and he simply jerks by on the other. I really do not think that Ty ever tried to spike a baseman intentionally. He comes in so fast and throws his body so quickly that he cannot figure on the position of the baseman."

That was Ty's argument after one of the most controversial episodes of his career: the spiking of Philadelphia third baseman Frank Baker on August 24, 1909. That afternoon the first-place Athletics, who led the Tigers by a single game, began a crucial three-game set at

A side of Cobb not usually seen. Here he avoids a collision with Highlanders shortstop Kid Elberfeld, who has just booted the ball and is clearly in the basepath.

Bennett Park. In the bottom of the first, Ty walked and stole second. As Sam Crawford took a fourth ball, Ty suddenly lit out for third. The catcher's throw to third baseman Frank Baker had him easily. When Cobb hook-slid to his left in an attempt to avoid Baker's bare-handed tag, his right foot flashed out and nicked the infielder's forearm. Although Baker's wound was little more than a scratch and he stayed in the game, Connie Mack and all of Philadelphia went ballistic. Mack called Cobb the dirtiest player in the history of baseball, while others talked of running him out of the league. Although a photograph clearly showed Baker awkwardly leaning over the bag, and league president Ban Johnson declared Ty to have been within his rights on the play, Philadelphia sportswriters didn't let the issue die. A minor scrape quickly evolved into a case of felonious assault. What really upset them was that the Tigers had swept the series, capturing a lead they never surrendered. The controversy produced an outpouring of letters with Philadelphia postmarks, many threatening death and dismemberment when Ty next visited the City of Brotherly Love.

The Baker spiking once again focused attention onto Ty's spirited play, which disgruntled opponents were increasingly describing as dirty. It was, complained many, of a piece with his abrasive personality.

When he was seven Mordecai Peter Centennial Brown stuck his right hand into his uncle's corn shredder. He emerged with a severed index finger and a paralyzed little finger—and a natural knuckleball. "Three Finger" Brown went on to accumulate 239 lifetime wins, including 13 over rival pitching great Christy Mathewson. Brown, who set a record with a miniscule 1.04 ERA in 1906, completely mystified the Tigers during the 1907 and 1908 World Series, shutting them out for 20 innings and winning 3 games—one for each digit.

47

Lou Criger, who caught Cy Young in Cleveland and Boston, was another gritty player who took advantage of every opportunity to agitate Cobb. Unlike many of his contemporaries, the veteran backstop generally held his own against the game's most aggressive base runner, although in this 1909 shot (right) Ty has managed to slide in safely under Criger's unprotected shins while umpire Billy Evans rushes in to make the call.

According to Detroit catcher Henry Beckendorf, his contortionist teammate was "the hardest man in the league to get. He is fast and he can throw his body like an eel."

48

Cornelius McGillicuddy, better known as Connie Mack, was born during the Civil War, began managing his Philadelphia Athletics shortly after the Spanish-American War, and was still managing them at the start of the Korean War in 1950. A lean, dignified man who was never called anything but "Mr. Mack," he won and lost more games than any manager in history. After the Baker incident, Mack called Ty the dirtiest player ever. Some thought Mack was guilty of sour grapes because Cobb's heroics helped the Athletics lose close races to the Tigers in 1907 and 1909.

The Baker spiking, as captured by Detroit News photographer William Kuenzel. The incident caused The Sporting News to editorialize: "The list of [Cobb's] victims is too long to attribute the injury of all to accident or the awkwardness of the victim." Responded Joe S. Jackson of the Detroit Free Press: "Cobb is being criticized, right and left, and being pictured as a murderer of his fellows, mostly by men who have not seen the plays on which he is being attacked."

"His trouble is he takes life too seriously," complained the venerable Cy Young. "Cobb is going at it too hard."

Ty never made any apologies about his aggressiveness or intimidating tactics. "When I played ball," he stressed in his autobiography, "I didn't play for fun. To me it wasn't parcheesi played under parcheesi rules. Baseball is a red-blooded sport for red-blooded men. It's no pink tea, and mollycoddles had better stay out. It's a contest and everything that implies, a struggle for supremacy, a survival for the fittest. Every man in the game, from the minors on up, is not only fighting against the other side, but he's trying to hold onto his own job against those on his own bench who'd love to take it away. Why deny this? Why minimize it? Why not boldly admit it?"

Ty had had much the same Darwinian philosophy as a minor leaguer in Augusta and Anniston, and no one had complained. But then, no one really cared about the bushes. It was a different story in big-league cities, where dozens of sportswriters, eager to beat deadlines and the competition, daily manufactured reams of copy out of whole cloth. The most damaging of these was the allegation that Ty filed his spikes. The story was fabricated by New York writers in 1908 when a couple of Detroit players—Germany Schaefer probably was one of them—joked around on the bench before a game with the Highlanders. Subscribing to Mark Twain's philosophy to never let the truth get in the way of a good story, writers such as Bugs Baer turned Cobb into a villain, then used the spike filing fiction as an example of his take-no-prisoners approach to the game. When Ty clipped Baker a year later, it was already an article of faith among many that he sharpened his spikes to a razor's edge before each game, which presumably made it easier for him to disembowel innocent infielders.

Although Ty appreciated the psychological effect of the sharpened-spikes stories, choosing not to discount them until after he had retired, he always bristled when described as a dirty player. He played hard, as did most players, albeit with more flair and effectiveness. Like any player protecting his place on the diamond, he settled quarrels in time-honored fashion. Head-hunting pitchers like Carl Mays and Dutch Leonard might suddenly find themselves fielding a

Cobb Wept Because He Had Spiked Barry.

49

When the Tigers next played the Athletics in Philadelphia after the Baker incident, hundreds of policemen were on hand to guard Cobb from venomous fans. Despite the death threats, Ty played with customary gusto, at one point cutting Jack Barry's leg with a hard slide into second. As Barry left the field for stitches, the Philadelphia shortstop indicated to fans that the spiking was not intentional. This cartoon in the Detroit Saturday Night would have you believe that Cobb later blubbered over the episode in his hotel room, which would have been way out of character.

50

Charles Conlon, an amateur shutterbug, took what many regard as the greatest baseball action photograph. One afternoon in 1909, Conlon—a friend of Highlanders' third baseman, Jimmy Austin—was stationed along the left field foul line at Hilltop Park when Cobb suddenly took off for third. Austin, who had moved in to guard against a bunt, awkwardly backed into the bag just as Ty arrived with customary fury. Conlon, more concerned with his friend's health than shooting a photograph, froze as Austin toppled over on his face. Austin was unhurt, but in the excitement Conlon couldn't remember whether he had tripped his box camera. To be safe, he changed the plates. That night Conlon developed the film at home and discovered what he had inadvertently captured.

drag bunt along the first-base line, giving Cobb a clear shot at stomping on their toes or hip-checking them into the stands. Or, on plays at the plate, catchers who strategically placed their iron masks in the base path might one day have their vital organs squeezed into pulp by a pair of scissored legs. Cobb, who admitted to spiking only two men deliberately in twenty-four years, normally didn't go out of his way to hurt anyone. But he also knew the rules of the game, both written and unwritten, and played accordingly.

"They always talk about Cobb playing dirty, trying to spike guys and all," said Sam Crawford. "Cobb never tried to spike anybody. The base line belongs to the runner. If the infielders get in the way, that's their lookout. Infielders are supposed to watch out and take care of themselves."

Opponents echoed Crawford. "I wouldn't say Cobb played dirty," said Joe Wood, who broke into the big leagues with Boston in 1908. "Cobb always told me and other fellows he played against, 'All you've got to do is give me room to get in there and it'll be all right, but if you don't give me room I'll cut my way in.' Fair enough." Ray Fisher, a Vermont farm boy who joined the Highlanders in 1910, also remembered Cobb as a tough but fair competitor. "I pitched against him a lot," he said. "I know one time I had to cover first, and I had trouble getting my foot on the bag. I had my leg out. He jumped over the bag. He could've stepped on me. He had a perfect right to." Of course, avoiding a confrontation didn't make for good copy, so innocuous but telling episodes like this never made it into the papers.

After the Baker spiking, Ty needed more controversy like he needed an extra set of elbows. But fewer than two weeks later, he got into a late-hours argument with the Black elevator operator inside Cleveland's Hotel Euclid. Thinking the man was "uppity" and "insolent" Ty slapped him in the face, which prompted a Black night watchman named George Stansfield to join the fray. After Stansfield hit him with his nightstick, Ty pulled a knife and slashed at him. Badly cut, Stansfield managed to knock Cobb silly with a blow to his head, at which point hotel employees moved in. By the time the incident came to light, the Tigers had left town, leaving behind a civil lawsuit and criminal charges. Frank Navin's attorneys quickly got Stansfield to settle out of court and, in late November, plea-bargained Cobb's case down to the lesser charge of assault and battery, for which he was fined $100. But for the rest of the regular season and the World Series, Ty had to avoid traveling through Ohio for fear of being arrested.

Death threats in Philadelphia and an arrest warrant in Cleveland—now *this* was the Ty Cobb the press and the public loved to hate. But, as he would so many times during his career, Ty used the mounting controversy as a form of amphetamine. Nothing stirred him to the heights of his ability more than the idea that the world was against him. That September in Philadelphia, with hundreds of policemen on hand to protect him from the record number of fans, some of whom were reportedly there to shoot him dead, Ty played with his customary fervor as the Tigers escaped town with their lead—and necks—intact. On the evening following the first game, Ty emerged from the hotel lobby, looking to take his usual after-dinner walk. Before he knew it, he was surrounded by scores of angry Philadelphians. Rather than retreat, Ty lit his cigar and slowly strolled down the sidewalk, parting the hostile crowd like Moses splitting the Red Sea. Despite the mumbling and curses in his wake, no one dared touch him. You didn't have to like the cocky son of a bitch, some in the crowd grudgingly agreed, but you had to admire his style. Before the series ended Cobb had won over the fans, diving over the outfield rope into the overflow crowd to make a circus catch of a fly ball, then

51

Ty takes a breather at Cleveland. During a series there in September 1909, he stabbed a hotel watchman, causing Cleveland police to seek an arrest warrant to charge him with felonious assault. The mess wasn't cleared up until late November, meaning Ty had to avoid traveling through Ohio for the rest of the season and the World Series.

COBB VS. THE AMERICAN LEAGUE

The following list, courtesy of Larry Amman, shows Cobb's lifetime batting average against all American League pitchers that he had at least 20 at-bats against. In the case of Hall of Famers (identified by an asterisk), his performance is listed regardless of how few at-bats he had against them. Note that the teams and seasons following a pitcher's name includes only those years where he faced Cobb.

Pitcher-Team(s)		AB	H	Avg.
Nick Altrock+	Chi 1905–09, Was 1909–24	49	18	.367
Doc Ayers	Was 1913–19	66	25	.379
Jim Bagby	Cle 1916–22	118	47	.398
Bill Bailey+	StL 1907–12	66	18	.273
Stan Baumgartner+	Phi 1924–26	23	4	.174
Bill Bayne	StL 1919–24, Cle 1928	36	5	.139
Hugh Bedient	Bos 1912–14	28	16	.571
*Chief Bender	Phi 1905–14, Chi 1925	82	30	.366
Joe Benz	Chi 1911–19	51	14	.275
Heinie Berger	Cle 1907–10	20	9	.450
Fred Blanding	Cle 1910–14	38	17	.447
Ted Blankenship	Chi 1922–28	50	17	.340
Joe Boehling+	Was 1912–16, Cle 1916–20	38	17	.447
Garland Buckeye+	Was 1918, Cle 1925–28	26	6	.231
Fred Burchell+	Bos 1907–09	20	5	.250
Bullet Joe Bush	Phi 1912–17, Bos 1918–21, NY 1922–24, StL 1925, Was 1926	152	58	.382
Ray Caldwell	NY 1910–18, Bos 1919, Cle 1919–21	120	45	.375
*Jack Chesbro	NY 1905–09, Bos 1909	54	23	.426
Eddie Cicotte	Bos 1908–12, Chi 1912–20	143	54	.378
Ray Collins+	Bos 1909–15	112	35	.313
Rip Collins	NY 1920–21, Bos 1922, Det 1927	33	12	.364
Sarge Connally	Chi 1921–28	42	14	.333
Jack Coombs	Phi 1906–14	73	29	.397
Fritz Coumbe	Bos 1914, Cle 1914–19	30	13	.433
*Stan Coveleski	Phi 1912, Cle 1916–24, Was 1925–27, NY 1928	163	59	.362
Dave Danforth+	Phi 1911–12, Chi 1916–19, StL 1922–25	77	22	.286
Dave Davenport	StL 1916–19	35	12	.343
Dixie Davis	Chi 1915, StL 1920–26	57	13	.228
Jimmy Dygert	Phi 1905–10	41	14	.341
Howard Ehmke	Bos 1923–26, Phi 1926	28	11	.393
*Red Faber	Chi 1914–28	164	55	.335
Cy Falkenberg	Was 1905–08, Cle 1908–13, Phi 1917	58	23	.397
Alex Ferguson	NY 1918–21, 1925, Bos 1922–25, Was 1925–26	50	26	.520
Ray Fisher	NY 1910–17	59	16	.271
Russ Ford	NY 1909–13	71	32	.451
Rube Foster	Bos 1913–17	49	15	.306

+ Left-hander

52

Pitcher-Team(s)		AB	H	Avg.
Curt Fullerton	Bos 1921–25	23	8	.348
Bert Gallia	Was 1912–17, StL 1918–20	58	20	.345
Milt Gaston	NY 1924, StL 1925–27,			
	Was 1928	40	15	.375
Fred Glade	StL 1905–07, NY 1908	30	5	.167
Bill Graham+	StL 1908–10	41	13	.317
Dolly Gray+	Was 1909–11	57	21	.368
Sam Gray	Phi 1924–26	30	13	.433
Vean Gregg+	Cle 1911–14, Bos 1914–16,			
	Phi 1918, Was 1925	68	25	.368
*Clark Griffith	NY 1905–08, Was 1912–14	4	1	.250
Bob Groom	Was 1909–13, StL 1916–17,			
	Cle 1918	95	26	.274
*Lefty Grove	Phi 1925–26	15	5	.333
Rip Hagerman	Cle 1914–16	24	10	.417
Sea Lion Hall	Bos 1909–13	26	11	.423
Earl Hamilton+	StL 1911–17	100	38	.380
Harry Harper+	Was 1913–19, Bos 1920,			
	NY 1921	75	28	.373
Slim Harriss	Phi 1920–26, Bos 1926–28	88	31	.352
Bob Hasty	Phi 1919–24	45	11	.244
Fred Heimach+	Phi 1920–26, Bos 1926,			
	NY 1928	36	13	.361
Otto Hess+	Cle 1905–08	43	12	.279
Bill Hogg	NY 1905–08	39	17	.436
Ken Hollaway	Det 1927–28	21	9	.429
Harry Howell	StL 1905–10	47	11	.234
*Waite Hoyt	Bos 1919–20, NY 1921–28	98	26	.265
Willis Hudlin	Cle 1926–28	21	5	.238
Tom Hughes	NY 1906–10	53	20	.377
*Walter Johnson	Was 1905–27	328	120	.366
Sad Sam Jones	Cle 1914–15, Bos 1916–21,			
	NY 1922–26, StL 1927,			
	Was 1928	121	38	.314
*Addie Joss	Cle 1905–10	94	25	.266
George Kahler	Cle 1910–14	37	12	.324
Ray Keating	NY 1912–18	24	8	.333
Dickie Kerr+	Chi 1919–25	47	16	.340
Ray Kolp	StL 1921–24	22	6	.273
Dutch Leonard+	Bos 1913–18	67	25	.373
Dixie Leverett	Chi 1922–26	30	14	.467
Glenn Liebhardt	Cle 1906–09	27	7	.259
*Ted Lyons	Chi 1923–28	75	24	.320
Firpo Marberry	Was 1923–28	26	8	.308
Carl Mays	Bos 1915–19, NY 1919–23	116	39	.336
Jake Miller+	Cle 1924–28	25	6	.240
Willie Mitchell+	Cle 1909–16	58	20	.345
George Mogridge+	Chi 1911–12, NY 1915–20,			
	Was 1921–25, StL 1925	137	47	.343
Cy Morgan	StL 1905–07, Bos 1907–09,			
	Phi 1909–12	32	10	.313
Guy Morton	Cle 1914–24	71	19	.268
Rollie Naylor	Phi 1917–24	64	33	.516
Doc Newton+	NY 1905–09	25	10	.400
Buck O'Brien	Bos 1911–13, Chi 1913	22	9	.409
Al Orth	NY 1905–09	23	9	.391
Frank Owen	Chi 1905–09	20	7	.350

+ Left-hander

Continued on next page

George Sisler made his professional mark as one of the game's greatest hitters, but as a collegiate pitcher he won 50 games without a loss for the University of Michigan. The left-hander started as a pitcher with the St. Louis Browns in 1915, splitting 8 decisions before shifting full time to first base. In one of those games, a complete-game 6–5 loss to Detroit on September 5, Sisler held Ty hitless in 5 at-bats. As a gimmick Sisler and Cobb pitched against each other in the final game of the 1918 season. Sisler pitched one scoreless inning, then smacked a double in his only time at bat against Ty.

Philadelphia's Eddie Plank, the game's winningest southpaw until Warren Spahn held Ty to a .343 career average. Plank was a fidgety curveballer who seemingly waited forever before delivering a pitch. "I hated to see Plank out there as much as any man I faced," said Ty.

54

COBB VS. THE AMERICAN LEAGUE, continued

Pitcher-Team(s)		AB	H	Avg.
Casey Patten+	Was 1905–08, Bos 1908	24	11	.458
Barney Pelty	StL 1905–12, Was 1912	43	20	.465
*Herb Pennock	Phi 1912–15, Bos 1915–22,			
	NY 1923–28	142	52	.366
Scott Perry	StL 1915, Phi 1918–21	34	17	.500
Bill Piercy	NY 1917–21, Bos 1922–24	33	14	.424
*Eddie Plank	Phi 1905–14, StL 1916–17	201	69	.343
Jack Powell	NY 1905, StL 1905–12	70	24	.343
Jack Quinn	NY 1909–12, 1919–21,			
	Chi 1918, Bos 1922–25,			
	Phi 1925–26	91	43	.473
Bob Rhoads	Cle 1905–09	79	24	.304
Ed Rommel	Phi 1920–26	89	31	.348
Dutch Ruether+	Was 1925–26, NY 1926–27	28	11	.393
*Red Ruffing	Bos 1924–28	26	6	.231
Allan Russell	NY 1915–19, Bos 1919–22,			
	Was 1923–25	69	23	.333
Reb Russell+	Chi 1913–19	60	23	.383
*Babe Ruth	Bos 1914–19, NY 1920–28	67	22	.328
Jim Scott	Chi 1909–17	64	28	.438
Joe Shaute+	Cle 1922–28	64	19	.297
Jim Shaw	Was 1913–21	61	28	.459
Bob Shawkey	Phi 1913–15, NY 1915–27	140	59	.421
Urban Shocker	NY 1916–17, 1925–28,			
	StL 1918–24	95	35	.368
Ernie Shore	Bos 1914–17, NY 1919–20	52	22	.423
*George Sisler+	StL 1915–26	6	0	.000
Charlie Smith	Was 1905–09, Bos 1909–11	29	14	.483
Frank Smith	Chi 1905–10, Bos 1910–11	74	22	.297
Allan Sothoron	StL 1914–21, Bos 1921,			
	Cle 1921–22	56	28	.500
Jesse Tannehill+	Bos 1905–08, Was 1908–09	27	10	.370
Tommy Thomas	Chi 1926–28	48	16	.333
Hank Thormahlen+	NY 1917–20, Bos 1921	31	9	.290
Sloppy Thurston	StL 1923, Chi 1923–26,			
	Was 1927	68	26	.382
George Uhle	Cle 1919–28	101	37	.366
Elam Vangilder	StL 1919–27, Det 1928	81	32	.395
*Rube Waddell	Phi 1905–07, StL 1908–10	76	27	.355
Dixie Walker	Was 1909–12	32	15	.469
*Ed Walsh	Chi 1905–16	123	42	.341
Jack Warhop	NY 1908–15	110	49	.445
Carl Weilman+	StL 1912–20	97	23	.237
Doc White+	Chi 1905–13	139	48	.345
Lefty Williams+	Chi 1916–20	59	15	.254
Hal Wiltse+	Bos 1926–28, StL 1928	26	13	.500
Ernie Wingard+	StL 1924–27	37	18	.486
George Winter	Bos 1905–08	28	14	.500
Smokey Joe Wood	Bos 1908–15, Cle 1917–20	70	30	.429
John Wyckoff	Phi 1913–16, Bos 1916–18	38	13	.342
*Cy Young	Bos 1907, Cle 1909–11	97	33	.340
Tom Zachary+	Phi 1918, Was 1919–25,			
	1927–28, StL 1926–27, NY 1928	111	37	.333
Paul Zahniser	Was 1923–24, Bos 1925–26	24	7	.292

+ Left-hander

Ty considered Plank's Hall of Fame teammate, Albert "Chief" Bender, the "brainiest pitch-er" he ever saw. Bender was a 6-foot-2 half-Chippewa Indian with a high leg kick and an overhand delivery that made him seem even bigger on the mound. Ty, who had no shortage of gray matter himself, touched the right-hander for a .366 average during the 11 seasons they faced each other.

offering five dollars to the man whose straw boater he had crushed. He even shook hands with Baker after stealing third base.

The Tigers faced the Pittsburgh Pirates in one of the most eager-ly anticipated World Series, giving the country a chance to see the game's two greatest players go head-to-head. In one corner, of course, was Cobb, the American League's top batsman, base stealer, and head-line maker. In the other was his National League counterpart, short-stop Honus Wagner, a veteran of the first modern World Series in 1903, when Pittsburgh was upset by the Boston Pilgrims. The 35-year-old "Flying Dutchman," who had just won his seventh of an eventual eight batting championships, was an unlikely looking hero. He was squat, chunky, and extremely bowlegged, as if his pins had buckled from carrying around all that talent. His large hands hung like baked hams from his long limbs, but he had tremendous range and a rocket launcher for a throwing arm. Wagner also ran the bases with as much success as Cobb. In fact, Wagner would retire in 1917 with 722 career steals, a National League mark that would stand until Lou Brock broke it in 1967. Almost everyone had a good word to say about Wagner, a good-humored, sociable man who enjoyed drinking beer and spinning stories.

Pittsburgh shortstop John "Honus" Wagner often is mentioned in the same breath as Cobb and Ruth as being the greatest ballplayer of all-time. A career .327 hitter, his 8 batting titles are second only to Cobb's 12. "The Flying Dutchman" had more in common with Cobb than his admirers cared to admit. Like Ty, he was a bigot—albeit a quiet one—and also superstitious. For instance, he hated being photographed with his favorite bats, believing the camera drained them of base-hit potential. In fact, moments after hearing the shutter close on this particular picture, the startled *Wagner* flew into a rage and flung his now useless bat at the photographer.

Cobb and Wagner met before the start of the 1909 Series and discovered one other common denominator: both used a split-hands grip.

56

It was a rugged Series. At one point George Moriarty, the fearless third baseman that Detroit had acquired at mid-season from New York, snatched the hat off Pittsburgh's Tommy Leach and unaccountably started whacking him over his bald head with it. And game six, which Detroit won in dramatic fashion to knot the Series at three games apiece, featured several spikings and collisions. But the most enduring episode was one that, like many stories involving Cobb, is more imagination than fact.

According to legend, Ty reached base in the first inning of the first game and immediately yelled to Wagner: "Hey, Krauthead, I'm coming down on the next pitch!" Then, the story continues, Ty set off for second, where Wagner impassively put the young pup in his place by slapping the ball into his face and knocking out a couple of teeth.

Such braggadocio certainly wouldn't have been out of character for Cobb, who during his short career had already endeared himself to the opposition by often broadcasting his intentions before stealing a base. But, like Babe Ruth's famous "called shot" in the 1932 World Series, the incident was a postgame invention, something that its authors decided would help illustrate the "comeuppance" the brash

SERIES OF DISAPPOINTMENTS

Much to the chagrin of teammates, fans, sportswriters—and most of all, to himself—Cobb never was able to break loose and dominate play in a World Series in the same fashion that he did during the regular season. Still, his composite performance in three dead-ball World Series (a .262 average in 17 games) compares favorably with those of fellow Hall of Famers Stan Musial (.256 and 1 home run in 23 games), Ted Williams (5 singles and a .200 mark in his lone World Series), and Willie Mays (.239, no home runs, and only 6 RBI in 20 games).

Why the lackluster numbers for Cobb? Beyond the obvious fact that the Tigers were facing one of the truly great pitching staffs of all time in the Chicago Cubs, Ty always maintained that his lack of experience and maturity contributed. After all, he was just twenty-two when he played in his *last* World Series game. Even a storied post-season performer like Babe Ruth (.326 with 15 home runs in 41 games) needed time to gain his stride. Ruth, in his first 17 World Series games (as a pitcher with Boston in 1915–16 and 1918, and then as an outfielder with New York in 1921–23), hit a collective .188 with just 1 home run and 15 strikeouts in 48 at-bats! However, to be completely fair to Ruth, it should be noted that during this period he also won all three of his Series starts.

The following chart breaks down Cobb's postseason record on a game-by-game basis, including date, result, and the pitchers he faced.

1907 vs. CHICAGO

Game-Date	Result	Pitcher(s)	AB	R	H	2B	3B	HR	RBI	BB	SO	SB	HBP
1/Oct. 8	3–3 tie	Overall, Reulbach	5	0	0	0	0	0	0	0	0	0-0	0
2/Oct. 9	CHI 3–1	Pfiester	3	0	1	0	0	0	0	0	0	0-0	1
3/Oct. 10	CHI 5–1	Reulbach	4	0	1	0	0	0	0	0	1	0-0	0
4+/Oct. 11	CHI 6–1	Overall	4	1	1	0	1	0	0	0	0	0-0	0
5+/Oct. 12	CHI 2–0	Brown	4	0	1	0	0	0	0	0	2	0-1	0
		Totals	20	1	4	0	1	0	0	0	3	0-1	1

1908 vs. CHICAGO

Game-Date	Result	Pitcher(s)	AB	R	H	2B	3B	HR	RBI	BB	SO	SB	HBP
1+/Oct. 10	CHI 10–6	Reulbach, Overall, Brown	4	2	2	0	0	0	1	0	0	0-0	0
2/Oct. 11	CHI 6–1	Overall	4	0	1	0	0	0	1	0	0	0-0	0
3/Oct. 12	DET 8–3	Pfiester, Reulbach	5	1	4	1	0	0	2	0	0	2-3	0
4+/Oct. 13	CHI 3–0	Brown	3	0	0	0	0	0	0	0	1	0-0	0
5+/Oct. 14	CHI 2–0	Overall	3	0	0	0	0	0	0	1	1	0-0	0
		Totals	19	3	7	1	0	0	4	1	2	2-3	0

1909 vs. PITTSBURGH

Game-Date	Result	Pitcher(s)	AB	R	H	2B	3B	HR	RBI	BB	SO	SB	HBP
1/Oct. 8	PIT 4–1	Adams	3	1	0	0	0	0	0	1	0	1-1	0
2/Oct. 9	DET 7–2	Camnitz, Willis	3	1	1	0	0	0	0	1	0	1-1	0
3+/Oct. 11	PIT 8–6	Maddox	5	0	2	1	0	0	2	0	1	0-0	0
4+/Oct. 12	DET 5–0	Leifield, Phillippe	3	0	1	1	0	0	2	0	0	0-1	1
5/Oct. 13	PIT 8–4	Adams	4	1	1	0	0	0	0	0	0	0-0	0
6+/Oct. 14	DET 5–4	Willis, Camnitz, Phillippe	4	0	1	1	0	0	1	0	1	0-0	0
7+/Oct. 16	PIT 8–0	Adams	4	0	0	0	0	0	0	0	0	0-0	0
		Totals	26	3	6	3	0	0	5	2	2	2-3	1

+ Game played in Detroit

and controversial young star was expected to receive from the beloved Pittsburgh paterfamilias.

Based on contemporary newspaper reports, the truth was more prosaic. In the fifth inning of the first game, Ty successfully stole second, with Wagner's sweeping tag of a low throw innocently nicking him in the face as he hook-slid into the bag. Afterward, Detroit trainer Harry Tuthill sewed three stitches into Ty's lip. Compared to the bruises, blisters, scars, cuts, and strawberries that typically covered Ty's hands, arms, legs, and hips at the end of the summer, his split lip was as inconsequential as the nick on Frank Baker's forearm.

Wagner indisputably outplayed Cobb in the Series. The Pirate hit .333 and stole 6 bases, while Ty was held to a .231 average and 2 stolen bases, including a theft of home in the second game. Unlike the two previous Octobers though, the Tigers managed to be competitive, taking the Pirates to a seventh game. But for the third straight year, the Tigers closed out the postseason ingloriously by getting shut out at home. Babe Adams, a 12-game winner in the regular season, spun a 6-hitter to win his third game of the Series, 8–0, on a blustery Saturday afternoon in Detroit. "We do all right in the World Series," complained Ban Johnson, "except when that damn National Leaguer, Jennings, gets into it. Then we get hell beaten out of us."

Hughie Jennings' team remains the only American League club ever to lose three World Series in a row. Viewed objectively, however, the Tigers of 1907–08–09 were not a great squad but rather a collection of scrappy ballplayers taking their lead from two big cats. That Cobb and Crawford were toothless at the plate accounted in part for

Although Cobb was an unrepentant bigot, he was capable of befriending individual Blacks. One was a young mascot nicknamed "Lil' Rastus," seen here flanked by a pair of patronizing Tigers in 1909. Ballplayers had discovered the homeless boy, whose real name was Ulysses Harrison, trying to find shelter inside Bennett Park a year earlier. When the Tigers unreeled a long winning streak, the superstitious Cobb kept him around as a good-luck charm, lodging him in the clubhouse and sneaking him aboard trains and into whites-only hotels during road trips. Ty, reported sportswriter Harry Salsinger, was the "Ethiopian's main defender and patron." Ty took Lil' Rastus home to Augusta following the 1909 season, promoting him to domestic servant.

Detroit's sorry World Series record of just 4 wins (and a tie) in 17 outings, but unreliable pitching and pitiful catching were just as much to blame. "I was too young when that part of my career happened," Ty later said. "I regret I never got a crack at a World Series during my peak years."

At the time, though, no one was betting against a Cobb-led team scratching and clawing its way into several more World Series. In just 4 full seasons, Ty had already won 3 batting titles and contributed to a like number of pennants. Moreover, half of the league was scared to death of Cobb, said Jennings. It must have been discouraging to fans and players in other American League cities to realize that, at twenty-two, this combative, sulphurous terror hadn't even entered his prime.

Meanwhile, as the elm and maple trees arching Detroit's cobblestoned streets changed colors in the autumn of 1909, Ty overcame his annual disappointment by doing what every American with enough money was doing.

He bought a new car.

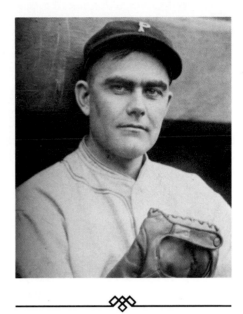

Pittsburgh's 27-year-old rookie right-hander, Charles "Babe" Adams, was the unexpected hero of the 1909 World Series. National League president John Heydler, who had watched Washington pitcher Dolly Gray frustrate the Tigers earlier in the season, suggested to Pittsburgh manager Fred Clarke that Adams, a 12-game winner during the regular season, had a similar style and might prove effective. Heydler's hunch paid off. Adams, a fastballer with a good curve and pinpoint control, beat Detroit three straight times—all 6-hitters— including an 8—0 victory in the finale.

Action in the sixth game of the 1909 World Series: Detroit first baseman Tom Jones slides safely into third base after Pittsburgh left fielder Fred Clarke misplays his single. The Tigers hung on to win a raucous 5—4 squeaker, forcing a seventh game at Bennett Park.

CHAPTER FOUR

You Auto Be in Detroit

My godfather was in Detroit and wrote me that he had paper on the walls, shoes, meat every day, fresh bread, milk, water in the house, beer on the corner, soup and plenty of money. From that time I was crazy to come.

The above words, written by a Polish immigrant to Detroit at the same time Ty Cobb broke in with the Tigers, reflected the passion with which the rest of the world regarded the city in the early part of the century. The genesis of such passion was the automobile, which by 1910 was lifting the world into the modern age and radically changing the face of Detroit.

The first person to drive an automobile on city streets was Charles Brady King on the nippy evening of March 6, 1896. "Turn that peanut roaster off before it spooks my horses!" a startled brewery teamster yelled at the 32-year-old engineer, who maneuvered his four-cylinder contraption down St. Antoine, made a right onto Jefferson Avenue, and then dropped into the deep well of obscurity. Three months later, Henry Ford, the 33-year-old chief engineer of the Edison Illuminating Company and a devoted tinkerer, drove his horseless carriage through downtown and straight into the history books, becoming in time the most recognized name in the world and the acknowledged architect of the greatest socio-economic revolution ever.

As the Tigers started their pursuit of an unprecedented fourth straight pennant in the spring of 1910, Ford's brand-new Highland Park plant began full production of the Model T. The ungainly but dependable vehicle had captured the public's imagination—and a good share of the marketplace—since its debut eighteen months earlier.

Ford clearly had a better idea. When Ransom Olds opened the city's first auto factory near the Belle Isle bridge in 1899, his hand-crafted vehicles had sold for $2,382. A union carpenter made only twenty-five cents an hour then, so Ford decided to leave such pricey vehicles to the "sports" and produce a car the average working man could afford. That strategy wasn't exactly foreign to many of the hundreds of carmakers in business in 1910. The Sears-Roebuck Company, for instance, offered a Sears Motor Car in its catalog for as low as $395.

Ford's genius was in passing on to the consumer the savings he realized through improved mass-production. Contrary to legend, Ford didn't invent the assembly line. He perfected it—first at the Highland Park plant, then at the massive Rouge Complex. As the time required to build a Model T continued to drop, so did its price. Between 1908 and 1924 the price of Ford's "family horse" shrank from $850 to $290. By World War I half of all cars in use were Model Ts, and before Ford quit building them in 1927 more than 15 million of the beloved "flivvers" had rolled onto America's primitive, pot-holed roads.

The mammoth electric sign atop the Temple Theatre on Monroe Street, where Ty often went to see the country's top vaudeville acts, implored pedestrians to "Watch The Fords Go By." Detroiters also watched Maxwells, Oldsmobiles, Franklins, Appersons, Paiges, Cadillacs, Buicks, Hudsons, Huppmobiles—and life as they once knew it—rumble past. In 1900, 4,192 automobiles were produced in the United States. Only a handful were spotted on the streets of Detroit, a horse-and-buggy town whose population at the turn of the century was a growing but still comfortable 286,000 people. Domestic auto production reached 187,000 vehicles in 1910, however, and Detroit's population kept pace by practically doubling. These were the peak years of immigration, with hungry, unskilled but hopeful men and their families arriving daily from Syria, Italy, Poland, and other countries. The steady stream would become a flood in 1914, when Henry Ford announced his famous "five dollar day" for factory workers.

Cobb's career as a Tiger coincided with the city's transformation into "Dynamic Detroit." When he arrived in 1905, the tranquility of a conservative, mid-sized community dominated by the scions of Yankee merchants and railroad and lumber tycoons was just beginning to be shattered by the babble of unfamiliar people and machines. By 1910 fashionable residential districts such as Woodward and Cass avenues had changed irreversibly, as gas stations, car dealerships, and

As more and more Americans were learning, an automobile created a previously unheard of freedom. Out of uniform and behind the wheel of his 1910 Owen, Ty could even escape fame. "More than 500,000 people saw Ty Cobb perform in Bennett Park this summer," reported a local paper. "Daily, when the team is home, Cobb drives about the streets in his automobile and not one person out of 100 ever gives him a second look."

Downtown Detroit in 1910. The Pontchartrain Hotel, whose elegant bar was the unofficial headquarters of the fledgling auto industry, stands at left.

other businesses sprang up and stately homes were sold and subdivided into boardinghouses. Throughout the core city and its outskirts, century-old shade trees were being leveled, meadows and other open spaces developed, and cobblestoned streets widened and paved over, all in a desperate attempt to keep up with the demand for factories, housing, roadways, and parking space.

Detroit's population included the largest percentage of foreign-born in the country. In the numerous factories (some of which posted signs in eight languages) and ethnic neighborhoods, the symphony of dialects competed with the roar of machinery and the sing-song of the street peddlers. "Detroit is alive and knows it," proclaimed one journalist. "Detroit is American and proud of it. Detroit is glad to be Detroit." By the time Cobb left in 1926, Detroit's factories were producing several million cars a year, its size had ballooned from twenty-six to 139 square miles, and the population had passed the 1.5 million mark, making the Motor City the fourth largest in the country.

Life in this noisy, confusing, polyglot urban colossus was far from perfect. Workers constantly suffered from the "boom-or-bust" vagaries of a one-industry town. Acute shortages of housing, health care, schools, and basic services plagued the city. But life here was still better than what it had been in Russia, Armenia, Lebanon, or Greece.

A mixed bag of major and minor leaguers gather around Ty during spring training in Augusta in 1910. Standing at far left is Nap Rucker of Crabapple, Georgia, an old Augusta teammate who went on to win 134 games during a 10-year career with Brooklyn.

A colorful floral display in Grand Circus Park spelled out this optimism: "In Detroit Life Is Worth Living." Regardless of one's language, few could argue with that, especially for those with gasoline in their veins. In 1910 the informal headquarters for the automobile set was the elegant oak and brass bar in the lobby of the Pontchartrain Hotel, which had opened in the fall of 1908. Located at the southeast corner of Michigan and Woodward avenues, the hotel was for several years the starting point for the famous Glidden Tour, an annual cross-country car rally that did much to convince a skeptical public that, thanks to the internal combustion engine, horsepower no longer had to mean horse apples. Here the aroma of cigar smoke mingled with the smell of opportunity.

"Fortunes were made overnight in early Detroit," Cobb recalled fondly in his autobiography. "You could toss your money in almost any direction and not miss."

Although he was beginning to stake out a reputation as a ballplayer, Ty kept his ears open, his mouth shut, and what little money he had in his pocket. He went to the Pontchartrain Hotel bar after games and listened to the architects of the new industrial age wheel and deal and argue the relative merits of the new machines. Engaged in these conversations were men such as David Buick, a plumbing contractor who thought of cars as bathtubs with engines and wheels; the two-fisted Dodge brothers, John and Horace, who had started out as uneducated factory hands and now built car bodies for Henry Ford; and others whose names were becoming associated with their products, Louis Chevrolet, the Fisher brothers, and the

Stanley twins. As countless stockowners were learning, you didn't have to be a manufacturer, either, to make it big. James Couzens, a bookkeeper who had invested $2,500 in Ford stock in 1903, cashed out in 1919 for $29,308,857. His sister's original $100 investment paid off $355,000 in just a few years.

Ty became close to two classic success stories. One was Walter O. Briggs, who started off as a young man checking coal cars in the Michigan Central Railroad yards for five dollars a week. He later joined boyhood friend Barney Everitt in a trim and painting shop, buying the business in 1909. The rough-hewn 32-year-old renamed it the Briggs Manufacturing Company and won contracts to build car bodies for Ford, Hudson, Packard and other automakers. In time the Briggs empire would include sixteen plants and 40,000 employees. Ty liked Briggs, "his interest in baseball, also his rugged outspoken ways," he said years later. "While I liked Walter I would have to say I loved John Kelsey."

Cobb and Kelsey had become acquainted on the Detroit Athletic Club baseball team when Ty was recuperating during the 1906 season. Kelsey, a pitcher and third baseman on D.A.C.'s 1892 national amateur champions, had gained considerable adulation as a financial angel, spending tens of thousands of dollars to keep the aging club alive even as his own business ventures were failing. Kelsey spearheaded the effort to build a magnificent seven-story D.A.C. clubhouse on Madison Avenue. When it opened in the spring of 1915

Hugh Chalmers, president of the auto company that bore his name. Considered one of the industry's first marketing geniuses, even he couldn't have predicted the enormous free publicity the first annual Chalmers Award would generate.

65

Two members of the auto set: Walter O. Briggs and John Kelsey. Both baseball-loving industrialists bought quarter-shares of the Tigers in 1920.

Briggs   Kelsey

(taking the auto crowd away from the Pontchartrain bar), many naturally thought its initials stood for "Detroit Automobile Club." Kelsey, elected president of the august group, never strayed far from his workbench beginnings. One of the many anecdotes illustrating his unaffectedness concerned a trip to New York, years after he had made his fortune producing wheels and brake systems for the auto industry. When businessmen dropped by Kelsey's hotel room to finalize a multi-million-dollar transaction, they discovered the wealthy owner of the Kelsey Wheel Company in his underwear, washing his socks in the bathroom sink.

Because of their love of the game and close friendship with Cobb, Briggs and Kelsey bought quarter-shares of the Tigers for $250,000 apiece in 1920. After Kelsey died in 1927, Briggs purchased his stock and became half-owner of the club. Eight years later, when Frank Navin was thrown from a horse and killed, Briggs bought out his widow to become sole owner. He then spent nearly two million Depression dollars converting Navin Field into Briggs Stadium, a 52,000-seat all-purpose sports facility that was one of the finest in the country. Not bad for someone who used to self-consciously sip ten-cent sherry flips at the lower end of the Pontchartrain bar with his ballplayer friend "because we could not afford [to] buy drinks for a number of them, though we would accept their proffer if they asked us," recalled Cobb.

By the winter of 1909–10 Ty was financially able to follow up on several tips (and, despite his well-deserved reputation as a nickel-nurser, presumably pick up a tab or two himself). After the World Series with Pittsburgh he had signed a new three-year contract for

66

The principals in the Great Automobile Race of 1910.

Cobb and Lajoie took delivery of their new Chalmers before a World Series game in Philadelphia.

67

$9,000 a year, a salary second only to Honus Wagner. (By comparison, the hourly wages in auto plants ranged from nine cents for unskilled labor to forty cents for experienced hands.) Perhaps taking a cue from Wagner, who owned a Regal Motor Car dealership in Carnegie, Pennsylvania, Cobb opened a small showroom in Augusta. He also started buying stock in General Motors. Within a decade his automobile stock, coupled with other shrewd investments, would make him independently wealthy and the first millionaire athlete.

More immediate rewards, however, were right down the road. Hugh Chalmers, president of the two-year-old Detroit auto company that bore his name, announced before the 1910 season that the winner of the batting championship in each league would receive a new Chalmers "30," a luxury car that normally retailed for a cool $2,700. This kind of promotion would cause barely a ripple of excitement today, of course, but in 1910 the opportunity to win an exotic prize worth what many ballplayers made in a year had fans, players, and sportswriters handicapping the contenders all season. Philadelphia outfielder Sherry Magee wound up winning the Chalmers in the National League without much suspense. But in the junior circuit, what some called "The Great American Automobile Race" developed between Cobb and Cleveland's Napoleon "Nap" Lajoie, throwing much-needed drama into an otherwise ho-hum year.

First, the pennant race. There was none. Despite leading the league in scoring for the fourth year in a row, the Tigers never contended, finishing in third place. Unlike the hungry Athletics, who rode the arms of Jack Coombs and Chief Bender to the pennant and a

The only man to get more ink than Ty Cobb in Detroit was Henry Ford, the folk-hero industrialist who was probably the most famous man in the world. The creator of the cheap but reliable Model T didn't invent the assembly line, but his mass-production techniques helped put the world on wheels. All told, more than 15 million of his "mechanical cock-roaches" rolled off the assembly line between 1908 and 1927, including these 8,900 vehicles—one day's production—positioned for a publicity photo in 1915.

World Series win over the Cubs, the Tigers often played like placated pussycats. One of the few times the team snarled all summer occurred not long after the city had finally removed its ban on Sunday ball, which allowed Detroit to join Chicago, Cincinnati, and St. Louis as the only major-league towns where the cries of "Kill the umpire!" could disturb legally the sacred air of the Sabbath. Bluenoses, who considered it a sacrilege for a working man to visit Bennett Park on his only day off, had their worst fears realized during a Sunday game with Boston. George Moriarty attempted to steal home in the bottom of the ninth, resulting in some banging and bruising at the plate. Red Sox catcher Bill "Rough" Carrigan responded by squirting tobacco juice into the prone base runner's eye. Moriarty slugged Carrigan in the jaw, and within seconds the two clubs were a knot of windmilling fists. Players and fans battled all the way to the clubhouse. As Navin stood on top of the dugout shouting in vain for order, a small army of Tiger cranks laid siege to the Boston dressing room, pounding on the door and threatening to lynch Carrigan. After about an hour, the Boston backstop escaped by slipping into a groundskeeper's overalls and boots, smearing his face with mud, and walking unmolested through the unsuspecting mob.

This was excitement, of a sort. But the *real* race, the one that captivated baseball fans and whose result remained undecided until long after the season ended, was just heating up. At the beginning of September, Cobb led Lajoie by just three percentage points, .362 to .359. Through October the two jockeyed for the lead, with the nation's newspapers reporting various "official" and "unofficial" averages. Most days it was a tossup as to who was on top. The American League office didn't help the confusion, issuing a notice that "the result probably will not be known until [league secretary] Rob McRoy gives out his figures."

Ty gambled that the figures showing him holding an eight-point lead as of October 6 were correct. He decided to sit out the final two games of the season against Chicago. Lajoie figured he needed a herculean effort to pass Cobb. What he didn't expect was help from the opposition.

If someone had polled American Leaguers on who they wished to see win the Chalmers, the 35-year-old Lajoie would have won hands down. The graceful second baseman was well-liked by practically everyone. Many remembered how the gifted ballplayer, who had dropped out of school when he was ten to work in a Rhode Island

69

The booming auto industry was responsible for Detroit's explosive growth during Cobb's career in the city. The Motor City's numerous car factories gave hundreds of thousands of unskilled immigrants like Francesco Petrella (posing proudly with his family and Model T on Independence Day) the opportunity to enjoy a standard of living unimaginable in Poland, Italy, or Greece. Detroit was more than soot-stained factories, of course. The wealth created there made it into a dynamic community where, as these postcards of Belle Isle and Grand Circus Park prove, life indeed was worth living.

mill, had given the fledgling American League instant credibility when he jumped over from the National League in 1901. The line-drive-hitting right-hander won his first of 3 batting titles that year with a .422 average, still the American League record. Lajoie was held in such high esteem the Cleveland club named itself the "Naps" after him. By contrast, Ty was easily the most unpopular man in baseball, despised as much for his brilliance as for his disposition. Many fans weren't pulling for Lajoie as much as they were pulling against Cobb.

This became obvious in Cleveland's season-ending doubleheader in St. Louis on Sunday, October 9. The last-place Browns were managed by Jack O'Conner, a former catcher who had played several years in Cleveland when the team was in the National League. O'Conner, nicknamed ironically "Peach Pie," despised the Georgia Peach. Before the first game he instructed rookie third baseman Red Corriden to play Lajoie extra deep every time he came to bat.

On Lajoie's first at-bat, he hit a long drive to center field that some observers claimed was misjudged deliberately by outfielder Hub Northern. It was scored a triple. On his next seven trips to the plate, noticing that Corriden was playing on the fringe of the outfield grass, Lajoie bunted down the third-base line. The first six times the slow-footed Lajoie beat them out for hits, Corriden not even making a throw on some, and the seventh time he was credited with a sacrifice. On his final at-bat Lajoie grounded to shortstop Bobby Wallace, long considered the league's finest glove man at that position. Wallace threw wildly to first and Lajoie was awarded a hit by the official scorer, who explained that even a good throw wouldn't have retired him.

Lajoie finished the doubleheader with 8 hits in 8 at-bats. "Larry Does Great Work at St. Louis," one out-of-town paper reported. Afterward Lajoie received several congratulatory telegrams, including one signed by several Tigers.

The transparent strategy enraged those writers on the scene. The five St. Louis dailies spoke of an "open scandal," whereby "certain St. Louis players allowed Napolean Lajoie to obtain base hits with the aim of letting him beat out Cobb for the batting title . . . Lajoie and others say there was no trickery—just cleverness and misjudgment combined."

The misjudgment turned out to be on the part of O'Conner, who explained, "Lajoie outguessed us." American League president Ban

"The threat in a bunt is a marvelous weapon," explained Ty, shown demonstrating his technique at Chicago's Comiskey Park about 1911. Cobb was known to bunt two or three times in a row to lure the infielders in, then fake another bunt and drive the ball straight at one of them.

On July 24, 1911, Ty joined several American League stars in an exhibition game to benefit the family of Cleveland pitcher Addie Joss. The 31-year-old Joss had died that spring of tubercular meningitis, cutting short a brilliant career. Pictured are: (bottom row, from left) Germany Schaefer, Tris Speaker, Sam Crawford, Jimmy McAleer, Cobb, Gabby Street, and Paddy Livingston; (top row) Bobby Wallace, Frank Baker, Joe Wood, Walter Johnson, Hal Chase, Clyde Milan, Russ Ford, and Eddie Collins. Ty arrived late and had to play in a borrowed uniform. For the record, the All-Stars defeated Cleveland, 7–2, raising $13,000.

Johnson didn't buy that. As the public waited for the official averages to be computed, new information about Lajoie's final-day performance came to light. During the doubleheader St. Louis coach Harry Howell had repeatedly visited the press box, asking how Lajoie's bunts were being scored. At one point a note arrived in the press box promising a new suit of clothes to the scorer if he would be lenient toward the Cleveland batter. After holding hearings and absolving Lajoie and the rookie Corriden of any blame, Johnson had O'Conner and Howell thrown out of the league.

On November 21 the league office released the final official averages. Cobb had won the batting title by the slimmest of margins:

	At-Bats	Hits	Avg.
Cobb	509	196	.385
Lajoie	591	227	.384

Lajoie went to his grave insisting that he had won the disputed batting championship, a belief proved correct long after all the principals in the controversy were dead. In 1981 Paul MacFarlane of *The Sporting News* reconstructed the 1910 batting race game by game. He reported that, among other minor errors in both players' records, the American League had mistakenly credited Cobb with an additional 2-for-3 performance on September 24. The recalibrated figures revealed that Lajoie had actually outhit Cobb, .383 to .382. Despite then-commissioner Bowie Kuhn's decision not to alter the record book, some

Ty's mother, Amanda, visited her famous son in Detroit in the summer of 1911. Ty holds Ty Jr., while Charlie humors their second child, Shirley Marion, born that June.

Auto racing was another expression of virility for young men like "Wild Bob" Burman, racing his Buick against an airplane at a Daytona Beach Speed Festival in 1910, and Cobb, getting set to master his machine at Indianapolis. Always a fast driver, even on city streets, Ty eased his foot off the pedal after Burman and another friend, Bob McNey, were killed in racing accidents.

revisionists have since credited Lajoie, not Cobb, with the 1910 batting title, tainted "hits" and all.

As it turned out, neither Lajoie nor Cobb lost anything of real value at the time. Hugh Chalmers, delighted with the windfall of free publicity the controversy had brought his product, gave both men a new Chalmers before the final results were released. It was the most sporting gesture of the whole affair.

Despite the aroma surrounding it, the first Chalmers Award (it would continue in a revised format for three more years) highlighted the growing association between ballplayers and motor cars. The automobile had replaced the diamond stickpin as a symbol of status and conspicuous consumption. Sam Crawford was an impressive man-about-town in his polished Cadillac, while several Pittsburgh players used their $1,825 winning shares to purchase new Regals after the 1909 World Series. Club owners were ambivalent about what the new machine age meant for the game. They feared many fans would decide to motor off in search of love, adventure, or other attractions outside of the ballpark. They also worried about their star players getting injured in an accident. After Honus Wagner crashed into a railroad crossing gate, *The Sporting News* urged owners to "forbid this fad, a result of players' natural craving for speed and undue risk."

For true adventure, nothing could compare with motoring. However, only a small percentage of Americans owned an automobile in 1910. It was still an expensive, unreliable machine, though sales were climbing steadily, prices were coming down, and mechanical advances were being made almost daily. The field was wide open. In 1911, 270 manufacturers were producing 400 models, including such exotic-sounding vehicles as the Grabowsky "Power Wagon" and Faulkner-Blanchard "Gunboat Six."

These early vehicles could be dangerous. Until the widespread use of Charles Kettering's electric self-starter (introduced on the 1912

Cadillac), motorists had to turn a crank to start the engine, a muscle-numbing procedure that could easily snap a forearm, shatter a jaw, or rip an arm out of its socket. Tires blew frequently. A set of four cost several hundred dollars but typically lasted only several hundred miles. In 1909 a mile-long stretch of concrete highway, the country's first, was laid on Woodward Avenue in Detroit, but only a tiny fraction of the country's other two million miles of rural roads were paved, some with nothing more than crushed seashells. Rain and snow made them impassable, forcing more than one stranded motorist to endure the barb, "Get a horse!," while some farmer pulled him out of the mud.

Driving conditions were scarcely better in the city. One of the great untold stories of early twentieth-century America was the chaos caused by the coming of the automobile. Cars, trucks, buggies, horses, wagons, streetcars, pushcarts, bicycles, pedestrians—all were knotted at intersections like balls of hopelessly tangled yarn. Despite the soaring number of accidents and fatalities, traffic control was practically nonexistent in 1911. Years later Detroit's mayor admitted the city had been purposely lax on traffic offenders. The reasoning: since its citizens were putting the world on wheels, they deserved slack. Thus the driving, unimpeded by traffic signals, patience, or common sense, often resembled a thrill show.

Ty, frequently spotted tooling around town in a succession of luxury models, was a regular offender. During the 1911 season, on one of the few occasions when a patrolman actually issued him a ticket for speeding, Ty received a suspended sentence from a sympathetic judge. "He told the judge he wasn't going any faster than when he steals second base," a local paper reported.

Young, vibrant, self-made, and adventurous, Ty and the automobile seemed to personify America in these throttle-down, big-shouldered years before World War I. Even Ty's diamond exploits coexisted on the same page as the motor car, since most papers published box scores and the latest auto news in an "Automobile and Sports" section. Throughout his twenties, Cobb caused Frank Navin fits by regularly taking laps at speedways in Atlanta, Indianapolis, Savannah, and other places, sometimes exceeding speeds of 100 miles per hour. Navin once had to step in at the last moment to cancel a heavily promoted ten-mile race in Atlanta between his star ballplayer and Dodgers' pitcher Nap Rucker.

The start of the first Indianapolis 500 in 1911. Ty once drove umpire Brick Owens around "the greatest race course in the world" at speeds reaching 100 miles per hour. Owens released his white-knuckled grip only long enough to lean over the side of the car and throw up.

73

Three Winners

Tyrus Raymond Cobb
Oldsmobile Sport Model
C. G. Spring Bumpers

THE

C. G. SPRING CO.

OF MICHIGAN

CHRISTIAN GIRL, Pres.   DETROIT, MICH.

DETROIT BRANCH
FOR
BUMPER SALES AND SERVICE

2660 E. GRAND BLVD.   EMpire 6315

For all of his connections in the Motor City, Ty did few commercial endorsements for automakers and their suppliers. The reason? Through the 1920s, automobiles sold themselves.

In 1911, Barney Oldfield, the veteran driver who had set several early speed records, announced he was considering retirement. Exploding tires, failed brakes, and other mechanical or human failures had caused more than 200 drivers and mechanics to die in the previous seven years. The famous racer's nerves were frayed almost beyond repair. "The motor racing game has outlived its usefulness," he said. "The science of speed has reached a point where any manufacturer can produce a car which will satisfy any buyer."

Cobb's response, in effect, was to take several bone-jarring laps around a racetrack, wipe the bugs off his teeth, and just laugh. "The point was: they'd never strapped themselves behind the wheel of a powerful Mercedes, Pope-Toledo, White Streak, Thomas Flyer, Lozier or Fiat and experienced the hair-raising thrill of mastering the roaring beasts," is how he once explained his fascination with speed. "Those who feared for my life were the pedestrian type. You have to do it to appreciate it." Ty's personal best for a "flying kilometer" was a forty-five-second mile at the brickyard in Indianapolis, driving a National "40." Despite the protestations of friends and family, Ty didn't slow down until a wreck killed a friend, race driver Bill McNey, at the Savannah raceway.

Cobb's heavy foot was the perfect metaphor for the 1911 edition of the Tigers, who won their first 12 games and accelerated to a blistering 21–2 start. Ty's 40-game hitting streak was finally stopped by Chicago's Ed Walsh during a sweltering Independence Day doubleheader at Bennett Park. That was just a momentary setback. One week later, in an important series against the Athletics, Ty kicked his competitive zeal into overdrive. On July 11 he scored from second on a fly ball, and the following day he made the veteran Philadelphia battery of Harry Krause and Ira Thomas look like helpless rookies as he swiped second, third, and home on consecutive pitches in the first inning.

Such exploits had fans talking of another World Series with the Chicago Cubs, who were setting the pace in the National League. However, like the Cubs, the Tigers faded badly and finished runner-up. Injuries to key players such as rookie first baseman Del Gainor, and continued dissension over Jennings' preferential treatment of Cobb, caused the huge early lead to dissipate. On the field, Cobb and Crawford presented the most feared one-two punch in the game, a threat to bang out back-to-back triples or pull off a double steal. Off the field they refused to speak to each other. Before the season Jennings and team captain George Moriarty had implored the two to bury the hatchet. Crawford figured he knew the perfect spot—Ty's swollen head—but the two agreed to shake hands, although friction in the clubhouse never disappeared. Meanwhile, Philadelphia passed

The American League's three leading batters of 1911, conveniently arranged according to finish: Cobb (.420), "Shoeless Joe" Jackson (.408), and Sam Crawford (a career-best .378). One of the more enduring Cobb myths has Ty purposely ignoring Jackson in the latter stages of the season, so confusing the illiterate Cleveland rookie that he fretted and stopped hitting, which allowed Ty to zoom past him for another batting title. Ty and Grantland Rice both repeated this tale in their autobiographies, using it as an example of Cobb's prowess in psychological warfare. But Jackson biographer Donald Gropman has pointed out that Jackson never led Cobb during the 1911 season; if anything Jackson gained ground in the last week. Although Jackson's .356 career average is third best, he never won a batting title, finishing runner-up to Cobb in 1911, 1912, and 1913.*

Detroit for good on August 4, finishing 13$^{1}/_{2}$ games in front. Connie Mack's white elephants then went on to stampede the New York Giants for their second straight championship.

Thanks in part to the introduction of a more lively cork-centered ball, averages and home runs jumped noticeably that summer. Several players, including Crawford and Cobb, enjoyed their finest all-around season. Wahoo Sam posted career highs in hits (217), runs (109), and batting average (.378). He also knocked in 115 runs, second in the league, and stole 37 bases.

But those numbers paled alongside Cobb's. Ty won his fifth straight batting title, hitting .420 with 248 hits, 47 doubles, and 24 triples. He scored 147 runs and knocked in 144. Not only were these all league highs, they would turn out to be personal bests. Ty, who also led in total bases and slugging, swiped 83 bases, easily outdistancing Clyde Milan to capture his third stolen base crown. In addition, he hit 8 home runs, second only to Philadelphia's Frank Baker (who would earn his sobriquet as "Home Run" Baker after hitting 2 more against the Giants in the World Series).

All in all, it was an extraordinary season statistically for Ty, one of the finest ever put together. Before the season the Chalmers Award had been restructured. Now a committee of sportswriters representing all major-league cities voted an automobile to the player in each league who "should prove himself as the most important and useful . . . to his club and to the league at large in point of deportment and value of services rendered."

With 64 points, Ty easily outdistanced Ed Walsh (35 points) and Eddie Collins (32) for the American League award. Although there

75

was no doubt about the value of his "services rendered," the voters apparently didn't attach much weight to the issue of deportment either. For, temperamentally, Ty remained as unstable as a feather in a tornado, someone with an almost uncanny ability to get under the skins of all those around him. Exactly how much of the abuse he inspired was deserved was open to debate. New York sportswriter Heywood Broun, for one, thought it was a case of small minds attached to feeble limbs:

> *Whether you like or dislike this young fellow, you must concede him one virtue: what he has won, he has taken by might of his own play. He asks no quarter and gives none. Pistareen ball players whom he has "shown up" dislike him. Third basemen with bum arms, second basemen with tender shins, catchers who cannot throw out a talented slider—all despise Cobb. And their attitude has infected the stands. Why do they so resent Cobb when he plays the game at every point on the field, giving his best at every moment, and makes life miserable for those less willing?*

Cobb may have pondered that question as he drove away yet another new Chalmers in the fall of 1911. Given his "vying nature," and his age (only twenty-four), long stretches of rough road loomed. However, his approach as he embarked on the most tumultuous seasons of his career would remain that of the speedway and the basepaths: full-bore and straight out, leaving doubters and detractors to choke on his dust.

ATHLETICS VS. TIGERS, MAY 31, 1911, BENNETT PARK, DETROIT, MICH.

McInnis BAKER BARRY Collins

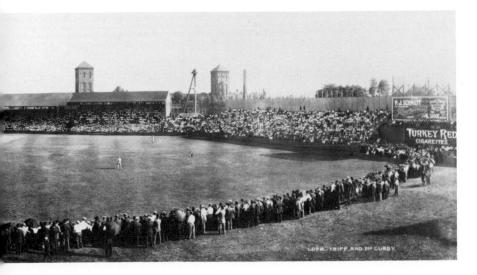

A panoramic view of Bennett Park, filled to over-flowing for a game with Philadelphia on May 24, 1911. The Tigers bolted to an incredible 21–2 start, but the Athletics passed Detroit in late August and never looked back. Connie Mack's club went on to win its second straight World Series, thanks to the "$100,000 Infield" of first baseman Stuffy McInnis, third baseman Frank "Home Run" Baker, shortstop Jack Barry, and second baseman Eddie Collins.

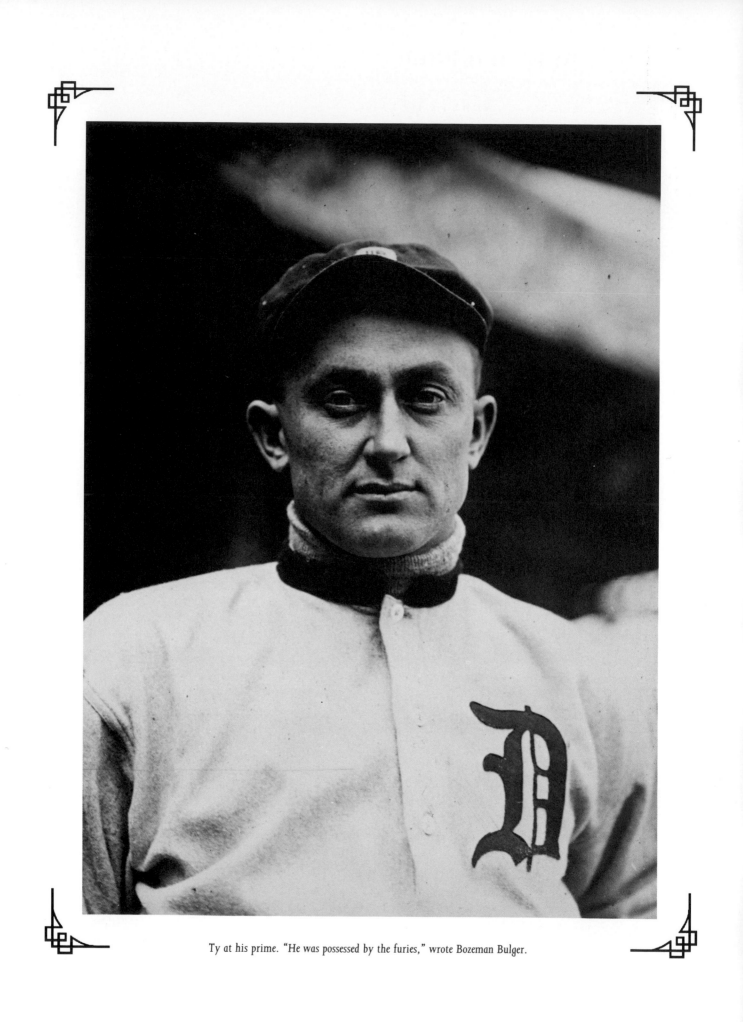

Ty at his prime. "He was possessed by the furies," wrote Bozeman Bulger.

CHAPTER FIVE
Glory Days and Others

A swing—and a smash—and a gray streak partaking
Of ghostly manoeuvres that follow the whack;
The old earth rebounds with a quiver and quaking
And high flies the dust as he thuds on the track;
The atmosphere reels—and it isn't the comet—
There follows the blur of a phantom at play;
Then out from the reel comes the glitter of steel—
And damned be the fellow that gets in the way.

A swing and a smash—and the far echoes quiver—
A ripping and rearing and volcanic roar;
And off streaks the Ghost with a shake and a shiver,
To hurdle red hell on the way to a score;
A cross between tidal wave, cyclone and earthquake—
Fire, wind and water all out on a lark;
Then out from the reel comes the glitter of steel,
Plus ten tons of dynamite hitched to a spark.
                              —Grantland Rice, Cobb

Probably nobody in New York City in 1912 hated Ty Cobb more than Claude Lucker, whose favorite pastimes included screaming slurs at the Detroit star whenever the Tigers visited Hilltop Park. The exact roots of his hostility remain unknown, but it was probably a case of one of life's victims venting his frustrations and bitterness at a convenient target—a thin-skinned star whose slow burn made for great sport.

Lucker, a former printing press operator, undoubtedly thought he had a right to be bitter. A year earlier an accident had severed one of his hands and lopped three fingers off the other. Forced to quit his printing job the middle-aged Lucker found work as a flunky for a minor Tammany Hall official named Thomas Foley. (Such safety nets as disability insurance and Social Security were unheard of then.) His friends were the low-rent cronies at downtown Tammany Hall, the center of New York's corrupt Democratic machine. Enduring stares and barbs, Lucker wasn't above using his handicap as an excuse for his loutish behavior.

Butt-heads like Claude Lucker have always attended sporting events, and they always will. However, player abuse was worse at the turn of the century. In the absence of ushers and security guards, spectators had no restraints. Police were always on hand, but they were usually highly partisan and—especially in New York—frequently joined in the fun. Catcalls, insults, threats, and an occasional thrown bottle were accepted hazards of the ballplayer's trade. There were legions of Cobb-haters in every park, and Ty dealt with them the only way

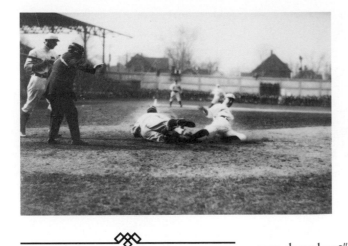

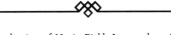

Ty scores the first-ever run at Navin Field, stealing home on Cleveland catcher Ted Blankenship.

80

An early view of Navin Field. It opened on April 20, 1912, the same day as Fenway Park in Boston.

he could: embarrass the home nine to the best of his ability. But on the afternoon of May 15, 1912, Claude Lucker outdid himself, pushing Cobb over the edge and setting in motion one of the wildest chain of events in sports history.

The trouble started shortly after the opening pitch of the Wednesday game between the Tigers and Highlanders. Lucker, seated about a dozen rows behind the visitors' dugout, directed an unceasing stream of invectives at Cobb. After Ty muffed a fly ball in the bottom of the first inning, Lucker screamed, "You look a little dopey. Hey, Cobb, are you doped up?"

Although the two men traded insult for insult, Ty did his best to avoid a confrontation. In the bottom of the second inning, he lingered in the outfield area rather than go back to the dugout and endure another point-blank blast of Lucker's taunts and insults. After New York was retired in the bottom of the third, Ty swung by the first-base stands, looking to ask New York club officials to have Lucker removed from the park. Unable to find anyone, Ty returned to the Tigers' bench, yelling at Lucker, "I was out with your sister last night." Lucker yelled something back.

"You going to let that bum call you names?" asked Sam Crawford.

"I don't know how much more I can take," admitted Cobb, who sat there simmering as epithets rained down. Newspapers delicately avoided the exact wording of Lucker's razzing, but it's known that less-than-flattering comments about the morals of Ty's mother finally set him off. Hughie Jennings later explained that, among other things, Lucker had called Ty a "half-nigger," an insult no Southerner would stand for.

CHAS. LUCKER.

"I heard the remark," said Jennings, "but I knew it would be use-less to restrain Ty, as he would have got his tormenter sooner or later. When Ty's Southern blood is aroused he is a bad man to handle." The unlucky Lucker would quickly discover that. As the Tigers trotted out to take the field in the bottom of the fourth, Ty suddenly turned on his heel, vaulted over the grandstand railing, and rushed up several rows to confront his nemesis. As the crowd stood to get a better view, and Detroit players stepped outside their dugout brandishing bats, Ty went to town on the shocked Lucker.

"Everything was very pleasant," the *New York Times* reported, "until Ty Cobb johnnykilbaned a spectator right on the place where he talks, started the claret, and stopped the flow of profane and vulgar words. Cobb led with a left jab and countered with a right kick to Mr. Spectator's left Weisbach, which made his peeper look as if someone had drawn a curtain over it. . . . Jabs bounded off the spectator's face like a golf ball from a rock." Lucker's account to police was more pro-saic. "He struck me with his fists on the forehead over the left eye and knocked me down. Then he jumped on me and spiked me in the left leg and kicked me in the side, after which he booted me behind the left ear."

Park police finally broke up the assault. Lucker was led away, bloodied and sputtering, while Ty was tossed from the game. Despite the shocking violence of the beating, which made headlines across the country, the main working press defended Ty's actions. The reaction of Hugh S. Fullerton, who noted that the police in New York's three major-league parks were "among the violent rooters," was typical. Cobb, he wrote, "goes around the circuit year after year, singled out as the special mark by every violent fan, and he has learned to endure almost any kind of abuse possible. If the epithets and accusations made by the Highlander fan towards Cobb was half as bad as the

On May 15, 1912, Ty climbed into the third-base stands at Hilltop Park and administered a fearful beating on Claude Lucker, an obnoxious, foul-mouthed fan. Although Lucker was physical-ly handicapped, he got what he deserved according to Cobb: "When a spectator calls me a 'half-nigger' I think it is about time to fight." Atlanta's mayor agreed, congratulating the Georgia Peach for upholding "the principles that have always been taught to Southern manhood."

81

Just four days before the Lucker incident, Cobb
stood at home plate at Hilltop Park and received
an impressive trophy for being the majors' leading
hitter in 1911 from George "Honey Boy" Evans,
a popular black-face comedian.

Cobb's suspension over the Lucker incident caused
the first players' strike in history. On May 18,
1912, Jennings frantically rounded up several
sandlotters to play a scheduled game in
Philadelphia. The ersatz Tigers lost by 22 runs.
At one point during the rout Jennings counseled a
distraught outfielder to forget trying to catch the
balls and to just "play them off the walls."

Detroit players claim, it was a case for violence. The wonder to me is
that other spectators could sit and listen without taking a hand in it
and beating up and throwing out the person using such language."

Unfortunately for Cobb, the league president didn't agree. Ban
Johnson, who happened to be in the stands that day, suspended Ty
immediately without hearing his side of the story. The following afternoon's game in Philadelphia was rained out, which gave the Tigers
plenty of time to grouse about Johnson's high-handed decision. On
Friday the Cobbless Tigers dropped a 6–4 decision to Philadelphia,
after which they displayed a rare show of solidarity with their temperamental teammate by sending a telegram to Johnson at his
Chicago office. It read:

*Feeling Mr. Cobb is being done an injustice by your action in suspending
him, we, the undersigned, refuse to play in another game until such action is
adjusted to our satisfaction. He was fully justified, as no one could stand
such abuse from anyone. We want him reinstated or there will be no game.
If players cannot have protection, we must protect ourselves.*

Meanwhile, in Detroit Frank Navin fretted over the automatic
$5,000 fine he would have to pay if he didn't field a team for
Saturday's game. He instructed Jennings and his coaches, Joe Sugden
and Jim "Deacon" McGuire, to fan out over Philadelphia
and gather a squad of substitutes, in case they were needed. As Bugs Baer later put it, any sandlotter who could
"stop a grapefruit from rolling uphill or hit a bull in the
pants with a bass fiddle" was given a chance. The scrubs
were signed for ten dollars apiece and hustled out to
Shibe Park, where a large crowd was gathering to see if
the Tigers were really going to follow through on their
threat to strike. When informed that Cobb's suspension
stood, Sam Crawford, George Mullin, Donie Bush, and
company marched off the field, turned in their uniforms,
and joined the amused Philadelphia bugs in the stands to
watch the raggedy band of sandlotters battle the two-
time champion Athletics.

It remains the most absurd major-league game ever played.
Twenty-year-old Aloysius Travers, like most of the scrubs recruited
from nearby St. Joseph's College, volunteered to take the mound when
he learned the pitcher earned an additional fifteen dollars—combat
pay, as it were. As Mullin surrendered his uniform to Travers in the
clubhouse, he said, "Kid, you can steal anything, but don't steal the
glove." Mullin didn't know his man. Travers was a theology student
who later became a Catholic priest.

Nothing short of divine intervention could have saved these ersatz Tigers. Aware of what awaited them, they had to be coaxed from the dugout and onto the field. Travers' only pitch was a roundhouse curve that was "not fast enough to dent butter," observed one writer. He did attempt one fastball in the first inning—to Frank "Home Run" Baker, of all people—and Baker sent it rocketing toward Opal Street, three blocks away but foul. This prompted Deacon McGuire, who at age forty-eight found himself pressed into duty behind the plate, to rise from his creaking knees and visit the mound.

"You wanna get killed, kid?" asked McGuire. "Just throw your regular stuff. It ain't good enough to hit."

It was a beautiful day for a game: sunny and about 75 degrees. Buoyed by the weather and the spectacle on the field, the crowd cheered the misfits on. One of the scrubs fielded a ground ball with his face, losing two teeth in the bargain. "This ain't baseball," he sputtered. "This is war." Travers staggered the distance, giving up 26 hits and 24 runs. He walked 7 and struck out 1. To add to the merriment, his teammates chipped in 9 errors. "It's a circus," declared Donie Bush, sitting in the upper pavilion. "I'm glad I came."

The third baseman, a 30-year-old semipro named Ed Irvin, accounted for half of the strikebreakers' 4 hits. Irvin made the most of his abbreviated major-league career, cracking 2 triples in 3 at-bats before fading into obscurity with a lifetime .667 batting average. Neither hit did any damage. In fact, the scrubs' only runs came in the fifth on a throwing error by shortstop Jack Barry.

The master on the art of sliding: "The whole secret of sliding is to make your move at the last possible second. When I went in there I wanted to see the whites of the fielder's eyes."

83

Several players could have beaten Ty in a foot race, but no one took greater advantage of basic base-running principles. Instead of circling bases in a wide arc, Ty pushed his left foot against the inside of the bag, then crossed over with his right leg. The pivot, executed at full speed, saved precious seconds and made him appear faster than he was.

Ty kicks the ball out of St. Louis catcher Paul Krichell's mitt on July 4, 1912, one of four times during his career when he stole second, third, and home in the same inning. The only other player to steal his way around the bases as many as three times was Honus Wagner.

84

With clenched jaw and gritted teeth, Ty pounds the ground at Chicago. "His determination was fantastic," marveled one backstop. "I never saw anybody like him. It was his base. It was his game. Everything was his. The most feared man in the history of baseball."

Bill Leinhauser, a slightly built 18-year-old, wore Cobb's uniform and played center field. He went hitless in 4 at-bats and got conked on the head with one of the several fly balls driven his way. At one point during the fusillade Jennings called time to give his distraught outfielder advice. "Forget about catching them, son," he said. "Just play them off the walls." Leinhauser later became a cop in Philadelphia, and until his death in 1978 he never tired of telling people of the time he filled in for the great Georgia Peach.

With minimum effort, the Athletics chalked up an official win, 24–2. Jennings, pinch-hitting for one of his shell-shocked troops in the ninth inning, drew the curtain on this theatre of the absurd by taking a called third strike from Herb Pennock.

Ban Johnson exploded when he learned of the farce. He and Navin hurried to Philadelphia for a conference; meanwhile, Ty urged his striking teammates to go back to work. "You've made our point," he said. "With the publicity we've received, the facts are now on record with the public. I don't want you paying any more fines. You've got to go back on the field sooner or later, so do it now. I'll be all right. Johnson will lift my suspension soon."

Which he did. Each of the striking Tigers was fined $100. Ty paid fifty dollars and sat out the balance of a ten-day suspension.

As ugly and ludicrous as the Lucker beating and its aftermath were, the episode was perhaps the only time during Ty's long career when he had the almost universal approval of his teammates. Asked about the Lucker incident eighty years later, Red Hoff—then a 21-year-old pitcher sitting on the Highlanders' bench—spoke for most players when he replied, "He went into the stands and did his duty." The effect of the entire episode is that ushers eventually were installed inside all big-league parks.

Lost in the commotion was another superb offensive season for Ty, who hit .410 in 1912 to capture his sixth straight batting title. On April 20, he had christened Frank Navin's new concrete-and-steel ballpark by scoring its first run. He did it in typically dramatic style, swiping home in the bottom of the first against Cleveland's Vean Gregg, the first of a record 8 steals of home he would pull off that summer.

Stealing home had turned into a specialty. During his career he stole it 55 times (including 1 World Series theft), far outdistancing runner-up Max Carey, who had 33 during his 20 years with Pittsburgh and Brooklyn. To put Ty's feat in perspective, consider that the two

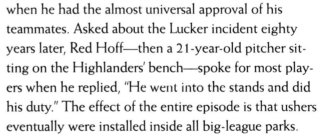

players ahead of him in career steals, Rickey Henderson and Lou Brock, have stolen home only 7 times between them!

No one will ever approach Ty's record for stealing home. Today's big-bang offense has cheapened the importance of a single run, and modern teams are smarter about defending against it. Third basemen play closer to the bag, while pitchers long ago abandoned the wind-up in favor of the set position. Both reduce the big lead a runner needs to get a jump on the ball. Plus, in the era of astronomical contracts few base stealers are willing to risk a career-ending injury through a home plate collision. For these reasons this once-popular offensive maneuver is virtually obsolete. Ty's stolen base mark is as safe as his .367 lifetime batting average.

Larry Amman of the Society for American Baseball Research has tracked all of Cobb's attempted steals of home, discovering some interesting figures. Of his 98 regular-season dashes for home, two-thirds occurred with two outs. Of these 66 all-or-nothing attempts, he was successful half of the time. Cobb made an additional 28 attempts with one out; 18 (a commendable 64 percent) were successful. Only 4 of his attempts were with none out. This is considered a bad percentage play, but Ty was successful the first three times he attempted it.

Analyzing Cobb's attempts further, we find that:

• He was more likely to try to pilfer home with his team ahead (28 steals in 53 attempts) than with his team behind (14 steals in 27 attempts). With the score tied, he was successful on 12 of 18 attempts.

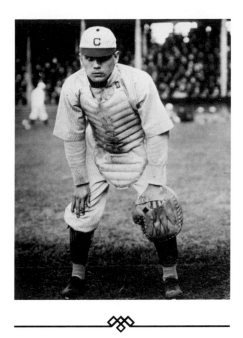

Cobb's reputation may account for the slightly spooked look on Cleveland catcher Nig Clarke's face.

85

Although one would hardly guess it by his reputation, Ty smiled— frequently. Here's proof.

In fact, this portrait was his favorite.

The Tigers were the last major-league team to abandon the once-popular Byron collar, finally changing their uniform style in 1915. Unlike most players, who folded down their collars or tucked them in at the neckline, Ty always wore his tunic-style, fastening the ends at the throat with a large safety pin. Fashion considerations aside (Ty was a big admirer of Napoleon and other military figures), the upright collar also had a practical purpose, keeping the brutal summer sun off Ty's fair skin.

• He was more aggressive in the early innings, stealing home 24 times in 46 attempts in the first three innings of a ball game. From the seventh inning on, he was more responsible (and successful), swiping home 14 of 19 tries—a sterling 74 percent.

• Although it's thought to be easier to steal home on a southpaw, because his back is turned to third base, fewer than one-third (16) of Ty's successful thefts came off left-handers.

Ty didn't take up cigarettes until retirement, believing they cut down his wind. But he saw nothing wrong with chewing tobacco, snuff, and cigars, all of which he used freely during his playing days.

As always, Cobb turned baseball logic on its ear. Conventional wisdom holds that stealing home should be attempted with a poor hitter at the plate, because a weak hitter is less likely to drive in a run. Moreover, that batter should be right-handed so as to obscure the catcher's view of the runner. Yet Ty was more likely to break from third with Bobby Veach—one of the game's best left-handed RBI men—at bat than any other player. "Cobb was using the element of surprise," a writer noted after one of the Peach's successful attempts. "No one thought he would try for home with a left-handed hitter up." Which, of course, is why he did it.

After five years of contending, the Tigers finished sixth in 1912. Despite the absence of a competitive team, a growing population base and a new ballpark helped Frank Navin once again turn a nice profit. Ty, whose contract ran out at the end of 1912, thought he was entitled to a larger share of the purse. When Navin turned down his demand for a three-year deal at $15,000 a season, Ty held out through the following April. Because of organized baseball's unique reserve clause, Ty was bound legally to play for the Tigers—or no one. Displaying his usual tenacity, he vowed to enter the business world rather than accept a lower figure. Navin and his star attraction finally came to terms on a one-year deal for $12,000, but only after Ty's old Georgia friend, Sen. Hoke Smith, made noises about investigating whether baseball violated federal antitrust laws. Ty hit a major-league-best .390 in 1913 for the sixth-place Tigers, then watched with satisfaction as a heretofore closed market suddenly opened for business.

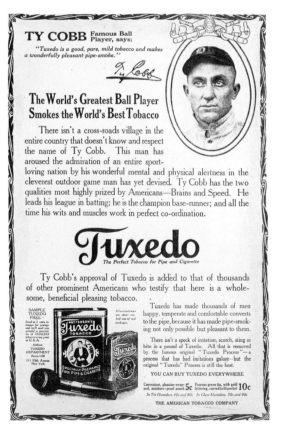

The reason was the formation of the Federal League, which remains the only serious challenge to the established major leagues in this century. The Feds started in 1914 with franchises in eight cities, many in direct competition with major-league teams. Before the Feds went belly-up after three seasons, they had succeeded in signing 172 players from American and National League rosters and driving up the game's salary structure. Although Ty received overtures from Chicago manufacturer James Gilmore and oil magnate Harry Sinclair, two of the new league's wealthiest backers, he never seriously considered jumping. Instead, he used the threat to leverage a $15,000 contract for the 1914 season from Navin. The following year he signed a three-year pact for $20,000 per annum.

This was a tremendous amount of money—and a point of considerable pride to Cobb. In early 1914, Henry Ford had shocked the industrial world by introducing the five dollar day for his unskilled workforce. As unbelievable as that figure seemed to the tens of thousands of laborers hurrying to Detroit, it was but a fraction of the $130 or so Ty made every time he played a two-hour game of baseball.

The teens were Cobb's salad days. After years of living in rented apartments and houses, he bought a spacious two-story home at 2425 William Street in Augusta. There he and Charlie and their children shared space with several domestic servants and pets. Life was comfortable. In addition to his regular-season salary, Ty drew fees from such endorsements as underwear, suspenders, chewing gum, motor parts, Coca-Cola, chewing tobacco, cigarettes, and a nickel candy bar named after him. He was the most famous and recognizable ballplayer in the country, his name and face appearing on bats, magazine covers, tobacco cards, gum tins, sheet music, paper fans, candy bar wrappers,

A year after Granddad Johnny died in August 1912, Ty and his grandmother visited a studio with Ty Jr. and Shirley.

87

After a lengthy holdout, Ty and Frank Navin came to terms on April 25, 1913, on a $15,000 contract that made Ty the highest-paid ballplayer ever. Ty's seemingly annual holdouts not only brought him the money he felt he deserved, they gave him a respite from spring training, which he hated.

The Nats' gnat, Clyde "Deerfoot" Milan, couldn't hit with Cobb, but he was as fast as his nickname suggests. In 1912 the little Washington outfielder stole 88 bases, shattering Ty's year-old record of 76. Milan pilfered another 74 bases in 1913, giving him the only 2 stolen-base titles of his 16-year career with Washington.

The famous Detroit outfield of 1915. From left: Bobby Veach, Ty Cobb, and Sam Crawford. The trio dominated the league's statistical categories, capturing the top positions in base hits, RBI, and total bases. The RBI title was the first of 3 in 4 years for Detroit's "other" outfielder, Veach, who for a dozen summers labored in the shadow of Cobb, Crawford, and later, Harry Heilmann. A lifetime .310 hitter, the colorless left fielder from Kentucky also at various times led the junior circuit in doubles, triples, and base hits.

Boston's equally famous outfield of Duffy Lewis (partially obscured by a throwing Sam Crawford), Tris Speaker, and Harry Hooper was arguably the greatest defensive trio ever, one of the reasons the Tigers finished 2½ games behind the Red Sox in 1915 and 4 games back in 1916. Donie Bush and Bobby Veach (far right) are the other Tigers in the picture.

and a patent medicine called Nuxated Iron, which—if the ad copy was to be believed—rescued baseball's number-one star from his early season listlessness. It's hard to believe that Ty could be ever so afflicted. Always restless, he spent his off-seasons barnstorming, hunting, golfing, and motoring. He followed the progress of his stock investments and engaged in minor entrepreneurial activities, including car dealerships and real estate. Like other famous athletes, he also took a turn on the vaudeville circuit and even appeared in a forgettable two-reeler called *Somewhere in Georgia*. So much for Professor Cobb's worry that his son would amount to nothing better than a muscle-worker.

Meanwhile, his family continued to grow. In addition to Ty Jr. and Shirley, he and Charlie had three more children over the next several years. Herschel was born in 1916, followed by Beverly in 1918 and Jimmy in 1921.

Ty admittedly lacked patience with people of all ages (the 1990s term "zero tolerance" leaps to mind), but his affection for children was the same as his father's: genuine, if often awkward. He frequently brought the frustrations of his job home with him. He had a short fuse and could be bitingly sarcastic. Plus, as the children grew, his high and often unrealistic expectations for them created tension within the household. But his sole surviving son, Jimmy, has always maintained that although his dad was a strict disciplinarian, he never physically mistreated them. Others who knew the family disagree.

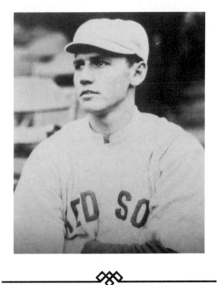

Pitcher "Smokey Joe" Wood, who joined Boston a year after Speaker, agreed with his teammate's assessment that Cobb was head-and-shoulders above his peers. "I don't think there's anybody that ever saw Cobb play in his heyday who wouldn't say, without a doubt: Cobb. If there'd been a higher league, he'd have been the only one in it." Ty would have gladly traded all the compliments for just one of the four world championships Boston won between 1912 and 1918.

89

Tris Speaker was a gambler, outdoorsman, Southerner, and consistently spectacular performer. Small wonder that he and Cobb were good pals. Speaker, who broke in with the Red Sox in 1907, snapped Ty's string of batting titles at 9 in 1916, the year he was traded to Cleveland. An outstanding all-around center fielder who hit— and prevented—more doubles than anybody in history, Speaker's misfortune was to play during Cobb's era. "Good as I was," he once admitted, "I never was close to Cobb, and neither was Babe Ruth or anybody else." Nonetheless, Speaker was brilliant enough to join Ty in the Hall of Fame's first class of inductees.

NO PLACE LIKE HOME

Ty Cobb stole home 55 times in his career (including one World Series theft), easily the most of any player in history. Here is a complete chronological listing of each of them, including date, inning, and the opposing battery. An asterisk (*) indicates that the theft was at the front end of a double steal; a double asterisk (**) indicates that it was at the front end of a triple steal.

Date	Opponent		Inning	Opposing Battery (Pitcher & Catcher)
1907 (2)				
+June 29	Cleveland		6	Heinie Berger & Howard Wakefield*
+July 5	Philadelphia		7	Rube Waddell & Ossee Schreckengost*
1908 (3)				
June 23	Chicago		1	Ed Walsh and Billy Sullivan*
+September 24	Philadelphia		1	Jack Coombs & Mike Powers*
September 27	Philadelphia		3	Jack Coombs & Mike Powers*
1909 (3)				
+May 13	New York		7	Rube Manning & Red Kleinow
June 16	Philadelphia		1	Chief Bender & Ira Thomas*
+July 22	Boston		7	Harry Walter & Pat Donohue*
1909 World Series (1)				
October 9	Pittsburgh		3	Vic Willis & George Gibson
1910 (3)				
+May 30	St. Louis	b	1	Bill Bailey & Jim Stephens
August 16	Washington		4	Bob Groom & Eddie Ainsmith
+October 5	Cleveland	b	3	Fred Blanding & Grover Land
1911 (5)				
+April 18	Cleveland		1	George Kahler & Syd Smith *
+May 1	Cleveland		6	George Kahler & Grover Land
+May 12	New York		7	Ray Caldwell & Ed Sweeney
+July 12	Philadelphia		1	Harry Krause & Ira Thomas
+August 18	Boston		1	Jack Killilay & Bill Carrigan**
1912 (8)				
+April 20	Cleveland		1	Vean Gregg & Ted Easterly*
+May 1	Chicago		1	Joe Benz & Bruno Block
+May 13	New York		1	Hippo Vaughn & Gabby Street*
+June 21	Cleveland		6	Fred Blanding & Steve O'Neill*
+July 1	Cleveland		3	Vean Gregg & Steve O'Neill*
+July 4	St. Louis	a	5	George Baumgardner & Paul Krichell*
+August 1	Washington		6	Bob Groom & Rip Williams
+September 6	St. Louis		8	Earl Hamilton & Paul Krichell*
1913 (4)				
+April 30	Chicago		8	Ed Cicotte & Ray Schalk
+May 18	Washington		7	Walter Johnson & Eddie Ainsmith
+May 20	Philadelphia		3	Duke Houck & Jack Lapp
September 15	New York		5	Jack Warhop & Ed Sweeney*

Date	Opponent	Inning	**Opposing Battery** (Pitcher & Catcher)
1914 (1)			
+June 9	Philadelphia	4	Bob Shawkey & Jack Lapp*
1915 (5)			
+April 28	St. Louis	3	Bill James & Sam Agnew**
June 4	New York	9	Ray Caldwell & Less Nunamaker
June 9	Boston	3	Ray Collins & Bill Carrigan
June 18	Washington	1	Joe Boehling & John Henry**
+June 23	St. Louis	8	Grover Lowdermilk & Sam Agnew
1916 (1)			
August 23	Philadelphia	8	Tom Sheehan & Val Picinich
1917 (1)			
September 26	New York	3	Jack Enright & Muddy Ruel
1918 (1)			
July 9	Philadelphia b	5	Scott Perry & Cy Perkins*
1919 (1)			
+August 23	Boston	3	Waite Hoyt & Roxy Walters**
1920 (3)			
May 18	Philadelphia	8	Pat Martin & Glen Myatt
+September 18	Boston	1	Elmer Myers & Wally Schang*
+September 19	Washington a	4	Harry Courtney & Patsy Gharrity
1921 (2)			
June 9	Washington	6	Eric Erickson & Patsy Gharrity*
September 16	Philadelphia	5	Roy Moore & Glenn Myatt
1922 (2)			
May 8	Boston	9	Allen Russell & Muddy Ruel*
+July 26	Washington	3	George Mogridge & Patsy Gharrity
1923 (1)			
October 2	Chicago	7	Paul Castner & Buck Crouse*
1924 (3)			
+April 22	St. Louis	3	Bill Bayne & Pat Collins*
+April 27	Chicago	5	Ted Lyons & Buck Crouse
+August 10	Boston	7	Buster Ross & Val Picinich
1926 (1)			
July 3	Cleveland	1	George Uhle & Luke Sewell
1927 (3)			
April 19	Washington	6	General Crowder & Muddy Ruel**
April 26	Boston	7	Tony Welzer & Grover Hartley*
July 6	Boston a	1	Del Lundgren & Grover Hartley**
1928 (1)			
June 15	Cleveland	8	George Grant & Luke Sewell

+ Home game   a First game of doubleheader b Second game of doubleheader

91

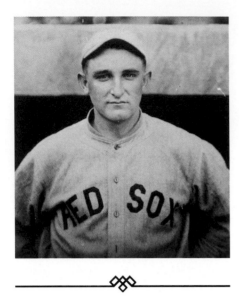

A thorn in the Tigers' side—or, more accurately, a fastball in the ribs—was Carl Mays, a surly, submarining right-hander who pitched on 6 pennant winners for the Red Sox and Yankees between 1915 and 1923. Mays, who had a well-deserved reputation for dusting off batters, hated Cobb. The feeling was mutual. Described as "a morose loner," Mays is best known as the man who in 1920 killed Ray Chapman with a pitched ball—an accidental beaning that has probably kept him out of the Hall of Fame.

Cobb's relationship with children has always taken a beating, with one writer saying that only a couple pictures of him with children exist. Actually, there are many, not all of them posed. Some exist only in the memories of old men who knew him away from the park. "I know people say Cobb was mean and rotten on the baseball field and off," said Jim Cullen, who lived in an apartment building on Woodward Avenue in Detroit, close to where Ty and Charlie rented during the season. "But he was always great with us. He would play with all the little kids whenever he was in town."

Jasper Miner, the sweet-tempered grandson of famed Canadian naturalist Jack Miner, remembers Ty as "a man's man" who took an interest in earnest youths. As regular hosts to Ty's family during the summer, and as frequent guests of Ty at Navin Field, the Miners were witnesses to more than one Cobb outburst. But like others who spent time with Ty regularly off the diamond, the family considered his radical mood swings one of those unfortunate prices of friendship and moved on from there. Jasper was impressed enough with Ty to try his hand as a catcher. Ty, knowing Jasper had a snowball's chance in Arizona of making a living playing pro ball, still arranged a tryout for him with the Philadelphia Athletics. "You don't hear at all about the good things that Ty did," said Miner. "As far as this family goes, he'd give you the shirt off his back."

But as Ty's own family was learning, some men are destined for fame, others for notoriety. Cobb experienced both. On the field, he was the unquestioned king of the diamond, the master of the unexpected. "A lot of times Cobb would be on third base and I'd draw a base on balls," said Sam Crawford, recalling some ancient mischief for Larry Ritter, "and as I started to go down to first I'd sort of half glance at Cobb, at third. He'd make a slight move that told me he wanted to keep going—not to stop at first, but to keep on going to second. Well,

A bat-throwing altercation with Mays produced this remarkable scene at Fenway Park on September 16, 1915. After catching a fly ball for the final out of the game, Ty slowly walked in from center field, through a crowd of several thousand infuriated Red Sox fans. They pelted him with bottles and paper wads and yelled insults and curses—and kept their distance.

Following the 1916 season, Ty became the first professional athlete to star in a commercial motion picture. *Somewhere in Georgia* was filmed in New York City in two weeks—and looked it. The story, written by Grantland Rice, had Ty playing a small-town bank clerk who is signed to a contract by the Detroit Tigers. Homesick for his girlfriend (played by Elsie MacLeod), Ty returns to Georgia, where he is kidnapped by villains. Not to fear. Ty escapes, commandeers a mule wagon, and arrives at the park just in time to win the game. Much to the relief of Detroit fans and noted critic Ward Morehouse (who called *Somewhere in Georgia* "absolutely the worst movie I ever saw"), he didn't quit his day job.

I'd trot two-thirds of the way to first and then suddenly, without warning, I'd speed up and go across first as fast as I could and tear out for second. He's on third, see. They're watching him, and suddenly there I go, and they don't know what the devil to do.

"If they try to stop me, Cobb'll take off for home. Sometimes they'd catch him, and sometimes they'd catch me, and sometimes they wouldn't get either of us. But most of the time they were too paralyzed to do anything, and I'd wind up at second on a base on balls. Boy, did that ever create excitement. For the crowd, you know; the fans were always wondering what might happen next."

Branch Rickey, then managing the St. Louis Browns, remembered: "One day he was on first base against us. The pitcher threw over to first and Cobb got back in time. But as the first baseman lobbed the ball back to the pitcher, Cobb was off in a flash streaking for second. The pitcher hurried his throw and it went into center field.

The Federal League of 1914–15 was an ambitious but short-lived attempt at a third major league. Its biggest star was Benny Kauff, a rough-hewn but likable outfielder from Ohio with a penchant for silk underwear, diamond rings, and colorful quotes. Kauff was the Feds' hitting and base-stealing champion in each of its two complete seasons. In 1914 he batted .370 and stole 75 bases for the first-place Indianapolis Hoosiers; the following year he batted .342 and stole 55 bases for the Brooklyn Federals. Kauff signed a contract with John McGraw in 1916 and vowed that he would "make Cobb look like a bush leaguer." His numbers, however, dropped considerably once he started playing with the big boys: a .287 average and 103 stolen bases in 5 years as a New York Giant.

George Herman Ruth's first appearance in Detroit, 1915. A superlative pitcher for the Red Sox for 6 seasons, the Babe's bat was as electrifying and hard to ignore as his personality. He won his first home run title in 1918 while still taking his regular turn on the mound. The following summer he set a single-season record with 29— 6 more than the entire Detroit team hit. A dramatic change in the way America loved its pastime was literally in the wind.

Ty wasn't considered overpoweringly handsome, but women such as soprano Frances Ingram (left) were attracted to him because of his fame. And, in sharp contrast to how he dealt with most men, Ty was unfailingly gracious to women.

94

Ty was a doting father. Home in Georgia after the 1914 season, he poses with Charlie, little Ty, and Shirley.

Cobb popped to his feet and headed for third. The throw had him beaten, but the third baseman dropped the ball. Cobb slid for the ball and kicked it into the dugout, then got up and jogged home with the winning run. It was a clear case of interference, but the umpires said it must have been an accident. They could not believe that any player could perform such a stunt on purpose."

The same disbelief held true for Ty's growing number of off-field confrontations. One of the most dramatic came on the heels of the Lucker incident. As Ty and his wife were driving to catch a train in Detroit in July 1912, three men jumped on the running board of their car. Although their identities were never established, it's thought they were thugs hired by Tammany Hall to avenge the Lucker beating. Whoever they were, one knife-wielding attacker slashed Ty's back before he fought them off with the .32-caliber automatic pistol he often carried. Leaving a terrorized Charlie behind, Ty chased one of the men down an alley. He caught up with him and then, flush with anger, pistol-whipped him until his face resembled hamburger. Cobb later confessed he may have killed the man, although no one will ever know.

A couple of years later, in June 1914, the same pistol figured prominently in another row. This time the affair revolved around twenty cents of spoiled fish that a merchant supposedly sold Ty's wife. Coming home with Washington manager Clark Griffith after a Saturday game with the Senators, Ty was told about an argument that

Charlie had had with William L. Carpenter, the owner of a local butcher shop. Carpenter asserted that Mrs. Cobb was mistaken, that the fish he had delivered earlier in the day had been fresh.

More unsavory than the fish was Cobb's reaction. Ty phoned the merchant and, convinced that he had insulted his wife, marched out the door, revolver in hand. As crimson-faced Charlie stayed home with several dinner guests, Ty left their rented cottage on Longfellow Avenue, drove to the Progressive Meat Market at 1526 Hamilton Boulevard, and forced Carpenter at gunpoint to phone Charlie and apologize. All the while Ty carried on a wordfest with a 20-year-old butcher named Harold Harding, who finally got Cobb's goat by calling him a coward. As the papers later reported, the ensuing "fist mill was interrupted by two patrolmen, who, with great reluctance, called the patrol wagon" and delivered Ty to the Bethune Avenue station.

There, Ty nursed a fractured thumb and declared his reputation ruined. "I'll be joshed out of Detroit and sent to the Federal League," he moaned. Instead he spent the night in jail, was found guilty of disturbing the peace, and paid a fifty dollar fine. The injured thumb limited him to just 97 games in 1914, but he still hit .368 to once again lead the majors.

Such shameful episodes added to Ty's reputation as a social miscreant and put a strain on his marriage. Charlie shunned public life, but her husband's periodic run-ins aimed the spotlight indirectly on her and her children. Soon Charlie and the kids were living most of the year at their Augusta home, where the results of Ty's propensity for violence and embarrassing confrontations could be mitigated by distance.

American Leaguers weren't as fortunate. By 1915 the Tigers had been rebuilt into a contender, and for the next two summers they battled the Boston Red Sox for the pennant. "Battle" they did. Detroit-

The best team of the war years was the Chicago White Sox, who led the league in patriotic flourishes. As seen here, the Sox dutifully drilled with bats and in 1918 introduced the playing of "The Star-Spangled Banner" to ballparks. They won a championship in 1917 and probably would have won more, if not for eight players committing baseball's most treacherous act.

Ty's off-field fight with New York infielder Charles "Buck" Herzog during spring training in 1917 was one of his most widely reported confrontations. The following day Giants manager John McGraw nearly came to blows with Cobb in the lobby of the hotel where both teams were staying. "If you were a younger man," Ty told the 44-year-old manager before walking away, "I'd kill you."

GETTING A GRIP ON SOME LEGENDARY LUMBER

Although Hillerich & Bradsby today shares the baseball bat market with three major manufacturers—Worth Sports Company, Rawlings, and Cooper—at the turn of the century the maker of the legendary "Louisville Slugger" was unchallenged as *the* producer of quality big-league clubs. Unlike most of its early competitors, H & B took great care in inspecting wood for solidity, body, and resiliency before declaring it "fit for the fracas." Honus Wagner, for one, considered his Sluggers "perfectly balanced" and "made of the best driving wood."

The world's premier bat manufacturer got its start in 1884 when John A. "Bud" Hillerich, the 18-year-old son of a Louisville cooper named J. Frederich Hillerich, turned a bat for Pete Browning of the Louisville Eclipse baseball team. This was the first Louisville Slugger. Ten years later the name was registered as a trademark. Thanks in part to word-of-mouth advertising by Browning and satisfied teammates, the firm, J. F. Hillerich & Son, was off and running, quickly outgrowing its small wood shop and moving into a separate bat factory in 1901. In 1911 a young hardware buyer, Frank W. Bradsby, joined the business as sales manager. It was probably Bradsby who, looking to explain the bat maker's nearly universal acceptance among big leaguers and sandlotters, wrote the following ad copy around 1913:

> *A player is more particular with his bat than he is with his watch or throwing arm—or mother-in-law. It must be just "so-so," and this is the reason why the Hillerich product is so successful.*
>
> *A bat, to be a "beaut," must have the proper "feel," hang and balance, and few sticks turned out solely by machinery have ever met these requirements. The Hillerich plant has men who have grown gray-haired in the service of taking the raw material from the machines, "feeling" it out, and then by hand turning it into shape, balance and the "so-so." The veterans have sons in the plant learning the same trick.*
>
> *To the layman, the Louisville Slugger resembles all other bats; but to the experienced swatter, the resemblance is remote. There is a balance and hang to the Hillerich that other factories have never been able to consistently duplicate.*

In 1916 the firm changed its name to the Hillerich & Bradsby Company. Eight decades later, the name remains the same, although the company now produces its Louisville Sluggers (and other sporting goods, including golf clubs and aluminum bats) at plants in Jeffersonville, Indiana, and Sante Fe Springs, California.

Much of the company's early success can be attributed to commercial endorsements by some of the game's most accomplished hitters. On September 1, 1905—two days after Ty Cobb made his major-league debut—Pittsburgh's Honus Wagner signed a contract giving the bat company permission to use his autograph on Louisville Sluggers, becoming the first in a long line of players to endorse the product. Cleveland's Nap Lajoie was signed in 1905, followed by Philadelphia's Harry Davis in 1908. By 1920 most of the top hitters in both leagues had signed exclusive contracts with Hillerich & Bradsby.

Ty broke into the majors using homemade bats that he and his next-door neighbor, Joe Cunningham, had turned on a lathe in the Cunninghams' tool shed. These were small, heavy clubs made of ash. These favorites, some of which had accompanied his travels as a Royston Red, Anniston Nobleman, and Augusta Tourist, were sawed in half by malicious Detroit teammates early in the 1906 season. Although Ty later claimed to have switched to Louisville Sluggers and used them "exclusively" throughout the rest of his career, he probably experimented with a mix of factory-made bats between 1906 and 1908, winning his first 2 batting titles in the process. There were, after all, any number of bat manufacturers happy to donate their product for field testing by a budding star. Any Sluggers that Ty did swing during his first four seasons in the American League probably were either unsigned or Nap Lajoie models.

97

Cobb picks out a club. "Ty has as many different bats as milady has hairpins," reported Baseball Magazine in 1920.

On October 13, 1908, Cobb became the fourth player to have his decal pasted to the barrel of a Louisville Slugger. The terms of Ty's contract, however, were different from the others. Instead of accepting the standard seventy-five dollar endorsement fee ("a chunk of real money," he said), he exchanged the use of his name for a bin of specially constructed bats.

Specifically, Ty wanted his bats made of prime ash from Kentucky and Tennessee forests, considering it a stronger wood than the popular hickory and hackberry. He also wanted the wood to have a straight and fine grain, not a heavy grain. "And try to find wood with small whirly knots in it," he requested. As he later explained, this was "indicative of trees that have had a long, slow growth, producing the most resilient and stoutest timber."

On his regular trips to the factory Ty would whack each of his finished bats against the ground. "If it rang tenor," he said, "I'd put that one aside to keep. If I got a dull 'thump,' that one I discarded."

In those days no one wore batting gloves. Since Cobb disdained the sticky feel of resin on his hands, throughout his career all of his bats had several twists of tape wrapped about eight to ten inches up the handle to improve his grip. Some argue that, especially for a gifted hitter like Cobb, the effect of a custom-made bat is more psychological than anything. But in 1909, the first season Ty used his own autograph-model Louisville Slugger, he won the Triple Crown and led the Tigers into a third straight World Series.

On September 12, 1911, the Ty Cobb name was registered as a trademark under certificate No. 83,408. That year his picture started appearing in advertisements in trade journals, most notably *The Sporting Goods Dealer*. In 1921 the company began advertising Louisville Slugger bats to the general public, with ads appearing in *Boys' Life, The American Boy, The Youth's Companion,* and *The Sporting News*. Advertising, coupled to Ty's string of batting titles, made the Ty Cobb model 40Tc bat the company's most popular model through the 1920s.

Ty used the same model bat from 1911 to 1924. It featured a medium-sized barrel that gradually tapered to a medium handle and knob. The length was $34^1/_2$ inches and the weight, which ranged from 40 to 44 ounces, was evenly distributed. This created a large hitting surface—not that Cobb needed it. Years after Ty retired, an old Hillerich lathe hand named Henry Morrow produced a bat that showed Ty's "sweet spot," the place where batters try to consistently hit the ball. "Sure enough," one H & B executive recalled, "there was this place on the bat that was a well-worn hollow that showed how Cobb had met the ball squarely over and over." Ty reduced the weight over the years, dropping to a 38- to 40-ounce bat by the time he won his last batting title in 1919.

On May 5, 1924, Ty ordered a new model. The style was the same, except that this bat was slightly smaller and, at 35 ounces, lighter than his old model. Later that summer Ty returned to a 38-ounce version of his original stick. The following June Ty placed another order. Again it was similar in style to the 1911 bat only this time the barrel was slightly smaller and the end had been sawed. The effect was a nearly squared-end bat that was a quarter-inch shorter. Cobb used this 34-inch, 40-ounce club for a while, then switched to his lighter 1924 model for the balance of his career in Detroit. He returned to his 1911 bat after he signed with Philadelphia, typically employing 37- and 38-ounce versions of it for his final two years in the majors.

While many modern ballplayers go through hundreds of bats each year—a result of the trend toward thinner handles and thicker barrels, not to mention wide-open pocketbooks—players in Cobb's day could make a batch of bats last for years. Hall of Fame shortstop Joe Sewell, for instance, used the same bat for fourteen seasons! Ty wasn't as stingy, although he did everything he could to keep his favorite clubs in tip-top condition. To "set" the seams, he would soak them in neat's-foot oil or chewing tobacco, then clamp them in a vise and rub them with a large hollowed-out steer bone.

"My own favorite prescription was a chewing tobacco called Navy Nerve-Cut," he recalled, "the juiciest kind I ever discovered. Using the steer bone, I rubbed in Navy by the hour." Such loving care paid off, as Ty finished his career in 1928 using a Louisville Slugger that, based on the long-discontinued trademark, was judged to be at least thirteen years old.

After Ty invested in a Grand Rapids sporting goods store prior to World War I, his autograph appeared on the dealer's line of bats.

"Every great batter works on the theory that the pitcher is more afraid of him than he is of the pitcher." So spoke Ty, who in the last years of the decade reclaimed the title of league's top batsman with a string of remarkably consistent seasons: .383 in 1917, .382 in 1918, and .384 in 1919. Although he improved on these figures in 2 of the next 3 seasons, he never won another batting title.

100

Ignore the typo that has Ty batting .224 in 1908. Storeowners subscribing to The Sporting Goods Dealer obviously knew better, because through the early '20s they continued to order—and sell—more Ty Cobb bats than any other model.

Boston contests typically featured beanballs, locomotive-style slides, and all other weapons available to hard-nosed competitors hungry for a postseason check.

The Red Sox, world champions in 1912, were just setting out on a run that would produce three more championships in the next four years. Boasting the greatest defensive outfield of all time in Harry Hooper, Duffy Lewis, and Tris Speaker, the Sox also featured the best mound staff: Smokey Joe Wood, Babe Ruth, Ernie Shore, Dutch Leonard, and Carl Mays. Although the staff regularly aimed a few pitches each game at Ty's noggin, it was Mays—a surly, submarining right-hander who is most famous for throwing the pitch that killed Ray Chapman—who Ty detested more than anyone on the Boston club.

Matters came to a head in the opener of a showdown four-game series in Boston on September 16, 1915. Mays threw at Cobb each time he came to the plate. Finally, in the eighth inning Ty responded by firing his bat at him and calling him a "yellow dog." Ty stepped back in after order was restored—and was hit on the wrist with Mays' next pitch. The Fenway faithful showered him with pop bottles as he took first base.

The Tigers retired the Red Sox in the ninth to preserve a 6–1 victory, the final out coming on a fly ball to Cobb. Immediately, thousands of angry, frustrated fans carpeted the field. They surrounded Ty, who coolly walked in from center field as curses, paper wads, and bottles filled the air. "None of the mongrels in the crowd had the nerve to attack him," marveled Eddie Batchelor, "each waiting for somebody else to strike the first blow." Cobb's remarkable show of courage, however, couldn't prevent Boston from taking the next three games and the pennant.

Hughie Jennings later labeled 1915 his biggest disappointment. The Tigers, propelled by 20-game winners George "Hooks" Dauss and Harry Coveleski, and outfielders Sam Crawford and Bobby Veach (who tied for the league lead with 112 RBI), became the first team to win 100 games but not the pennant. Ty, his competitive instincts kicked into overdrive by a pennant race and the pursuit of personal glory, was more brilliant than ever. He scored 144 runs, won his ninth straight batting title with a .369 mark—breaking Honus Wagner's record of 8—and set a single-season base-stealing mark of 96. Ty, who stole second for the team and third for himself, departed from tradition and played every game of the schedule, seeking to rack up as many steals as possible.

"I've always regretted I didn't make it a hundred steals that year," he later reflected. "With a little greater effort, I believe I could've gotten those four additional bases." As it was, the record—which seemed invincible—wound up standing for nearly a half-century.

Ty was caught in a relaxed mood by a Navin Field fan sometime during the 1917 season.

101

The following year, Ty found himself in another kind of uniform. As with many veterans of "the war to end all wars," Ty was shipped to France too late to participate in the fighting. This was a shame, said Hughie Jennings, who considered him "the most fearless man I have ever known. He was afraid of nothing." Jennings always thought it was the North's good fortune that Cobb hadn't been born forty years earlier. "He would have been a whole Confederate army."

Babe Ruth and the swing that captivated America.

CHAPTER SIX

Damned Yankee

How dear to my heart was the old-fashioned batter
  Who scattered line drives from the spring to the fall.
He did not resemble the up-to-date batter
  Who swings from his heels and then misses the ball.
The up-to-date batter I'm not very strong for;
  He shatters the ozone with all of his might.
And that is the reason I hanker and long for
  Those who doubled to left, and tripled to right.

The old-fashioned batter,
  The eagle-eyed batter,
The thinking-man's batter,
  Who tripled to right.
                                    —George E. Phair

In 1916, the Tigers again made a bid for the pennant, and again they fell just short, finishing 4 games behind first-place Boston and 2 back of second-place Chicago. To top off another disappointing season, Ty saw his string of batting titles snapped at 9. Despite Cobb's .371 average, Tris Speaker—who had been dealt from Boston to Cleveland before the season—bested that with a .383 effort. Ty's stolen base total dropped to 68, but he easily outdistanced runner-up Armando Marsans of St. Louis, a refugee from the Federal League.

The following April the United States finally entered the war that had been draining Europe of its young men for nearly three years. As if to warm up for the real thing, Ty got involved in one of his most widely publicized frays. That spring the Tigers trained in Waxahachie, Texas. On March 31, the club traveled to Dallas to open a series of exhibitions with the New York Giants, managed by the feisty John McGraw. Ty, who had played eighteen holes of golf that morning, arrived just before game time. This earned him an earful from the Giants' Art Fletcher and Charles "Buck" Herzog, who shouted that the Tiger star was a "showoff" and a "swellhead."

Ty singled his first time up and yelled to second baseman Herzog that he was coming down on the next pitch. The throw had him easily, but Cobb's flashing spikes sliced Herzog's trousers and drew blood. As the two thrashed about in the dirt, Fletcher ran over from his shortstop position to get in his licks. Within seconds Giants, Tigers, and park policemen were

George "Buck" Weaver, a.k.a. "The Ginger Kid," reportedly was the only third baseman Ty wouldn't bunt on. Weaver's career, like that of the rest of the Chicago Black Sox, abruptly ended on September 28, 1920, when a Cook County grand jury indicted eight players for conspiring to throw the 1919 World Series. The Black Sox's final game together had been a 2–0 victory over the Tigers the previous afternoon.

knotted around second base, but order was quickly restored. Cobb was given the thumb by umpire Bill Brennan, a decision that brought a storm of protest from the 5,500 fans who had come to see a favorite son of the South.

Both clubs were staying at the Oriental Hotel. That evening, Herzog interrupted Ty's dinner and challenged him to finish their business in one hour inside Ty's room, giving Cobb time to clear away the rugs and furniture and to sprinkle the floor with water. Herzog, who boxed some in the army, arrived wearing tennis shoes, a fateful decision. Several Giants and Tigers jammed the fourth-floor hallway to get a better view of the show, but only Heinie Zimmerman and Oscar Stanage were allowed into the room as seconds. Detroit trainer Harry Tuthill refereed the match, which according to everyone present was won by Cobb. As he planned, the slippery floor negated Herzog's superior boxing skills. Ty, who was wearing leather street shoes for a better grip, had Herzog stretched backwards over the bed and was hammering him when Tuthill finally declared the affair over.

But it wasn't. McGraw, enraged when he discovered the condition of his badly mauled infielder, accosted Cobb the following morning in the lobby. As a crowd of stunned hotel guests looked on, McGraw "became so vituperative that I had to restrain myself from repeating the performance of Room 404," Ty said.

Ignoring the pleas of local chambers of commerce and the taunts of the New York team, Ty refused to take the field for the rest of the Tigers-Giants tour. Instead, he traveled to Cincinnati, where he continued his conditioning with the Reds. The Giants and Tigers finally part-

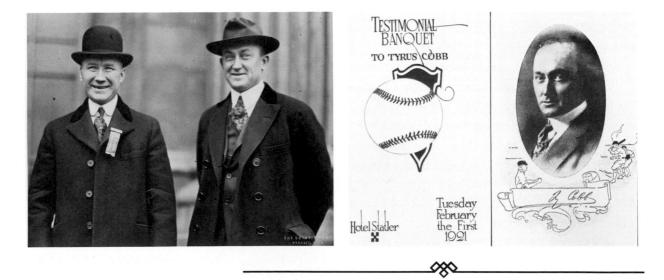

With fired manager Hughie Jennings by his side, Ty officially took over the reins of the Tigers on February 1, 1921. As part of the elaborate day-long ceremonies in Detroit, Cobb received the keys to the city and was toasted by 600 people at a testimonial dinner.

ed company in Kansas City, where McGraw and Company dashed off a telegram to Cobb: "It's safe to rejoin your club now. We've left."

"That was the one way the Giants could have the last word," Cobb retorted in his autobiography. "By mail."

Ty reclaimed the batting championship in 1917, hitting a resounding .383, 30 points higher than anyone else in the majors. He also easily outdistanced everyone in baseball in hits, doubles, triples, total bases, and slugging percentage. Although he added his sixth, and final, stolen-base crown with 55 thefts, his days as a dominant base-stealing threat were just about at an end. To use an automotive metaphor, at thirty his wheels simply had too many miles on them. "The shock when he hits the dirt is terrific, especially in mid-season when the ground is hard," observed Vic Tomlinson, the physical director of the Detroit Athletic Club. "Anyone who wants to get an idea of the bump that a man sliding to a base receives can easily do so by running at top speed and then jumping with all his might flat on the ground. . . ." After averaging 61 stolen bases during his first dozen full seasons, Ty slipped to 34 steals in 1918, then averaged but 15 steals a season for the final decade of his career.

His two last batting titles bracketed an abbreviated military career. As hundreds of thousands of Yanks went "over there" during 1918, the provost marshal of the armed forces issued a "work or fight" order for all men of draft age. Baseball players were classified as nonessential to the war effort, so the regular season ended a month earlier than usual. Ty batted .382 in the curtailed 1918 campaign (once again outdistancing his closest competitor by 30 points), then became one of the twenty-five current and former Tigers to serve in the military during the war.

105

Two views of some of the "Cobbmen" at spring training in San Antonio in 1921, Ty's first as manager. From left: Cobb, Allen Conkwright, Lu Blue, Joe Sargent, Johnny Bassler, John Bogart, Bert Cole, Donie Bush, and Bob Fothergill. Although Ty earnestly tried to pump much-needed life into his troops, players soon complained of a lack of communication with their new boss.

The heart of the Yankees' lineup in 1921, the first of 3 straight pennant-winning seasons. Left to right: first baseman Wally Pipp, left fielder Babe Ruth, shortstop Roger Peckinpaugh, right fielder Bob Meusel, and third baseman Frank Baker.

Despite managing the club and playing in 128 games, Ty found time to perform his famous fall-away slide for a motion picture camera sometime in 1921.

Given his combative personality, Cobb and the military seemed a perfect fit. Hughie Jennings, for one, considered Ty the most fearless man he had ever known, one who would have impaled the Kaiser on a *picklehauser* if he'd gotten to Europe in time to do some real fighting. Instead, Ty arrived overseas, a captain in the Chemical Warfare Service, fewer than three weeks before the armistice.

He did have a life-threatening experience though. After receiving just a week of instruction at a base near Claumont, France, Ty and his fellow CWS officers—including former pitching great Christy Mathewson—were expected to train enlisted men in the proper use of their gas masks. During one botched training exercise, poison gas was released into a chamber before Cobb and Mathewson, the officers in charge, gave the signal. By the time the chamber door was finally opened, several men had inhaled a lethal dosage. Ty was only mildly sick, but the accident may have led to the tuberculosis that killed Mathewson seven years later.

The accident was the most eventful experience of Ty's three-month hitch. He caught the first troop ship home from France and arrived in New York on December 16. Just a couple of days away from turning thirty-two, he told reporters on the dock that he was tired of baseball and wished "to quit while I'm still good."

Instead, he held out almost all of spring training in a dispute with Frank Navin, who saluted his returning doughboys by trying to force pay cuts on them. Cobb refused, finally signed his sixth straight $20,000 contract, then went on to capture his twelfth and final batting title with a .384 average. Also making 1919 a memorable year for Ty were a postgame confrontation at Navin Field, when he kicked a mouthy fan in the groin and then faced down several of the victim's pals, and the insatiable postwar demand for American cotton, which allowed Ty to sell his futures for a whopping $155,000 profit.

The biggest story of 1919 took place that fall in Chicago, where eight players changed the color of their socks for a few pieces of silver. But their betrayal wouldn't surface until the following year. For now baseball fans couldn't stop talking about the game's newest sensation, a converted pitcher who had just set a new season's home run record with 29. George Herman "Babe" Ruth, the *New York Times* enthusiastically announced, had "supplanted the great Ty Cobb as baseball's greatest attraction." Although followers of thinking-man's baseball disagreed, their protests were already being drowned out by the din of shouting headlines and the jazzed-up pace of American life.

The 1920 season unfolded in predictable fashion for Cobb. As he had for each at-bat through fifteen big-league summers, Ty would approach the plate, tap each foot with the bat, then yank the peak of his cap low over his forehead. His eyes, thus shielded, would dart around the field until he had determined the opponent's defense and settled on a strategy. The shortstop shading toward second? Perhaps he would punch it through the hole between third and short. The right fielder playing too far off the line? Maybe he should try to pull the pitch. A tough lefty on the mound? Okay, maybe a drag bunt was in order. . . .

What Ty didn't know as his mind whirred and clicked and processed information was that his style of hitting was endangered. The old-fashioned thinking-man's batter was being shoved out of the spotlight and into the orchestra pit by a muscular stagehand named George Herman Ruth.

The phenomenon that came to be known as Babe Ruth was one of those unforeseen marriages of man, moment, and media with which American cultural history is rife. Ruth, the son of a Baltimore saloon-keeper, was born in 1895 and consigned to an orphanage when he was seven. An incorrigible schoolboy and a natural athlete, he moved from the playground to the International League's Baltimore Orioles, who in turn sold him to the Boston Red Sox in 1914. According to teammate Harry Hooper, by 1916 Ruth was "already the best lefty in the league." A batter's reputation meant nothing to him, Hooper added. "He was

The 1922 Cobbmen batted .305 and moved up three notches in the standings to third. Rookie infielder Fred Haney (second from right in the middle row) soaked up all he could about hitting from his boss and wound up batting .352.

107

Ty at bat in Washington in 1922. That season, aided by a controversial scoring decision, he hit .400 for the 3rd time in his career.

Babe Ruth and New York owner Jacob Ruppert at the World Series in 1923, the year the Yankees moved into their brand-new stadium and officially became the Bronx Bombers.

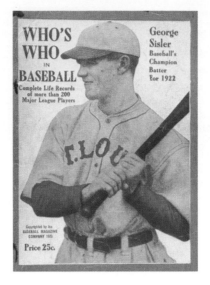

In 1917 Baseball Magazine called George Sisler "Ty Cobb's probable successor," a prediction that missed coming true by a nose. In 1920 the St. Louis Browns' spray-hitting first baseman collected 257 base hits, still the single-season record, as he won his 1st batting title with a .407 average. In 1922 the converted pitcher won his 2nd batting championship with a torrid .420 mark, eclipsing Ty's record 40-game hit streak in the process. Nicknamed "Gorgeous George," Sisler also was an outstanding defensive player, gifted runner (he won 4 stolen-base crowns), and heady batter. For years he set up certain pitchers by purposely striking out on high inside pitches, gambling they would throw him the same pitch in a tight spot. However, in 1923 a severe sinus infection affected Sisler's optic nerve and caused him to miss the entire season. He was never the same hitter after that.

probably too dumb to know the difference. But he was one of the few men who could throw a fastball past Cobb with any regularity."

Or hit the long ball consistently. Forget the glittering pitching stats: 23 wins and a league-low 1.75 ERA in 1915, 24 wins in 1916, and a record $29\frac{2}{3}$ consecutive scoreless innings in World Series play. Ruth's bashing—home run titles in 1918 and 1919 while still taking a regular turn on the mound—is what turned heads and caused Yankees owner Jacob Ruppert to write the money-poor Red Sox a check in excess of $100,000 for Ruth's services before the 1920 season.

Aiding Babe—and all hitters—that summer were significant rule changes. Prior to 1920 (the so-called dead-ball era) a ball was kept in play until it practically disintegrated in a pitcher's hand. By the middle innings it was a dark, lopsided sphere with the resiliency of squash, making power hitting next to impossible. Now a fresh ball was introduced into play several times a game, handing batters an unprecedented advantage. In addition, trick pitches such as the spitter and emory ball were outlawed starting in 1920 (although a grandfather clause allowed a few veteran pitchers to continue throwing them). Adding to the mayhem were the shorter outfield fence distances of the new ballparks being built. The inviting fences tempted even long-time choke hitters to pull and uppercut the ball.

Even without Ruth, these changes eventually would have killed the place-hitting and base-stealing game Cobb had dominated for so long. But Ruth's remarkable performance his first summer in New York accelerated the change. That year he slugged a staggering 54 home runs (including 10 against Detroit), more than any other *team* hit! Each seemed to soar farther than the last. Moreover, he hit .376 (fourth in

The Cobb home in Augusta.

the league) and broke existing records for runs scored, walks, and RBI. His .847 slugging percentage remains the single-season standard. In August, as the dreary and punchless Tigers fought to stay out of the basement, Ruth checked into Navin Field and powered 3 long home runs in two days, prompting the record number of Tiger fans to go wild. Detroiters gave the new superman of baseball "the welcome due a conquering hero," observed Harry Salsinger. "He got the applause, the shrieking adoration of the multitude, in Cobb's own city. Cobb, standing aside, could feel deeply how fickle the adoration of the sport-loving public is. He saw before him a new king acclaimed. . . ."

King indeed. Helped substantially by modern myth-making machinery—mass-circulation magazines, radio, movies, sophisticated national advertising, and countless daily newspapers—the irrepressible Ruth was the beneficiary of postwar America's fascination with the cult of personality. The 1920s produced Valentino, Grange, Dempsey, and Lindbergh, heroes whose fame fed on itself. In this league of media all-stars, the Babe rose to the top. His breathtaking metamorphosis into the country's foremost cultural icon flabbergasted even those who knew him well.

"You know, I saw it all happen, from beginning to end," Harry Hooper recalled years later. "But sometimes I still can't believe what I saw: this 19-year-old kid, crude, poorly educated, only slightly brushed by the social veneer we call civilization, gradually transformed into the idol of American youth and the symbol of baseball the world over—a man loved by more people and with an intensity of feeling that perhaps has never been equaled before or since. I saw a man transformed from a human being into something pretty close to a god. If somebody had predicted that back on the Boston Red Sox in 1914, he would have been thrown into a lunatic asylum."

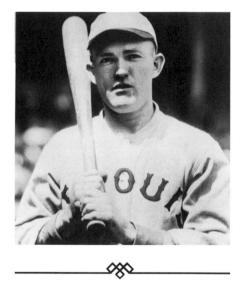

St. Louis also was home to Cardinal second baseman Rogers Hornsby, a moody, straight-shooting Texan who combined average and power better than any man in history. "The Rajah" won 6 straight batting titles between 1920 and 1925, then added number 7 later in the decade for the Boston Braves. Hornsby, who had hit 36 round-trippers in his first 6 seasons, was the consummate beneficiary of the lively ball. In his 3 .400 seasons (1922, 1924, 1925) he averaged 35 home runs and twice won the Triple Crown. His .424 average in 1924 remains the modern record and his .358 lifetime mark is second only to Cobb.

110

Knowing Jack Miner (top left), said Ty, "was one of the finest things that happened to me." The famous naturalist operated a bird sanctuary in Ontario, Canada, across the river from Detroit. Starting in 1917 and continuing for nearly a decade, Ty and his family were regular guests of the Miners, with Ty Jr. often spending summers there. Miner's conservation practices didn't prevent him from inviting Ty on moose hunting expeditions into the Canadian wilderness.

Ruth more than personified the shift from skill to power in the national pastime; his widely publicized hedonism embodied the entire Roaring Twenties, a decade he and his fellow free-swinging Yankees were to dominate. With the "war to end all wars" behind them (15 million killed) and Prohibition in front of them (15 million served), Americans in New York and Detroit and every other big city and backwater burg rejected accepted standards of social behavior in favor of dancing the Charleston, joyriding in one of Henry Ford's flivvers, and getting "blotto" on a hip flask of illegal gin. Even women, that forgotten half of Victorian society, revolted, bobbing their hair, shortening their skirts, and jamming cigarettes into their mouths. Why, in 1920, they even voted for the first time! To those who remembered the quieter and simpler times, when radios didn't spit out jazz and airplanes didn't roar overhead, when social life centered around front-porch conversation and not back-seat rendezvous, the world as they once knew it was going to hell in a handbasket. That included the beloved national pastime, whose most enduring image—a blurry Ty Cobb, gritted teeth and all, jamming his spikes into a bag—had been eclipsed by a spindly legged, moon-faced man-child taking mincing steps around the bases as another one of his wallops landed a Pullman's jump from the plate.

All of Ruth's heroics couldn't put the Yankees in the World Series in 1920. Instead, the Cleveland Indians, overcoming the accidental death of shortstop Ray Chapman in August, grabbed the pennant and beat Brooklyn in the Series. For Ty, it was a bittersweet win. He was happy for Cleveland manager Tris Speaker, but envious of his old friend's participation in one more fall classic.

Nearly thirty-four, that chance seemed more distant than ever to Ty. Hobbled by a knee injury, he hit a mere .334 in 1920, his weakest performance since 1906. More discouraging were the prospects for

COBB AND COKE

It was perhaps inevitable that two of America's greatest cultural icons—Ty Cobb and Coca-Cola—would enjoy a long, satisfying relationship. Both were products of the state of Georgia, born just a few months and a few whistle-stops apart in 1886. And both grew up to become integral parts of the national experience after the turn of the century.

Arguably the most successful product in the history of commerce (the company estimates that the soft drink is consumed hundreds of millions of times around the world daily), Coca-Cola was created on May 8, 1886, in Atlanta, Georgia, when a pharmacist, John Smith Pemberton, stirred up a batch of syrup inside a three-legged brass pot in his back yard. Satisfied with the taste, he took a jug of it to the local pharmacy. There it was mixed with carbonated water and placed on sale as a soda fountain drink for a nickel a glass.

Pemberton never realized his concoction's financial potential, selling off shares of the business until his death in 1888. Atlanta businessman Asa G. Candler, his brother John, and a couple of Pemberton's original partners (including bookkeeper Frank M. Robinson, who named the drink and penned the now-famous Coca-Cola script logo), made the syrup a success. Under their direction, the company started its tradition of heavy promotion, the Coca-Cola trademark showing up on everything from souvenir fans to complimentary calendars. Innovative approaches to advertising included placing colorful signs in trolley cars and loaning ornate leaded glass chandeliers to soda shops. After World War I, an investment group headed by Atlanta banker Ernest Woodruff bought the company for $25 million.

Ty's first commercial endorsement was a newspaper advertisement in September 1907 that had the 20-year-old star stating, "I drink Coca-Cola regularly throughout all seasons of the year." He did more than drink it, of course. He also started investing in it. Upon the advice of Woodruff's son, Robert, in 1918 Ty borrowed $10,800 from the Trust Company of Georgia and bought his first 300 shares (at thirty-six dollars a share) of Coca-Cola stock. The value skyrocketed after the distinctively flavored soft drink broadened its distribution beyond the South, selling the beverage nationally then overseas during the 1920s. A mushrooming network

of regional bottling plants, aided by massive advertising and innovative marketing (the company introduced the contoured bottle in 1916, the six-bottle carry-home carton in 1923, and the metal open-top cooler in 1929), helped account for the sales boom.

As Ty also continued to prosper during the decade, drawing annual salaries in the $50,000-75,000 range and earning tens of thousands of dollars more in endorsements and dividends, he could afford to purchase additional shares. He passed along stock tips to his teammates and urged them to invest, although few had the inclination or resources. "I remember when I first came along as a kid, making $4,000 a year, and he was telling me to buy General Motors and Coca-Cola stock," said second baseman Charlie Gehringer, who broke into the majors in 1924. "Which was good advice. But you had to live, too, besides buying stock."

Ty Cobb at the Bat

Something's bound to happen. Everybody on edge—nerves a-tingle—head whizzing. Crack!! Good boy Ty!! Safe!! And then you shout yourself hoarse. When it's all over you're hot, thirsty and limp. A cold, snappy drink of

Coca-Cola

will put you back into the game — relieve the thirst and cool you off. Rooters and ball players swear by it.

Ty Cobb Says:

"I drink Coca-Cola regularly throughout all seasons of the year. On days when we are playing a double-header I always find that a drink of Coca-Cola between the games, refreshes me to such an extent that I can start the second game, feeling as if I had not been exercising at all, in spite of my exertions in the first."

Delicious—Refreshing
Thirst-Quenching
GET THE GENUINE
5c. Everywhere

Ty's first commercial endorsement was this 1907 ad.

Robert Woodruff, president of Coca-Cola, was one of Ty's closest friends.

Coca-Cola weathered the stock market crash and the Great Depression in good shape, never failing to pay a dividend. Much of the credit for that goes to Robert Woodruff, who became president of the company in 1923. It was Woodruff's objective to capitalize on the vast potential for the bottle business and place Coke "within an arm's reach of desire" of everyone. In 1928, Coca-Cola sales in bottles, including millions at ballparks, finally surpassed fountain sales. (Umpires considered bottles a nuisance. For decades, until owners banned pop bottles from their parks, more than one umpire was knocked unconscious by a glass missile thrown by an irate fan.)

Woodruff, a gruff, competitive fellow with a passion for the outdoors, got along famously with Cobb. They frequently hunted together on Woodruff's 30,000-acre estate, Ichauway, in south Georgia, betting on who would bag the most birds. During one hunting trip Ty confided he was considering the Tigers' managerial job. Woodruff, a good judge of people, advised against it.

"Why do you say that?" asked Ty.

"You're too damn mean," replied Woodruff.

In 1940 Ty bought a bottling plant in Twin Falls, Idaho, and set up his son, Herschel, as manager. Another son, Jimmy, also became associated with the plant after World War II. Later, Herschel and his wife acquired additional bottling plants in Bend, Oregon, and Santa Maria, California. Ty's role in these acquisitions is unknown.

However, his face remained familiar, as Coca-Cola introduced it to a new generation of sports fans on a set of "All-Time Winners" cardboard posters, first distributed in 1947.

Cobb died a multimillionaire. Estimates of his wealth—most of it tied up in stock, bonds, and real estate—ranged between $6 million and $12 million. According to *The Sporting News* in 1961, the value of his Coca-Cola stock alone was worth $1.78 million. Twenty years later, the *Baltimore Sun* determined that a share that had originally cost Ty forty dollars would then be selling for about 200 times that amount, or roughly $8,000. The real thing, indeed!

❖

Naturally, when the company released a set of "*All-Time Winners*" cardboard posters in 1947, Ty was among them.

Cobb may have been hated in the City of Brotherly Love, but the Philadelphia Carmel Company (actually based in Camden, New Jersey) included him in its series of premium candy cards, circa 1909.

Ty also was one of Colgan's "Stars of the Diamonds," appearing on the company's triangular advertising posters and as a circular card inside gum tins.

Turkey Red Tobacco premium card of Ty Cobb, circa 1910.

By 1911, Ty's familiar face could be seen throughout America on such novelty items as tobacco cards and paper fans.

The name of America's most famous confection was coined in 1896 when a salesman, delighted by the taste of the caramelized popcorn, exclaimed, "Now, that's a Cracker Jack of a treat!" Eleven years later the line, "Buy me some peanuts and Cracker Jack," was immortalized in the song, "Take Me Out to the Ball Game." In 1914 the company issued its first set of 144 baseball cards (available only inside boxes), then expanded it to 176 cards in 1915. Although more than 15 million cards were distributed, most went the way of the tin whistles, riddle books, and other miniature prizes that have always been found inside each box of the sticky treat. Those cards that survive are quite valuable. Today this Ty Cobb card is worth more than $2,000.

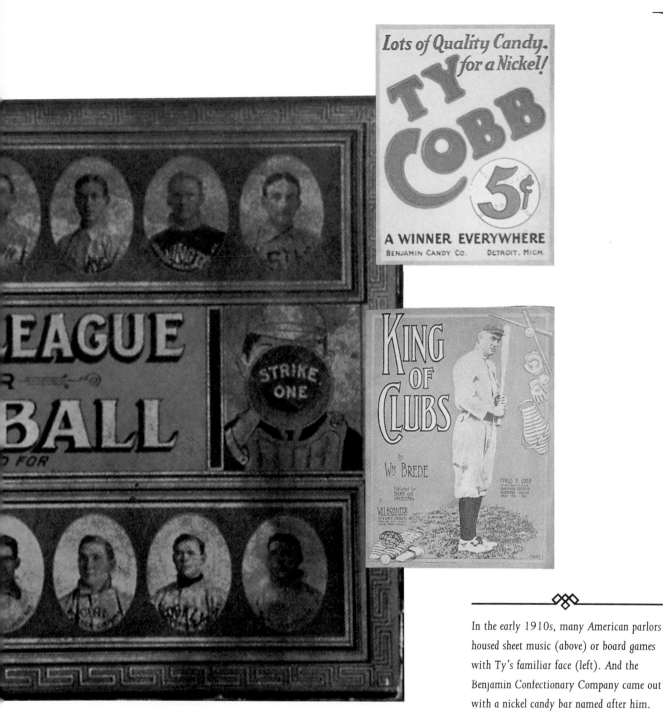

In the years leading up to *World War I*, Ty regularly made magazine covers and head-lines.

As this circa-1924 shot suggests, there was no mistaking who was the boss of the Tigers during Cobb's 6 years as manager.

A stereoscopic view of Cobb at bat at Chicago's West Side Park during the 1907 World Series.

Until the practice was discontinued after the 1921 model year, the barrels of selected Sluggers were adorned with colorful decals.

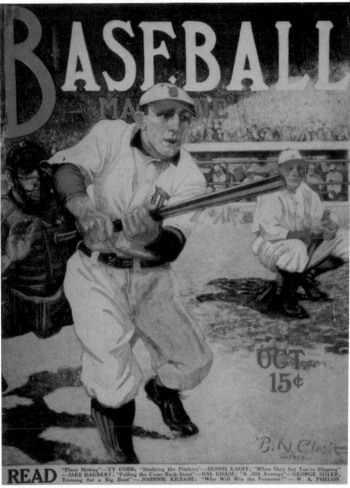

B.N. Clark's stylish portrait of Cobb "place hitting" appeared on the cover of the October 1917 issue of Baseball Magazine.

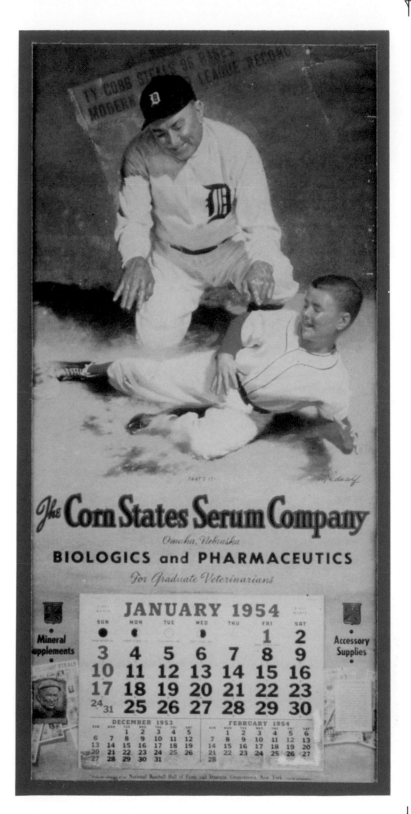

In 1954 the Corn States Serum Company of Omaha, Nebraska, offered customers a stylish calendar featuring Ty coaching a sliding little leaguer.

the seventh-place Tigers. Financially set, he even made noises about retiring. That November, while he was duck hunting and barnstorming in California, Hughie Jennings was fired. After fourteen years, the club would have a new manager. Navin called Cobb: Would he be interested in the job?

Ty said no. Throughout his career, he had stated time and again that the headaches of managing held no appeal for him. And Jennings, who at the end was a burned-out alcoholic, was a fresh warning of what could happen to even the best of them. But trusted friends and members of the press wore Ty down. Walter Briggs and John Kelsey, old buddies from the days of the Pontchartrain Hotel who had bought quarter-shares of the team the previous spring, wanted Cobb. And sportswriter Eddie Batchelor warned Ty that if he didn't take the job, he might find himself playing for another top candidate, Clarence "Pants" Rowland, the former White Sox skipper Ty considered an incompetent fraud. Mulling the offer over, Ty finally met with Frank Navin on December 18 at the Hotel Vanderbilt in New York. It was Ty's thirty-fourth birthday, but it was Navin who emerged after a four-hour meeting with the biggest gift: a new manager.

Ty was hardly celebrating. A huge raise to $35,000 made him the best-paid player in the game, but he always regretted his decision. "Rowland or no Rowland," he later said, "I wish now I'd never stuck my neck into the noose that the Tiger management represented."

No rope was present as Cobb officially took over the club in a gala civic lovefest on February 1, 1921. The decision was extremely popular in Detroit. Many assumed Ty's brilliance as a player would translate easily into that of a player-manager. Fans and players would soon find out different.

Ty's managerial debut was a soggy 6–5 win over Chicago at Navin Field on April 14, 1921. But from there the pitching-poor Tigers went into a tailspin that landed them in sixth place at season's end. The low point for Ty came June 13 at the Polo Grounds, when the versatile Ruth returned temporarily to the mound. He pitched 5 innings to get credit for an 11–8 Yankees victory, hit 2 home runs—including a monstrous 460-foot drive to right center field—and struck out Cobb. While the Tigers floundered near the bottom of the standings, Ruth led the Yankees to their first pennant with another astonishing year: a .378 average, 59 home runs, 177 runs, 171 RBI. Only Harry Heilmann, who hit .394, and Cobb, who hit .389, kept Ruth from capturing the Triple Crown.

Cobb could be kindly toward individual (and deferential) Blacks, as when one-time mascot Ulysses ("Lil' Rastus") Harrison returned to Navin Field in 1918. Cobb accepted without question the racial stereotypes of the day.

123

Ty always had all sorts of dogs around the house—hunting, show, and domestic.

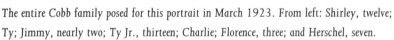

The entire Cobb family posed for this portrait in March 1923. From left: Shirley, twelve; Ty; Jimmy, nearly two; Ty Jr., thirteen; Charlie; Florence, three; and Herschel, seven.

124

The man who helped convince Ty to manage later regretted his advice. Cobb, said Detroit sportswriter Eddie Batchelor, "couldn't understand why anybody who had a good enough physique to be in the major leagues couldn't do approximately the things he did. He found that some of the fellows who could hit, field, and run the bases almost as well as he could didn't have the 'will to win' nor the interest in the game which made him great."

The sportswriter Cobb trusted most was Harry Salsinger, sports editor of the Detroit News from 1907 until his death in 1958. Salsinger, a warm, cultured man, wrote a syndicated biography of Ty in 1923, the same year they were photographed in the back yard of Ty's Augusta home with a pair of his prize shooting dogs. The two men corresponded regularly to the end of their lives. To Salsinger's often-expressed thought that they collaborate on his autobiography, Ty responded in 1953: "There are several false lights I have been placed in that I feel an urge to correct . . . I have never considered I could do such a thing with anyone better than yourself." Neither man lived to read what both called "the true record" of Ty's life.

Damned Yankee

Heilmann's unexpected batting title illustrated Cobb's chief managerial quality. "In all modesty," Ty later admitted, "I could teach hitting." No fooling. The first edition of the "Cobbmen" hit a blistering .316, still the American League record. Heilmann, a slow-footed first baseman/outfielder who had hit a composite .282 in his first 6 big-league seasons, blossomed under Cobb's tutelage. Ty tinkered with his stance and swing, moved him to right field permanently, then watched him emerge as the most feared right-handed hitter in the league. "Ol' Slug" would go on to win 3 more batting titles: in 1923 (.403), 1925 (.393), and 1927 (.398).

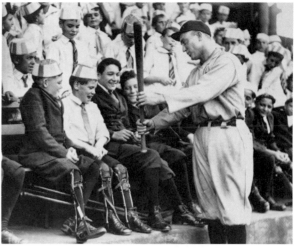

From the beginning Cobb used psychology to motivate his players. To impel easy-going Bobby Veach, he instructed Heilmann to start insulting him from the on-deck circle. The manufactured feud worked—to a point. Looking to show up his tormentor, Veach had career highs in home runs and RBI in 1921. However, at the end of the season Cobb returned to Georgia without explaining the strategy to Veach, as he had promised Heilmann. When Heilmann tried to apologize, Veach waved him away. "Don't come sucking around me with that phony line," he said. The two outfielders remained on the outs until Veach left the team three years later.

When he was about twenty-five, Ty joined the Masonic Order, an ancient society that his father had belonged to. He regularly visited Masonic temples in American League cities and participated in the Shriners' many charitable activities for handicapped children.

125

On a more successful note, that first spring training Ty reluctantly left behind a hustling infielder named Fred Haney, but not before concentrating as mightily on the young man's confidence as on his stroke. He encouraged Haney, no bigger than a plug of tobacco, to continue to work hard and to use his small size to his advantage by crouching at the plate. Haney came north with the team the following season and surprised everyone, except Cobb, with his .352 average.

Afterward, the feisty Haney had nothing but good things to say about Ty. The fact the infielder hustled and gave his best, day in and day out, was a big reason why, because if you worked hard every day, even if you were a utility player with minimal ability, Cobb had few complaints with you. But if your effort was lacking or your work habits sloppy, Ty could be unduly harsh in his criticism. Players resented Cobb's tirades, which after several frustrating seasons often degenerated into biting sarcasm. Ty felt a professional owed it to his owner, his manager, his fans, and his teammates—but most of all, to himself—to constantly strive for perfection. You may fall short, Ty would instruct, but it shouldn't be for lack of effort.

Unfortunately, Cobb's approach to the game was considered outdated, even then. He complained that players who were supposed to be fighting each other tooth-and-nail on the diamond had had

There is heavy suspicion that for a time Cobb and fellow major-league stars Tris Speaker, Rogers Hornsby, and Gabby Street belonged to the Ku Klux Klan. Several ballplayers admitted as much to New York sportswriter Fred Lieb. The Klan, seen here at a rally outside Atlanta, Georgia, in 1921, enjoyed a huge resurgence in the early '20s, especially in Detroit, where it burned a cross on the steps of city hall and just missed placing a Klan-backed candidate in the mayor's office. Given his prejudices and love of intrigue and ritual, Ty probably was a member—if only for a short while—in either Detroit or Georgia. However, no matter where he might have parked his pillowcase, it's improbable that he would have been foolish enough to slip his famous face inside of it at a rally.

126

their competitive drive dulled by lack of discipline and off-field fraternization, a no-no in Cobb's heyday, but a real problem in the wide-open '20s.

Nowhere was the exaggerated motion of the decade more pronounced than in Detroit, a boom town whose growing pains were exacerbated by Prohibition. The Motor City, described by one national publication as "soused and serene," had an estimated 25,000 speakeasies and an unknown number of amateur and professional bootleggers, who found it simple to smuggle Canadian booze across the one-mile-wide Detroit River. "It was absolutely impossible to get a drink in Detroit," recalled newspaperman Malcolm Bingay, "unless you walked at least ten feet and told the busy bartender what you wanted in a voice loud enough for him to hear you above the uproar."

The Detroit clubhouse had its share of rounders, whose escapades tried Ty's patience. Heilmann was a regular man-about-town, as were promising outfielder Heinie Manush and star pitcher George "Hooks" Dauss. Once a drunken Heilmann drove his roadster down the steps of a speakeasy and up to its bar, whereupon he casually ordered a drink. On another occasion after a long night on the town he legged out a triple, then vomited all over the bag. Ty, unimpressed with Ol' Slug's misery, left him in the game. In fact, having a hungover player take his medicine under the hot summer sun was a favorite Cobb disciplinarian tactic. When George Dauss reported red-faced for a 1924 start in New York, Ty sent him out to the mound anyway. Dauss was pounded for 7 runs before given the hook.

There also was the problem of what Ty had to work with. "Some of the young men that he expects to manipulate subtleties are better equipped for the use of the broad-axe than the rapier,"

THE TIGERS UNDER COBB

Season	Won	Lost	Pct.	Finish	GB	Pennant Winner
1921	71	82	.464	Sixth	27	New York
1922	79	75	.513	Third	15	New York
1923	83	71	.539	Second	16	New York
1924	86	68	.558	Third	6	Washington
1925	81	73	.526	Fourth	16.5	Washington
1926	79	75	.513	Sixth	12	New York

observed a writer close to the team. "Instead of comparing a player's brains with the average, Ty insists upon comparing them with his own. Naturally the player suffers in the comparison, since there are few so fast and original in their baseball thinking as the Georgia phenomenon."

A good share of Ty's original managerial thinking involved platooning, especially as it concerned pitchers. A firm and early believer in its advantages, he almost made a mockery of its use. Long before baseball had heard of middle relievers, set-up men, and stoppers, before pitchers were yanked after facing one batter, Cobb was often using four and five hurlers a game—usually with mixed results. He also thought nothing of repeatedly calling time and trudging in from the outfield to offer pitching advice. "Golly, he wore a path from center field to the pitcher's mound," recalled Charlie Gehringer. During each

With the growing recognition of America's Negro leagues, all sorts of stories regarding Cobb's performance against Black competition have surfaced. Catcher Ted "Double Duty" Radcliffe, for one, has maintained that he caught Cobb trying to steal 3 times in a single exhibition game. This is 2 fewer than the claim of Louis Santop, which Red Smith unquestionably repeated in his nationally syndicated column. Actually, Ty only played against Blacks once. That was in 1910, when he arrived late for an exhibition series in Cuba between a squad of barnstorming Tigers and an all-star team of Cuban and Black American players. Although the only thing that enthused him about the series was the money, he wound up hitting .370 (7 for 19) in the 5 games he played. He also struck out once against the mighty Cuban fastballer Jose Mendez and was thrown out trying to steal second by Bruce Petway, often named as the top catcher in the Black leagues. Ironically, Mendez (sixth from left) and Petway (third from right) played the 1919 season with the Detroit Stars, a charter member of the Negro National League. Three years later, a group of Tigers played a three-game set against the Black league's powerful Chicago American Giants, but Ty and several other Detroit regulars skipped the exhibitions. Displaying his usual paradoxical behavior in racial matters, however, Ty agreed to throw out the first pitch when the Detroit Stars opened a new ballpark in 1930.

Oscar Charleston personified the experience of the typical Black ballplayer in the first half of this century. Although the fleet, powerful center fielder was widely regarded as "the Black Cobb" during his 22 seasons in the Negro leagues, his name and achievements were unknown to most. Relegated to anonymity, he died as a broken-down baggage handler in Philadelphia. Charleston was a gifted but quick-tempered, no-nonsense ballplayer whose idea of a good joke was to drop-kick a third baseman into left field. "The catcher would catch the devil when Charleston's scoring," recalled one opponent, "because he would jump on you at your chest, knock you down. Or one of the infielders, he'd run over him. He didn't care what you did to him, because he'd get his revenge some way." Maybe he was the Black Ty Cobb, after all.

of Ty's first 4 seasons at the helm, the Detroit staff had the most relief appearances and fewest complete games in the league.

All this maneuvering underscored Ty's principal managerial fault. One day in New York, Eddie Wells, a young southpaw in a slump, found himself alone in the clubhouse with Cobb.

"Ty," he said, "I'm having a tough time."

"I know it," said Cobb.

"What in the name of sense do you think my trouble is?" asked Wells. "I can't seem to figure out what's wrong."

"Ed," replied Cobb, "that's something I know nothing about—pitching."

"And that was the truth," added Wells years later.

This lack of expertise cost pitching-poor Detroit the future Hall of Famer Carl Hubbell, whose screwball failed to impress Ty in a pair of spring training camps. Upon Cobb's advice, the slim left-hander was instead assigned to Detroit's farm club in Toronto. (Frank Navin, however, was the one who finally sold Hubbell to the New York Giants in 1928, after Detroit had exhausted its options on him. By that time Ty was no longer with the Tigers.)

Billy Evans, who started calling balls and strikes in the American League in 1906 when he was just twenty-two, arbitrated one dispute with Ty under the stands in Washington. Evans lost the fistfight, but he held no hard feelings. In 1946, he became general manager of the Tigers.

128

The Washington Senators, behind Walter Johnson, won pennants in 1924 and 1925, the only 2 flags the Yankees failed to capture during Ty's 6 years as manager.

Slick-fielding first baseman Lu Blue became a solid .300 hitter under Ty's tutelage. In 1924 he was clipping along at a .311 pace when a broken ankle sidelined him late in the summer, dashing the Tigers' pennant hopes.

Ty admittedly lacked patience with people of all ages, but his image as someone who was an ogre around youngsters is unfair. The truth is that his affection for children was the same as his father's: genuine if awkward.

Although Ty had promised to quit managing if he couldn't better the Tigers' seventh-place finish of 1920, he was encouraged enough by the 1921 season to give it another try. In 1922 the Tigers improved all the way to third, the wrecking crew hitting a composite .305. Leading the way was Cobb, whose .401 mark was aided by a controversial scoring decision. During a midsummer game in New York, Ty's grounder was misplayed by shortstop Everett Scott. The official scorer, Fred Lieb, scored it an error. The Associated Press scored it a hit. No one cared until the final averages showed Ty hitting .399. American League president Ban Johnson retroactively overruled the official scorer and gave Ty his third .400 season, a gift that still kept him runner-up to George Sisler's .420.

The Tigers emulated their manager the following season, finishing a distant second with an 83–71 record. New York, playing in their new stadium in the Bronx, won a third straight pennant and their first World Series. Once again, the headlines screamed RUTH. The Babe hit 41 round-trippers, drove in 151 runs, and just to prove he could hit for average, stroked the ball at a .393 clip. Only Heilmann's .403 was better. "The Ruth is mighty," wrote Heywood Broun, "and shall prevail."

To Ty, Ruth had become flypaper for all that was wrong with the modern game: the lack of discipline at the plate and off the field. That

The most reliable Detroit pitcher of the '20s was Earl Whitehill, a handsome and aloof southpaw whose stature increased after he married the girl who modeled for the front of the California Raisins box. The temperamental Whitehill once refused Cobb's orders to leave the game; on another occasion he fired an umpire's whisk broom over the stands to protest a call. Despite his temper—or maybe because of it—Whitehill enjoyed 13 consecutive seasons of double-digit wins for Detroit and Washington.

Harry Heilmann won batting titles in 1921, 1923, 1925, and 1927— the last 2 on the final day of the season.

the Babe's ceaseless wenching and drinking was being rewarded with universal public adoration was more than his spartan counterpart could stand. The reminiscences of Bill Kennedy, a young scorecard seller at Cleveland's Dunn Field in the early '20s, capture the essence of the two superstars' disparate public images.

"When the Tigers played the Indians we scorecard sellers would see Ty Cobb coming into the park around noon or so," he recalled. "Cobb was always indifferent to us, striding by us as though we weren't there. But Babe Ruth? We loved him. The proudest day of my life was when he gave me a pat on the back. A thrill supreme! And he would always say, 'Hello, kid.' He called everybody 'Kid.' He had a deep, wonderful, masculine voice, a la Wallace Beery, who could have played the Bambino in a movie.

"Anyway, the Babe always would go directly to Lefty Weisman, the Indians' trainer, for a rubdown before the game. While waiting for the scorecards to be printed one day, I opened the door to the locker room. There was the Babe, lying flat on his back on the massage table, his giant body completely naked. And Lefty slapping his hands, smacking them against the Babe with some kind of bottled lotion.

"There were about 12 or 13 reporters there, all with notebooks. They were asking the usual routine questions . . . but only halfheartedly. They were staring at another Ruthian achievement—his giant penis! Erect!

Detroit finished 6 games behind Washington in 1924, the closest the team would come to a pennant under Cobb. Still, Frank Navin was pleased. Playing in a park expanded to 40,000 seats, the club drew one million customers for the first time.

Judge Landis and the mountain that gave him his unusual name. Kennesaw Mountain in Georgia had been the site of a Union victory in 1864, fought not far from where various members of the Cobb clan hung their hats. Gray hats, of course. Appointed the first commissioner of baseball in 1920, Landis was vain, often hypocritical, and always dictatorial, but by the time he died in 1944 he had served his intended purpose, restoring integrity to the national pastime.

131

"I, too, was nonplussed. It reminded me of a tennis match, with reporters' heads turning with the gyrations of Lefty's skilled hands, resulting in the Babe's Tower of Pisa leaning in north and south directions. All the time the Babe was roaring with laughter at the embarrassment of the fourth estate. He just didn't give a damn! He was like a giant infant."

Like all infants, Ruth needed to be regularly disciplined. In fact, the supreme irony of the Cobb-Ruth rivalry is that, despite Ty's reputation as a villain, Ruth had more run-ins with authority. During his career he punched umpires, bullied managers and teammates, regularly reported for spring training out of shape, charged into the stands after hecklers, and was named in several paternity suits. He was suspended four times in 1922 alone and five more times in 1925, the year he had to cough up a record $5,000 fine. But while the world frowned at Cobb's indiscretions, it winked at Babe's indulgences.

Cobb's bench jockeying grew more vicious as the Babe's popularity grew. One of his favorite tactics was to call Ruth "nigger," a dig at his broad nose and dark complexion. (Actually, for years players around the league had nicknamed Ruth "Nig," a corruption of

Bancroft "Ban" Johnson revived the Western League in the 1890s at a time when other circuits were folding repeatedly. In 1900 he changed its name to the American League, declared it to be on a par with the country's only other major league, the National League, and commenced player raids on the "senior circuit." As president of the "junior circuit" between 1901 and 1927, Johnson had a reputation for being as bullheaded, arbitrary, and autocratic as the white-haired judge who would eventually usurp most of his power. He also had an understandably proprietary interest in his league, one reason his decisions often favored its biggest star, the temperamental Ty Cobb.

The two things Detroit produced like mad were cars and hard-hitting outfielders. In fact, three Tiger outfielders—Cobb, Heinie Manush, and Harry Heilmann—combined for 17 batting championships in 21 years. Another Tiger outfielder, Bob "Fats" Fothergill, never led the league in hitting but was a marvelous line-drive hitter all the same. An ex-footballer from Massillon, Ohio, his best seasons under Ty were .353 in 1925 and .367 in 1926. A minor claim to fame for the fun-loving Fothergill was that he was the last man to pinch-hit for the Peach.

132

Cobb's insult.) On several occasions, Cobb and Ruth nearly came to blows.

A typical exchange occurred in early 1923, with Ruth coming off a second straight miserable World Series against the Giants the previous fall. "We hear that little Johnny Rawlings ran you out of the Giant clubhouse," Cobb said. "Is that true?"

"It ain't a goddamned bit true," Ruth replied, "and you sons of bitches can go fuck yourselves."

For all his bravado, Ruth was more lover than fighter. All things considered, he would rather expend his mental energy mapping out a swell time at his favorite brothel, the House of the Good Shepherd in St. Louis, then debate his contemptuous rival. In the final analysis, it was pennants that counted, and Ruth and the Yankees had the last word. During Cobb's 6 seasons as manager, the Yankees won 4 pennants, the Tigers none.

The Tigers' best chance came in 1924. That year Detroit beat the Yankees in 13 of 22 meetings, including a final-week sweep that kept the Bombers from a fourth straight pennant. The most memorable contest between the two occurred June 13 at Navin Field, when their festering feud exploded into full fury.

That afternoon the first-place Yankees led 10–6 going into the ninth. As usual, the air had been turned blue with profanity and taunts. In the top of the ninth, the Tigers' Bert Cole first fired a fastball at Ruth's head and then drilled Bob Meusel in the back with a pitch—presumably on Cobb's orders. Meusel flung his bat at Cole and then charged the mound. Both benches emptied, and according to one report Cobb and Ruth plowed into each other like a pair of runaway trains at home plate. Before they could settle their differences once and for all, about 1,000 spectators joined in, including several neanderthals who tore seats loose from the concrete floor and tossed them onto the field. When order still hadn't been restored after thirty minutes of fighting, umpire Billy Evans forfeited the game to New York, 9–0.

The fired-up Tigers, helped by the 17-win performance of rookie southpaw Earl Whitehill, the Tigers' only reliable pitcher of the decade, stayed in the race to the end, despite a season-ending leg injury to first baseman Lu Blue in August and Heilmann's summer-long bout with sinusitis. Cobb, smelling a pennant, ignored his own aches and pains and played the full schedule of 155 games. He piled up 211 hits and 23 stolen bases (including 3 steals of home), commendable numbers for the balding 37-year-old warhorse.

"I knew Cobb was a pretty tough hombre during his stormy career," a St. Louis physician who examined him told Fred Lieb. "But, when I saw him stripped, my admiration for him increased many fold. His legs from his feet to his hips were a mass of scars and bruises, new ones and old—souvenirs of years of play. In some places, there was a

Discipline, always a problem, was compounded by Prohibition. Two of Ty's players, Heinie Manush (number 12 in photo, with lady's hand under his chin) and Harry Heilmann (number 9, and doing his best to hide his well-known face from the camera), join a beaming Bambino (seated, center) for a few illegal drinks in the basement of Detroit sportsman Alfred Tenge. The year is 1925.

"Imagine a town where anything went. . . ." That was Detroit during the Roaring Twenties, when marathon dancers and 25,000 blind pigs contributed to the jazzed-up pace of life.

133

Heinie Manush took over center field from Ty in 1926 and immediately won his only batting championship by 6 points over Babe Ruth. Traded to the Browns after the 1927 season, Manush went on to a .330 lifetime mark and a place in the Hall of Fame.

WHAT THE TIGERS NEED IS—

A little more of this

And a little less of this.

By Opening Day in 1925, local publications had figured out the real problem with the Tigers.

The Browns could have used more pitching help on May 2, 1925, the day Cobb slammed 6 hits, including 3 home runs. (Right) The last one sailed over the right-field pavilion at Sportsman's Park and onto Grand Avenue.

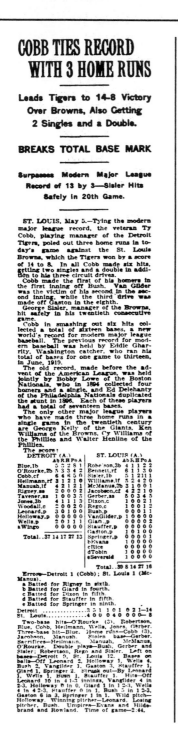

COBB TIES RECORD WITH 3 HOME RUNS

Leads Tigers to 14-8 Victory Over Browns, Also Getting 2 Singles and a Double.

BREAKS TOTAL BASE MARK

Surpasses Modern Major League Record of 13 by 3—Sisler Hits Safely in 20th Game.

ST. LOUIS, May 5.—Tying the modern major league record, the veteran Ty Cobb, playing manager of the Detroit Tigers, poled out three home runs in to-day's game against the St. Louis Browns, which the Tigers won by a score of 14 to 8. In all Cobb made six hits, getting two singles and a double in addition to his three circuit drives.

Cobb made the first of his homers in the first inning off Bush. Van Gilder was the victim of his second in the second inning, while the third drive was made off Gaston in the eighth.

George Sisler, manager of the Browns, hit safely in his twentieth consecutive game.

Cobb in smashing out six hits collected a total of sixteen bases, a new world's record for modern major league baseball. The previous record for modern baseball was held by Eddie Gharrity, Washington catcher, who ran his total of bases for one game to thirteen, in June, 1919.

The old record, made before the advent of the American League, was held jointly by Bobby Lowe of the Boston Nationals, who in 1894 collected four homers and a single, and Ed Delehanty of the Philadelphia Nationals duplicated the stunt in 1896. Each of these players had a total of seventeen bases.

The only other major league players who have made three home runs in a single game in the twentieth century are George Kelly of the Giants, Ken Williams of the Browns, Cy Williams of the Phillies and Walter Henline of the Phillies.

new scar over an old one. I decided then and there that Ty Cobb could take it as well as dish it out."

What he couldn't take was Frank Navin's perceived indifference. Ty moaned to the end of his days how the tight-fisted owner's refusal to buy Johnny Neun from Minneapolis to replace Blue had cost him the pennant. As it was, Navin, who had added an upper-deck grandstand before the season, was pleased. The team had won 86 games, its most since 1916, and finished third, just 6 games back of the champion Washington Senators. The excitement of a pennant race had allowed the Tigers to become only the third team to draw one million fans at home. And on the road the heavy hitting "Tygers" (they led the circuit in batting and runs) remained the league's top-drawing attraction, outside of the Yankees.

Ty figured to improve on the near-miss of 1924. Instead the team sank back into fourth place in 1925, despite a .302 team batting mark and a league-high 903 runs. Ty was drained, both physically and psychologically, by the demands of playing and managing. The dual roles meant he took each loss twice as hard. At night he lost sleep replaying that afternoon's game, second-guessing the moves he made—or didn't make.

Dissension was rampant, with players regularly complaining behind closed doors to Navin. They had cause, because Ty had grown increasingly bitter, sarcastic, and thin-skinned. "Nobody liked him as a manager," said Charlie Gehringer, the Hall of Fame second baseman who had signed with Detroit in the fall of 1923. "He was such a great player himself, he figured that if he told you something, there was no reason why you couldn't do it as well as he did. But a lot of guys don't have that ability. He couldn't understand that."

Although Gehringer's quiet nature often exasperated Cobb, who expected incessant chatter from his infielders, he spent considerable

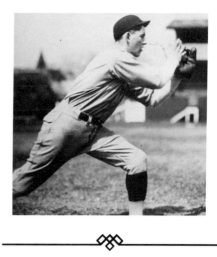

HEADING THE HIT PARADE

There are several ways to measure Ty Cobb's greatness as a hitter. Perhaps the most telling is his domination of the batting title. In his prime, the 16 seasons from 1907 to 1922, the King of Clubs won 12 batting titles and finished runner-up 3 times—a stretch without parallel in baseball history. The following chart lists the batting champion and runner-up in each of Cobb's 24 years in the league. Note that in Cobb's final 8 seasons, a pair of his pupils, Harry Heilmann and Heinie Manush, captured 5 batting crowns between them.

Year	Batting Champion	Avg.	Runner-up	Avg.
1905	Lew Flick, CLE	.308	Willie Keeler, NY	.302
1906	George Stone, STL	.358	Nap Lajoie, CLE	.355
1907	Ty Cobb, DET	.350	Sam Crawford, DET	.323
1908	Ty Cobb, DET	.324	Sam Crawford, DET	.311
1909	Ty Cobb, DET	.377	Eddie Collins, PHI	.346
1910	Ty Cobb, DET	.385	Nap Lajoie, CLE	.384
1911	Ty Cobb, DET	.420	Joe Jackson, CLE	.408
1912	Ty Cobb, DET	.410	Joe Jackson, CLE	.395
1913	Ty Cobb, DET	.390	Joe Jackson, CLE	.373
1914	Ty Cobb, DET	.368	Eddie Collins, PHI	.344
1915	Ty Cobb, DET	.369	Eddie Collins, PHI	.332
1916	Tris Speaker, CLE	.386	Ty Cobb, DET	.371
1917	Ty Cobb, DET	.383	George Sisler, STL	.353
1918	Ty Cobb, DET	.382	George Burns, PHI	.352
1919	Ty Cobb, DET	.384	Bobby Veach, DET	.355
1920	George Sisler, STL	.407	Tris Speaker, CLE	.388
1921	Harry Heilmann, DET	.394	Ty Cobb, DET	.389
1922	George Sisler, STL	.420	Ty Cobb, DET	.401
1923	Harry Heilmann, DET	.403	Babe Ruth, NY	.393
1924	Babe Ruth, NY	.378	Charlie Jamieson, CLE	.359
1925	Harry Heilmann, DET	.393	Tris Speaker, CLE	.389
1926	Heinie Manush, DET	.378	Babe Ruth, NY	.372
1927	Harry Heilmann, DET	.398	Lou Gehrig, NY	.373
1928	Goose Goslin, WAS	.379	Heinie Manush, STL	.378

Charlie Gehringer during his first spring training with Detroit, 1924. The gentle Gehringer, who went on to a 19-year Hall of Fame career as a Tiger second baseman, was particularly offended by Ty's rantings and ravings. "Nobody liked him as a manager," he said simply.

"The best thing that ever happened to me was when that son of a bitch released me." So said Carl Hubbell to Bill Moore one day in the '30s, by which time he had become the ace of the New York Giants' staff. Hubbell had languished in Detroit's farm system, mainly because Ty and others in the pitching-poor organization felt his screwball would be ineffective against major-league hitters.

time with his second baseman on train rides and inside hotel lobbies. "He even made me use his own bat, which was kind of a thin little thing," said Gehringer. "I said, 'Gee, I'd like a little more batting space,' but I didn't dare use another one. He would've shipped me to Siberia." Or the Tigers' farm-team equivalent, Oklahoma City.

Bill Moore, a big right-handed pitcher with control problems, had a confrontation with Cobb that spring training that he always felt

As a batter, Ty's chief nemesis during the 1920s was an obscure pitcher named Bill Bayne. The little left-hander lost one more game than he won during his 9-year career, the bulk of it spent with St. Louis. But he limited Cobb to a .139 average, his worst performance against any pitcher he faced at least 30 times. Bayne's handling of Cobb, much like teammate Hub Pruett's well-publicized success with Babe Ruth, defies easy explanation. One theory is that Bayne was a lefty with good control—the kind of pitcher that gave Cobb the most fits—and that he was used primarily in relief, denying Ty the extra at-bats it often took for him to solve a pitcher.

cost him a big-league career. One day the nervous rookie was erratically pitching batting practice to the regulars when Ty suddenly grabbed a bat and jumped into the box. After Moore delivered two across the plate, Cobb asked, "What would you do now with a couple of strikes?" Intentionally or not, the next pitch sent him sprawling into the dirt.

"Cobb got up spluttering, 'You son of a bitch!'" recalled Moore. "All sorts of words. I turned around to get another ball and I could just feel the hair rising on the back of my neck. I got so mad, I took the ball and threw it over the grandstand and yelled, 'Stick the ball up your ass!'"

Moore stormed into the clubhouse. Despite the scene, he made the trip north as the tenth pitcher on a weak staff. Considering the company, he figured to get plenty of opportunities to prove himself. On the second day of the season, during a lopsided loss to Chicago, Ty sent Moore to the mound. "Go in there and try to throw strikes," he instructed. Instead Moore walked the first three men he faced and pitched a ball to the fourth before he was yanked.

"Cobb didn't even come out to the mound," he said. "He just hollered for me to get out of there." Moore was immediately dispatched to the Tigers' farm club in Rochester, New York. He languished in the Tigers' system for several years, finally quitting during the depression and becoming a policeman in his native Corning, New York. He always blamed Cobb's capricious, vindictive nature as much as his own inability to throw strikes for his truncated major-league career. "From the day I told Cobb to stick that ball up his ass," he said, "I think I was cooked."

Ty never really cared what Moore or anybody else in the dugout thought of him. "The great trouble with baseball today," he complained, "is that most of the players are in the game for the money that's in it—not for the love of it, the excitement of it, and the thrill of it. Times seem to have changed since I broke in more than a generation ago."

Although the team was going nowhere, Ty could still rise to the occasion. Of course, the ever-scientific Peach knew when to pick his spots—such as May 4, 1925, when he brashly announced to Harry Salsinger and Sid Keener of the *St. Louis Star* that he was going to try for home runs for the first time.

Even allowing for a short right-field fence and a strong wind blowing out from the plate, the results were astonishing. In 6 at-bats Cobb collected 2 singles, a double, and 3 home runs, as the Tigers swamped the Browns, 14–8. All 3 round-trippers were pulled to right, the final one clearing the bleachers and landing on Grand Avenue. The 16 total bases set a big-league record while the 3 home runs tied a mark shared by four others. Scanning that evening's sports page, Cobb must have been pleased to learn none of them was named Babe Ruth.

The following day Cobb continued his Ruthian ways by singling and hitting 2 more home runs, giving him 9 straight hits and 5 homers in two days. Satisfied, Ty returned to "nipping" at the ball, finishing the year with a .378 average and 102 RBI in just 121 games.

On August 29, Ty was feted by 30,000 fans at Navin Field in ceremonies marking his twentieth anniversary in Detroit. Cobb contributed a couple of hits in a 9–5 win over Philadelphia, then changed into formal attire for that evening's banquet at the Book Cadillac Hotel. Among the gifts were a $1,000 grandfather clock and a check from the ball club for $10,000. Frank Navin was all smiles when he presented the check. But Ty had to hold back from decking his boss. Unbeknownst to the 600 guests roaring in the banquet hall, Navin's magnificent gift was in reality the balance of Ty's $50,000 salary. When negotiating Cobb's contract before the season, the two had

Rookie pitcher Bill Moore may have thought of using both barrels on Cobb in 1925, the year of his run-in with the short-fused manager.

137

After two decades in the game, ballpark ceremonies had become an almost ho-hum occurrence for Ty, who still participated in them with good grace. Here he makes idle talk with actress Hope Hawthorn, accepts a gift of classic books from a Congressional delegation, and in 1925, participates in activities honoring his 20 years as a Tiger.

Ty's final season in Detroit began with a case of "proud flesh" (a.k.a. pterygium), an eye condition that results in cloudy vision. He was operated on and had to wear smoked glasses. "Between that and managing under Frank Navin's ownership," said Ty, "baseball no longer was fun for me."

Waite "Schoolboy" Hoyt, the telling difference in the Yankees-Tigers baseball wars of the 1920s. "What we could have done with a couple of pitchers!" said Cobb. "If I'd had them, the Yankees would have had to wait a few years to become the terrors of baseball. In every other way but pitching, we spit in their eye."

agreed to a lump-sum payment so as to hide that Ty was making as much as the president of the American League. Navin's "phony act," Ty recalled, had soured one of the finest evenings of his life.

Although the owner was making a handsome profit, he frequently refused to buy the players Cobb recommended. "No one understands what a sincere manager suffers when he lacks just a few of the tools necessary to make a strong contender a champion," Ty said later. That winter Navin said no to a $45,000 purchase of San Francisco Seals outfielder Paul Waner, "who single-handed could have brought us two and maybe three pennants," argued Cobb. Waner, a future Hall of Famer, thus joined Jim Bagby, George Grantham, Flint Rhem, and a host of other promising minor leaguers and available veterans that slipped through Ty's fingers because of Navin's stinginess.

"It got so I couldn't stand to look at Navin," Cobb said later. Nonetheless, he returned in 1926 for a sixth season as manager.

Exactly why isn't clear. He didn't need the money nor the aggravation. And he had to be realistic about the Tigers' pennant chances. The best guess is that he looked forward to finishing the development of young players like Heinie Manush and Charlie Gehringer. Even that small pleasure was muddled by a severe case of "proud flesh," an eye condition that required surgery and caused him to wear smoked glasses at the start of the season. He took them off in time to see on June 8 Babe Ruth smote what may be the longest home run ever: a clout that soared beyond Navin Field's right-field wall and traveled an estimated 626 feet before landing on Brooklyn Avenue, two blocks away.

About this time Ty's vantage point shifted to the bench. He installed Manush in center field, and the 25-year-old Alabama native responded with a .378 average. Much of the credit went to Cobb, who worked to level his swing. Ty whistled from the dugout whenever he noticed Manush holding the bat below his waist, an arm position that caused him to uppercut the ball. Manush was one of the few bright spots in the Tigers' sixth-place season. Although the Yankees finished on top of the standings, Manush did his whistling mentor proud by going 6 for 9 in a season-ending doubleheader to edge Ruth for the batting title. It was the third time in 6 seasons that a Tiger batting champion had prevented the Babe from capturing the Triple Crown, one of the few accomplishments that would elude him during his career.

Throughout the summer Navin Field fans lustily booed Ty, who spent less and less time on the field. For the year he appeared in just 79 games, 61 as a starter, and most of those before July. Ty hit .339 in just 233 at-bats, although only the starting outfielders—Heilmann, Manush, and Bob Fothergill—bested his 62 RBI.

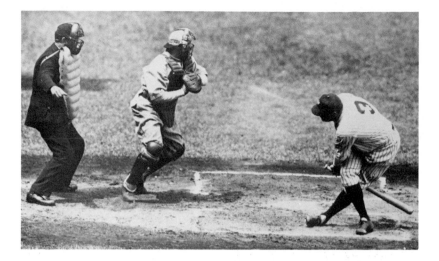

Ruth struck out 76 times in 1926, Cobb twice. While most Americans loved the new big-bang approach to scoring, others hankered for the old-fashioned hitter. After listening to a friend in the press box marvel over the muscular feats of one masher, Ring Lardner responded, "Swings good, but how far do you think he'd hit 'em with the old ball?"

Despite Cobb's production, many thought that familiar all-consuming urge to hustle was missing. As Ty explained to Eddie Batchelor, forcing himself to make the extra effort was more and more of a chore. "You might say that I am slowing up, not so much physically in that my muscles aren't capable of their former performance, or slowing up mentally in that my brain hasn't the same command over my muscles, but slowing up in my desire to force myself to the utmost to attain success that I already have achieved."

Ty understood that it was human nature to try harder to reach the peak than to stay there. Cobb had not only climbed to the top of his profession, he had stayed there for more than twenty years. Now, growing round, bald, and jowly, emptied of challenges and weary of the daily grind, he was ready to step down from the mountaintop and rest.

Or so he thought.

After 22 seasons as a Tiger, Ty joined Connie Mack's herd of white elephants.

CHAPTER SEVEN

Philadelphia Story

He may have his faults, but dishonesty is not one of them.
—Charlie Cobb, 1927

The Yankees lost the World Series to the St. Louis Cardinals in 1926, the final out of the decisive seventh game coming when Babe Ruth attempted to steal second base with two outs in the bottom of the ninth. That it was a one-run game at the time, with slugging Bob Meusel at the plate, made no difference to Ruth, whose reckless dash dominated post series talk. But a string of sensational developments shoved the Bambino's bonehead play to the back burner of the hot stove league.

On November 3, 1926, Ty Cobb announced his retirement from the Detroit Tigers. The Peach's numbers over 22 summers with the Tigers were unimpeachable: 3,902 hits in 2,805 games for a .369 average, 2,087 runs scored and another 1,828 batted in, 865 stolen bases, and a dozen batting championships. All were major-league records.

His record as a manager, however, was open to criticism. Eddie Batchelor later told fellow sportswriter Fred Lieb that "Ty lacked the patience to make allowances for men who didn't think as fast as he did, nor had his mechanical ability to play ball. Like so many great performers, he was impatient with stupidity, lack of ambition, and lack of what he considered normal baseball ability. The result was that he proved to be a poor teacher and that he never could get his team imbued with real team spirit."

Cobb would always defend his mediocre bench record of 479 wins and 444 losses over 6 seasons, a .519 winning percentage, maintaining that if he was not a managerial success, he

Hubert "Dutch" Leonard. After his allegations of corruption involving Cobb, Tris Speaker, and Joe Wood became public, he reportedly told sportswriter Damon Runyon, "I have had my revenge."

142

surely was not a managerial failure. "What we could have done with a couple of pitchers!" he reflected in his autobiography. "If I'd had them, the Yankees would have had to wait a few years to become the terrors of baseball. In every other way but pitching, we spit in their eye and showed them the scientific way to use a bat, a glove, and a ball."

Frank Navin said the decision to retire as an active player was entirely Cobb's, although the Tiger owner later admitted he had made up his mind early in the season that this would be Cobb's last as manager. Ty knew that if he didn't step down voluntarily, he would be fired. To reporters, he insisted age was responsible for his retirement. "I'm tired," he explained. "I can't take any chances any more. It's time to quit. I am going back to Georgia to be with my family."

One month later, Tris Speaker announced he too was retiring. Whereas Cobb's departure had not been unexpected, Speaker's was a shock. He had just managed the Cleveland Indians to a close second-place finish and played 150 games in the outfield. There seemed no plausible explanation for Speaker to surrender his $35,000-a-year job.

A disgruntled ex-Tiger in California was behind the resignations. Hubert "Dutch" Leonard, characterized as a slacker and a complainer, had nonetheless been an excellent pitcher during his 11-year major-league career with Boston and Detroit. In his 6 seasons with the Red Sox the left-hander had been an important member of three world championship teams, pitching 2 no-hitters and compiling a 1.01 ERA during the 1914 season, still the all-time low. Sold to Detroit in 1919, he became part of Hughie Jennings' rotation but gradually fell into disfavor after Ty took over as manager two years later. When Leonard couldn't come to terms with Frank Navin on a new contract after the 1921 season, he pitched semipro ball for two years in California. He returned to Detroit in August 1924, one of the few capable members of the Tigers' woeful mound staff.

By the middle of the 1925 season Leonard had compiled an 11–3 record. That didn't stop Cobb from accusing Leonard, who com-

Another scandal, this time involving an alleged game-fixing scheme in 1917, followed on the heels of the Cobb-Speaker case. In January 1927, Black Sox teammates Charlie "Swede" Risberg (seated in the rear with arms folded) and Charlie "Chick" Gandil (wearing bow tie) sat in the Chicago office of Commissioner Landis (rear, far left) and told what they knew.

While Landis dawdled, citizens of Augusta, Georgia, rallied to Ty's defense.

plained of a sore arm, of being a shirker, especially when it came to facing strong teams. "Don't you dare turn bolshevik on me," Cobb yelled at him one day in front of the team. "I'm the boss here." In what turned out to be Leonard's final big-league appearance, Cobb kept him on the mound despite getting pounded for 12 runs by Philadelphia. A few days later he put the 33-year-old pitcher on waivers.

No team claimed him. Leonard, who believed that Cobb and Speaker had conspired to waive him out of the league, swore revenge. In the spring of 1926 he contacted Navin and American League president Ban Johnson with allegations that he and Cobb had conspired to fix a game played between Detroit and Cleveland on September 25, 1919. Also in on the fix were Speaker and Smokey Joe Wood, the former pitching great then playing out his career in the Cleveland outfield. According to Leonard, on the afternoon of the game a Navin Field employee named Fred West was hired to place a bet totaling $5,500—including $2,000 put up by Cobb, $1,500 by Leonard, and $1,000 apiece by Wood and Speaker—with local bookmakers. Because of the size of the bet, West could only place $600 by game time. The Tigers, a 10–7 favorite, won the game, giving the players a $420 payoff. After paying West thirty dollars for his services, the players split the remaining winnings into equal $130 shares.

As proof Leonard produced letters written to him by Wood and Cobb. The correspondence seemed damning:

As always, America's favorite humorist provided the best line regarding the Cobb-Speaker affair. "If they had been selling out all these years," said Will Rogers, "I would like to have seen him play when they weren't selling!"

Cobb and Judge Landis in happier days. Although the commissioner eventually cleared Cobb and Speaker of Leonard's charges, players—and a considerable share of the press and public—were convinced of Ty's integrity. Most thought Landis had used the case to enhance his power.

144

THE WOOD LETTER

Cleveland, O., Friday

Enclosed please find certified check for sixteen hundred and thirty dollars ($1,630).

Dear Friend "Dutch":

The only bet West could get up was $600 against $420 (10 to 7). Cobb did not get up a cent. He told us that and I believed him. Could have put some at 5 to 2 on Detroit, but did not, as that would make us put up $1,000 to win $400.

We won the $420. I gave West $30, leaving $390, or $130 for each of us. Would not have cashed your check at all, but West thought he could get it up to 10–7, and I was going to put it all up at those odds. We would have won $1,750 for the $2,500 if we could have placed it.

If we ever get another chance like this we will know enough to try to get down early.

Let me hear from you, "Dutch."

With all good wishes to yourself and Mrs. Leonard, I am, always

[signed] Joe Wood

THE COBB LETTER

Augusta, Ga., Oct. 23, '19

Dear Dutch:

Well, old boy, guess you are out in old California by this time and enjoying life.

I arrived home and found Mrs. Cobb only fair, but the baby girl was fine, and at this time Mrs. Cobb is very well, but I have been very busy getting acquainted with my family and have not tried to do any correspondence, hence my delay.

Wood and myself are considerably disappointed in our business proposition, as we had $2,000 to put into it and the other side quoted us $1,400, and when we finally secured that much money it was about two o'clock and they refused to deal with us, as they had men in Chicago to take the matter up with and they had no time, so we completely fell down and of course we felt badly over it.

Everything was open to Wood and he can tell you about it when we get together. It was quite a responsibility and I don't care for it again, I can assure you.

With kindest regards to Mrs. Leonard, I remain, sincerely,

[signed] Ty Cobb

Ty and former teammate George Burns also testified.

Leonard agreed to sell his letters to Ban Johnson for $20,000, hush money equal to what the pitcher estimated he had lost in salary since being waived. In September, after league owners had met in private and voted to turn over the letters to Judge Landis, Johnson presented Cobb and Speaker with the case against them and urged them to quietly resign at the end of the season to spare embarrassment. While protesting their innocence, the two agreed. But when Landis continued the investigation on his own and rumors began leaking to the press, Cobb and Speaker demanded a formal inquiry where they and Wood (since 1923 the baseball coach at Yale University) could clear the air and save their reputations.

Four days before Christmas, Landis made the case public. Cobb and Speaker had both testified that, while having knowledge of the letters, they had done nothing wrong. The box score of the game indicated that, for four players supposedly throwing a game, they were woefully inept. Wood and Leonard hadn't played, while Cobb—who should have been thrown fat pitches to guarantee a Detroit win—had a poor day at the plate, with just 1 single in 5 at-bats. Conversely, Speaker—who should have been trying his hardest to lose—hit a single and 2 booming triples.

The story was front-page news for weeks, as the public waited for Landis to make a ruling. Cobb and his followers particularly resented the assault on his integrity. At a rally in Augusta, Georgia, citizens hung a banner that proclaimed "TY IS STILL OUR IDOL AND THE IDOL OF AMERICA." Umpire Billy Evans called Leonard "gutless," while former Tiger outfielder Del Drake said that "Cobb and Speaker were always on the square, working and hustling to beat the band." Former White Sox pitcher Dickie Kerr, commenting in Pine Bluff, Arkansas, was "not surprised" at Dutch Leonard's charges. "I met Leonard in San Francisco a year ago and he remarked that he would 'get even' with Cobb or 'die in the attempt,'" said Kerr. "He was sore because he was released by Detroit. He declared he had enough 'dope on Cobb to get him' and that he was going to use it."

The full truth will probably never be known, though it's clear circumstantially that a wager was placed on the game. Cobb was a close friend of Speaker, who was a notorious gambler, so he may have gone along with the idea against his better judgment. At any rate, the game of September 25, 1919, appears not to have been fixed. Certainly Cobb, by then the highest-paid player in the game and already a rich man, would not have jeopardized his future and reputation for the chance to win a few hundred dollars. Not that such shenanigans were out of the ordinary for ballplayers who were not nearly as well compensated as Cobb. Remember that just two weeks after the game in question eight members of the Chicago White Sox did the unthinkable, throwing the

145

Robert "Lefty" Grove was the ace of the Athletics' staff. The fireballer led the American League in strikeouts his first 7 seasons. In a 17-year career with Philadelphia and Boston he led the league in ERA 9 times and won an even 300 games. In his autobiography, Cobb included the short-fused pitcher on his all-time team, paying him his highest compliment. Grove "hated to lose as much as I did," he said.

Ty officially became an Athletic inside Connie Mack's Shibe Park office on February 9, 1927.

World Series to Cincinnati. Professional baseball was rife with incidents of gambling and game-fixing in the early years of the century, the major reason Judge Landis had been appointed commissioner.

While deliberating on what was known as "the Cobb-Speaker scandal," a second mud ball exploded in the commissioner's lap. Swede Risberg and Chick Gandil, two of the Black Sox expelled from the game for throwing the 1919 World Series, accused the Tigers of easing up in an important series with the White Sox during the 1917 pennant race between Chicago and Boston. In return, some Detroit pitchers and catchers were given cash by the Chicago team. Although the charges did not involve Cobb directly, they added to the foul aroma surrounding his own case.

Scores of witnesses paraded in front of Landis, who left Cobb and Speaker twisting in the wind a while longer as he tackled these new allegations. The gist of the testimony, and the story accepted by the commissioner, was that the Chicago players had indeed collected a cash purse for the Tigers in 1917—but for defeating the Red Sox in a crucial series, not lying down against the White Sox. This was a common practice, one that Landis then ordered a halt to.

On January 27, 1927, the commissioner handed down his decision in the Cobb-Speaker case. Frustrated by Leonard's refusal to leave his California farm and testify, Landis acquitted both men. "These players have not been, nor are they now, found guilty of fixing a game," he said. "By no decent system of justice could such a finding be made." Landis declared that Cobb and Speaker were both eligible to play for any team they wished. Within days Speaker signed with Washington.

Although cleared of any wrongdoing, Ty was far from satisfied with the way Landis had handled the ugly affair. The power-hungry judge had maneuvered so as to upstage and embarrass Ban Johnson, who soon afterward resigned as American League president. Cobb later confided that powerful legal friends of his had *"dictated and forced Landis' decision."* He went duck hunting to escape the press and con-templated taking "my pound of flesh" from the game through what promised to be an ugly lawsuit. As Ty stewed in the marshes of South Carolina, Connie Mack folded his lanky frame inside a Georgia-bound train, hoping to convince one of the game's biggest drawing cards to sign a Philadelphia contract.

The two met in Augusta. Now sixty-six, the grand old man of baseball was putting together what would be his last great champion-ship team. Ty had always respected Mack's integrity, noble manner, and baseball savvy, but he initially resisted Mack's overtures to return to the diamond.

"I've had enough," insisted Cobb. "I gave all I had and you've seen the way I was treated. If some wise guy fan should mention 'fix' to me from the stands, I'd probably go right up there after him."

"There isn't a fan who isn't for you, Ty," argued Mack. "We have a pennant contender in Philadelphia, and with you in the lineup, I just know we can win it."

After mulling over several other offers, Cobb decided to return for a twenty-third season wearing the white elephant of the Philadelphia Athletics. Setting more records held no appeal. The chance to play on a pennant winner, as well as the estimated $75,000 in salary and bonus, were factors. Most important, however, was vindi-cation.

"I could not and would not leave the game with the slightest cloud over my name," Cobb later said. "Even if I appeared in only one more major league game—on my own terms—I would have proved for the all-time record and generations of youngsters to come that baseball wanted Ty Cobb to the last."

That they did. Large crowds attended the Athletics' spring train-ing games in Florida, where Cobb joined 38-year-old Zack Wheat, an 18-year veteran of the Brooklyn Dodgers, and young Al Simmons in the outfield. Rejuvenated by the prospect of playing on a contending club, free from managerial worries for the first time in seven years, Ty smiled his way through his first day in an Athletics uniform. On March 7 he posed for countless photographs, chatted amiably with

147

Mickey Cochrane, Philadelphia's backstop from 1925 to 1933, was cut from the same cloth as Grove. "You have Grove pitching and Cochrane catching, and you lose 1–0, you're a little timid about going into that clubhouse," recalled Doc Cramer. Later, as player-manager for Detroit, Cochrane would accomplish what had eluded Cobb: the club's first championship.

reporters, even gently tossed a ball to Thomas Edison for the benefit of newsreel cameras. That the aging inventor nearly decapitated Cobb with a line drive from ten feet away couldn't spoil the moment.

Besides Mack, Cobb, Wheat, and Simmons, the 1927 Athletics featured four other future Hall of Famers: first baseman Jimmie Foxx, 40-year-old second baseman and coach Eddie Collins, pitching ace Robert "Lefty" Grove, and catcher Mickey Cochrane. "That whole gang were tough losers," Roger "Doc" Cramer once recalled. "You have Grove pitching and Cochrane catching, and you lose 1–0, you're a little timid about going into that clubhouse."

"An Old Friend in a New Suit," as the Detroit newspapers called Ty, enjoyed a festive homecoming when he returned to the city as a Philadelphia Athletic on May 10, 1927. A luncheon, motorcade, dinner, and a new car were all part of the festivities.

Grove and Cochrane had broken into the majors on the same afternoon in 1925 and quickly earned a reputation as the most volatile battery in baseball. Ty took a particular liking to the 24-year-old Cochrane, who as a rookie had one day taunted the legend from behind the plate.

"What are you going to do now, Ty?" asked Cochrane, as Cobb batted with a man on first and a two-strike count on him. Ty announced that he was going to hit-and-run.

"You're crazy," replied Cochrane, who called for a pitchout. But before the intentionally wide pitch could settle into his mitt, the old master reached out and slapped it to right field for a base hit. The

That afternoon at Navin Field, Ty exchanged a half-hearted handshake before the game with the man who had replaced him as manager, George Moriarty. Cobb doubled his first time up against Earl Whitehill, who later in the game tried picking him off first base. Making the futile tag is Lu Blue.

exhibition impressed the jug-eared, dark-faced catcher, whose own drive, intelligence, and fiery disposition matched Cobb's. Now teammates, it was perhaps inevitable that the two hard losers would become fast, lifelong friends.

Just as he had in Detroit, Cobb freely dispensed batting advice. He taught Cochrane to aim the ball at the pitcher's head, resulting in more base hits through the middle. He also showed Al Simmons how to move up on the plate against left-handers. Both saw their batting average jump more than 50 points in 1927. "How many guys do you know who could tell Simmons how to hit?" said Jimmie Dykes, who reached a rapprochement of sorts with Cobb.

Dykes, who came up to Philadelphia as a second baseman in 1918, had harassed Cobb through the years by standing on the middle of the bag as the teams changed positions. Ty, who superstitiously stepped on second on his way to and from the outfield, would "come running up and have to stop and touch the edge of the bag with his foot; then he'd give me a little blast," recalled Dykes. Cobb nicknamed the brash infielder "H.S." for "Hot Shit."

One day Dykes spotted him instructing Simmons at the batting cage and bent an ear. The next game the right-handed hitter employed some of Cobb's batting philosophy and stroked 3 hits. "After the game I'm sitting in front of my locker all smiles," said Dykes. "Cobb comes by, looks at me, and says, 'Well, rockhead, you're finally learning, aren't you?' From then on I could hit left-handers real well."

Cobb usually batted third and played right field for the Athletics. In his first regular-season at-bat, on April 12 at Yankee Stadium, he grounded out against Waite Hoyt. The Yankees blew past

Before his first spring training with the Athletics, Ty visited with his brother Paul and tried out his new home movie camera on a Florida beach. Paul, a decent minor-league first baseman, entered the real estate business after World War I and did quite well.

149

Ty followed up a season of personal vindication with a bountiful hunting expedition to Wyoming and northern Arizona. He and Charlie posed with some of the game he bagged, including two brown bears, two elk, two deer, and an antelope.

150

Cobb at bat in the 1928 season opener at Shibe Park. Playing half the year in new surroundings posed no problems for Ty. Displaying his usual consistency, he had a combined 3 home runs and 67 RBI during his 2 summers in Shibe Park—the same numbers he posted on the road.

Philadelphia, 8–3, in a game that was the season in a nutshell. For 1927 was the year of the Yankees, with the storied Murderers' Row bludgeoning its way to 110 regular-season wins and a 4-game sweep of Pittsburgh in the World Series. Ruth's shadow loomed larger than ever. He hit 60 home runs (a record that created little hysteria since everyone assumed he would just hit more the next season) and Lou Gehrig chipped in with 47. Philadelphia finished a distant second, 19 games out. Connie Mack caught some criticism for fielding so many graybeards. But nothing short of a natural disaster could have stopped the Yankees' juggernaut that summer.

Despite the disappointment of finishing runner-up, 1927 was a personal triumph for Cobb. Freed from the mental shackles of managing, Ty could concentrate totally on playing. A case in point was an early-season game at Boston, where he almost single-handedly engineered a come-from-behind victory. He had 3 hits, drove in 2 runs, and when pitcher Tony Welzer took his eyes off him for too long, he stole home, executing a classic hook slide around catcher Grover Hartley. Cobb iced the Athletics' 9–8 win with an unassisted double play, snagging Phil Todt's low line drive to short right field and then outracing the runner, Baby Doll Jacobson, to first base to end the game with a fillip.

In early May, Ty returned to Detroit. Headlines in local papers heralded Cobb as "A Friendly Enemy" and "An Old Friend in a New Suit." He almost missed the homecoming. A few days earlier he had gotten into a rhubarb with umpire Red Ormsby, who declared his home run foul. When Ty "accidentally" bumped Ormsby, he was tossed and placed on indefinite suspension by the league.

Detroiters went ahead with plans for Ty Cobb Day. On Tuesday, May 10, Ty was feted with a parade and luncheon. Midway through the event it was dramatically announced that Cobb's suspension had been lifted, making the police-escorted motorcade to that afternoon's game at Navin Field more than just a moot exercise.

A crowd of 27,410 turned out on an overcast afternoon and cheered as Ty graciously accepted a floral horseshoe, a silver service, and a new automobile from friends and fans. The ceremonies were carried live on radio station WWJ, which had started broadcasting Tiger games just three weeks earlier. In the top of the first inning another Ty who would one day become famous in the city—broadcaster Edwin "Ty" Tyson—aired the first live description of a Cobb at-bat in Navin Field, a double into the right field overflow off of Earl Whitehill. After taking the field in the bottom of the inning, Ty was besieged by autograph-seekers. Under the marbled sky, he patiently signed programs and slips of paper for fans, some of whom had undoubtedly booed him the previous summer when he was the Tigers' manager.

Although technically the enemy, Cobb was well-received on subsequent road trips to Detroit. The Tigers were going nowhere under his replacement, one-time teammate George Moriarty, so Detroit fans felt no guilt in boisterously pulling for an old favorite. On July 19 at Navin Field, Ty cracked a double off Sam Gibson, the 4,000th base hit of his career.

Cobb remained as unpopular as ever with the opposition. "Nobody liked him," insisted Willis "Ace" Hudlin, a 20-year-old sinkerball pitcher who joined the Cleveland rotation that season. "I didn't have to put up with him but a couple years. Only time he gave me trouble was at bat." On stealing bases, Willis recalled: "He'd let you know: 'I'm coming in.'"

Hudlin's teammate, right-hander George Uhle, said years later that umpires, perhaps awed by the aging Cobb, gave him the benefit of the doubt on close pitches—a common complaint about all great hitters in their twilight years. "His weakness was pitching inside on him. That was the one way you had the best luck with him. I hate to say it, but there weren't many umpires who'd call it a strike when it was a strike. He'd lean over home plate, and when it was on the inside corner, he would act as if the pitch was going to hit him."

In 1928, Frank "Lefty" O'Doul was a 31-year-old failed pitcher trying to make the New York Giants as an outfielder when he sought Ty's advice during spring training. Following Cobb's instructions to loosen his grip and to spray the ball to all fields, O'Doul went on to hit .349 lifetime with a pair of batting titles.

151

Shibe Park in the 1920s.

On April 19, Cobb stole home on Washington's General Crowder, one of 3 steals of home Ty manufactured that summer on his worn, 40-year-old wheels. All told, the majors' oldest everyday player had a fine season on the basepaths. He wound up swiping 22 bases, third best in the league and just 4 behind leader George Sisler of St. Louis.

Ty made several concessions to age. He took long showers after games and rested evenings in his hotel room, reading and unwinding to the soothing music of concert violinist Fritz Kreisler on his portable phonograph. "And I'd stay in that bed until almost noon the next day," he admitted. "I would breakfast in bed, entertain from my bed, and handle my outside business affairs from a bedside telephone. Only when it was time to leave for the park would I rise and dress." By pampering his tired body and conserving energy whenever possible, he would appear in 134 games, including 8 as a pinch-hitter. He still felt strong enough to swing a 37- or 38-ounce bat.

When first baseman Wally Pipp asked for a day off in 1925, Lou Gehrig replaced him and didn't leave the lineup for 14 years. Although the Yankees' clean-up hitter breathed Ruth's exhaust for much of that time, many considered Gehrig the most valuable and dependable member of New York's juggernaut. In 1927, the year of Babe's 60 home runs, Gehrig hit 47 (more than four other A.L. teams) with a .373 average and league-leading totals of 52 doubles and 175 RBI. The following year he cracked 27 homers (once again second to Ruth) with a .374 average and a league-best 47 doubles and 142 RBI. In New York's sweeps of the Pirates (1927) and Cardinals (1928), Gehrig had 10 hits—all but 1 for extra bases—and 13 RBI in 8 games.

Benched in the middle of the 1928 season, Ty, Tris Speaker, and Eddie Collins watch as a new generation of stars ably take their places. The young Athletics would go on to win 3 consecutive pennants and 2 World Series between 1929 and 1931.

Philadelphia Story

Ty was at his competitive best against New York, whose muscular, free-swinging lineup embodied the new age of jackrabbit ball. In one game he simmered in right field as Babe Ruth strode to the plate, playfully waved the Philadelphia outfielders back with his handkerchief, then struck out on three mighty swings. On his next trip to the plate, Cobb taunted the Yankees by waving a handkerchief himself. He beat out a bunt—then stole second and third.

In a year of monumental changes, when Charles Lindbergh became the first person to fly solo across the Atlantic and Henry Ford ended production of his beloved Model T, some writers unabashedly enjoyed these final glimpses of baseball as it had once been played, when the game—and life itself—seemed less frenzied. Joe Williams reported on one such moment during a New York-Philadelphia contest:

"Ty Cobb went around the bases in the sixth inning . . . but more enlightening was the method he used—old-fashioned stuff scorned in the Era of Ruth.

"He laid down a bunt, perfectly, which caught third baseman Joe Dugan totally by surprise. Cobb slid into first, beating Dugan's hasty throw. How long since you've seen a first base slide?

"Next, when Hale hit a short rap to center field, and when anyone else would have stopped at second, Cobb pumped his aged legs and went for third. Combs' throw to Dugan had him out cold. Locating the ball with a quick glance over his shoulder, Cobb slid left, then contorted himself to the right. There was a geyser of dust and when it cleared, he was seen to have half-smothered the throw with

The last man to pitch to Ty Cobb in a major-league game was Hank Johnson, who on September 11, 1928, induced the Georgia Peach to pop up to shortstop Mark Koenig in the ninth inning of New York's 5–3 win at Yankee Stadium. Six days later in Cleveland, Ty called it quits.

153

Despite all the mileage on his battered 40-year-old body, Ty still displayed flashes of his old brilliance. Here he legs out a triple at Cleveland as shortstop Joe Sewell's relay throw to third baseman Johnny Hodapp arrives late and wide of the bag.

COBB'S REPORTED ANNUAL COMPENSATION IN THE MAJOR LEAGUES

Season	Salary		World Series Share
1905	$ 375	a	
1906	1,500		
1907	2,400		$ 1,946
1908	4,800	b	871
1909	4,800	b	1,273.50
1910	9,000		
1911	9,000		
1912	9,000		
1913	11,332.55	c	
1914	15,000		
1915	20,000		
1916	20,000		
1917	20,000		
1918	20,000		
1919	20,000		
1920	20,000		
1921	35,000		
1922	35,000		
1923	35,000		
1924	38,000		
1925	50,000		
1926	50,000		
1927	75,000	d	
1928	40,000	d	
Totals	$547,607.55		$4,090.50

a   Joined Detroit on August 30. Salary of $1,500 prorated.
b   Includes $800 bonus for hitting .300.
c   Missed two weeks of season in holdout. Salary of $15,000 prorated.
d   Estimated.

When asked at the press conference announcing his retirement to name the pitcher who gave him the most trouble during his career, Ty picked Carl "Zeke" Weilman, the one-time ace of the St. Louis staff. In addition to being left-handed, Weilman's other advantages were height (he stood nearly 6-foot-6), a good fastball, and excellent control. Ty went hitless against him on 10 occasions and only twice had as many as 2 hits off him in a game. He batted a collective .237 in the 8 seasons they faced each other—not as bad as he fared against other hurlers. What Ty probably remembered most about Weilman is that he had beaten the Tigers 3 times in a five-game set back in 1915, the year Detroit lost the pennant to Boston by 2½ games.

his body, and as Dugan scrambled for the ball, Cobb was up and dusting himself off.

"The whole sequence was beautiful to see, a subtle, forgotten heritage from the romantic past."

Despite such nostalgic flourishes, the Athletics rarely solved the Yankees that summer. With the pennant lost, Ty played his final game of the season on September 22, leaving in the fifth inning after going hitless in 3 at-bats against the Indians. He showered, shook hands all around, then departed for his annual post season hunting trip.

He left behind some remarkable numbers: a .357 batting average, fourth best in the league; 104 runs scored; 93 RBI; and a miserly

12 strikeouts in 490 at-bats. This was vindication, and then some. While Ty enjoyed a bountiful big-game hunting expedition in Wyoming and Arizona, the baseball public wondered whether it had seen the last of the old warhorse.

The answer: no. Returning to Philadelphia after his hunting trip, he told reporters during a stopover in Detroit, "I am sound physically, but there is no telling what might happen if I tried to drag on." Mack, who attributed his club's strong showing to Cobb's leadership, wanted him back in 1928, but couldn't afford him at his 1927 salary. He told Ty he could pursue offers elsewhere.

After discussing employment with a couple of clubs, Cobb announced on March 1 that he had agreed to terms with Mack. The undisclosed salary, probably about $40,000, wasn't a factor in Ty's decision, which contradicted his professed desire to spend more time with family and spare his battered body from another season of painful slides and spills. The longing to play in one last World Series, although diminished somewhat by now, probably played a part. So did the chance, after a quarter-century of organized ball, to finally play alongside his old friend Tris Speaker, who had been released by Washington and signed to a one-year contract by Mack.

Like most sequels, this one was a sorry anticlimax. For the second year in a row, the Athletics opened the season with an 8–3 loss to the Yankees, who went on to grab the pennant by 2¹/₂ games. Much of the blame for the near-miss was assigned to Connie Mack's early-season insistence on playing his two slow-footed veterans in the outfield, where balls dropped in regularly. "If this keeps up," complained left fielder Al Simmons, who chased down several of the long drives that eluded Cobb and Speaker, "I'll be an old man myself by the end of the season."

155

No one personified the new breed of swing-from-the-heels power hitters better than Lewis "Hack" Wilson, the Chicago Cubs' squat, one-dimensional outfielder. Wilson, who would be the goat of the following year's World Series against the Athletics when he butchered two fly balls, led the National League in home runs 4 times between 1926 and 1930. Hack's hitting philosophy must have made Ty twinge: "I just go up there with the intention of knocking the ball out of the park and swing."

Although his reflexes in the field had slowed embarrassingly, Cobb still could inspire respect. In 95 games he hit for a .323 average, and in a June 15 contest against Cleveland he stole home for the 55th—and final—time in his career. Billy Rogell, then a young infielder with the Red Sox, remembered one game that final season: "He was in a terrible, terrible slump. . . . He hit a blooper into left field and he had to slide into second base. He hit the bag and that bag *flew*. He tore that bastard right off. He got up, sparks in his eyes. 'Jesus Christ,' I thought to myself, 'I don't want to tangle with that old bastard.'"

Such fire was all but extinguished on July 27, when Ty was hit in the chest by a George Connally pitch. That game against Chicago was his last regular-season start. The painful injury pushed the already ailing 41-year-old to the bench, alongside Speaker and Collins, where the three old-timers remained through August and September as

Three weeks after Ty announced his retirement, big boppers Ruth and Gehrig once again made the Yankees champions of the world. While straw boaters sailed onto the field in wild celebration of Babe's third home run of the final game, Japan-bound Ty took a moment to pose on a Honolulu dock with his family and say sayonara.

Philadelphia Story

Connie Mack used younger troops in a desperate battle with the Yankees.

At Yankee Stadium Cobb had his final big-league at-bat. On the afternoon of September 11, 1928, with the Athletics trailing the Yankees 5–3, he pinch-hit for Jimmie Dykes leading off the ninth. He failed to get around on right-hander Hank Johnson, popping a pitch back of third base, where shortstop Mark Koenig made the routine catch.

The record books slammed shut when Koenig squeezed his glove, although that wasn't apparent until six days later, when Ty announced his retirement inside his Cleveland hotel room. The statement he handed reporters read:

> *Never again, after the finish of the present pennant race, will I be an active player in the game to which I have devoted 24 seasons of what for me was hard labor. I make this announcement today because of the many inquiries constantly coming to me concerning my future plans.*
>
> *Friends have urged me to try it one more season so that I could round out a quarter century of continuous service in the American League, but I prefer to retire while there still may remain some base hits in my bat. Baseball is the greatest game in the world. I owe all that I possess in the way of worldly goods to this game. For each week, month, and year of my career, I have felt a deep sense of responsibility to the grand old national sport that has been everything to me.*
>
> *I will not reconsider. This is final.*

That was it. The statement made no mention of his final numbers, which for years would seem unmatchable. Rows of figures told only part of the story, anyway; it was Ty's hurricane-force personality that had made him baseball's centerpiece for much of his career. Ty was well aware of his place in baseball's history, a place that remained secure despite a sour curtain call. Even at the end, when his cement legs had him grounding into double plays and being thrown out by outfielders with popgun arms, the fact that he was, after all *Ty Cobb*, was enough for most fans, including a young Philadelphian named James A. Michener.

"They weren't what you'd call really good," the famous author, remembering the summer of '28 at Shibe Park, wrote many years later, "but by God they were Speaker and Cobb, and I saw them."

Ty in the autumn of 1955, shortly before turning sixty-nine.

CHAPTER EIGHT

The Long Way Home

I only know that summer sang in me
A little while, that in me sings no more.
—Edna St. Vincent Millay

In the spring of 1929, baseball prepared for a new season without its most storied competitor. Although few infielders or pitchers were mourning his absence, the notion of America's game being played without the Georgia Peach was newsworthy enough to dispatch a film crew to Cobb country.

"Well, Ty," asked the man from Movietone News, "how's it feel to be down here hunting in Georgia instead of training in a ball camp?"

"Wel-l-l," replied Ty in his familiar high-pitched drawl, "I had about twenty-five years of baseball and I'll have to admit that I got pretty well fed up on it. And I'm obliged to say that I'm very happy not to have on my mind having to report for spring training. I have played ball for so long, and it was such a task, I was really happy to get out. And I've been very happy since I've been out. I've had a lot of inquiries from people who wondered about my feelings, my ability to retire from the game, and they've wondered just how I *could* retire. Well, I'll be honest and tell you that baseball is quite a task and I feel that I've served a long time and now I'm looking forward to the things that I have wanted to do for so many years. As yet, I haven't had any desire to re-enter the game."

As the newsreel cameraman cranked away, Ty turned to one of his hunting dogs. "This old friend of mine here," he continued, "he's a dog, it's true, but he's a great friend. Now, he won't boo me and he won't criticize me. But I do want to say this, that I'm not finding any

In the 7 seasons following his retirement, Ty's two former employers—Detroit and Philadelphia—won 5 pennants and 3 World Series between them. Mickey Cochrane, seen here visiting with his old friend before a September 1934 game at Navin Field, was the catcher and inspirational leader on each of them.

160

fault with the fans or anyone because I feel deeply obligated to everyone for all the kindnesses and all the nice things they've done and they've said about me and my career as a ballplayer. Of course, that's a closed incident as far as actively engaging in baseball. But I do want to have the fans realize that I still appreciate them."

That two-minute newsreel, part of the usual between-features fare, is how millions of fans in movie palaces across America got their first glimpse of the great Ty Cobb in retirement. The 42-year-old Peach sounded not only gracious and contented, he sounded practically *genial*. But Ty could no sooner learn to enjoy a life of idle retirement than his dogs could learn to tap dance. His restless and competitive nature wouldn't allow it. As the years passed, much of his time would be spent coming to grips with his unsavory reputation, his disintegrating family, and, ultimately, his own mortality.

Initially, however, Ty reveled in his freedom from the daily rigors of baseball. He traveled widely and indulged a variety of pastimes, including big-game hunting, fishing, golf, and even polo. In 1929 he and Charlie visited the European continent, England, and Scotland in grand style. In Scotland Ty fulfilled a lifelong dream by visiting Keith, "the big league of upland bird hunting, a pilgrimage place for the world's finest shotgun artists." There he impressed Sir Isaac Sharpe, the world-famous trainer of hunting dogs, with his superior shooting

Ty Jr., photographed in the 1920s, was a handsome, sensitive youth who grew weary of his father's expectations for him. As a boy he played sports like football and baseball but hated them. By the time Cobb had retired, he and his first-born were constantly at odds with each other—an eerie parallel to Ty's relationship with his father.

ABOVE THE CROWD

By Stookie Allen

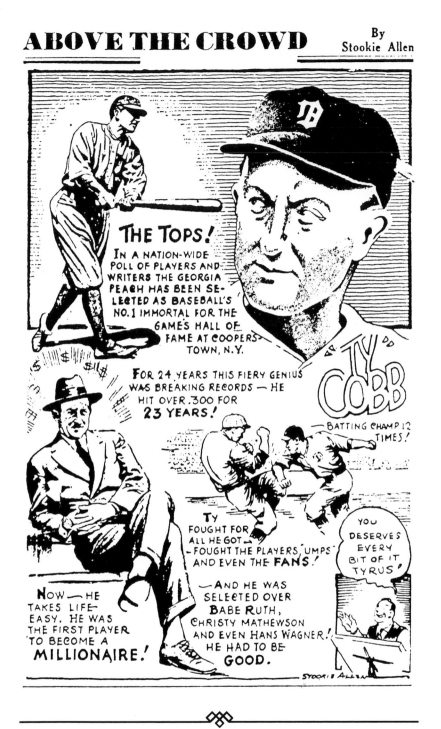

THE TOPS!

IN A NATION-WIDE POLL OF PLAYERS AND WRITERS THE GEORGIA PEACH HAS BEEN SELECTED AS BASEBALL'S NO.1 IMMORTAL FOR THE GAME'S HALL OF FAME AT COOPERSTOWN, N.Y.

FOR 24 YEARS THIS FIERY GENIUS WAS BREAKING RECORDS — HE HIT OVER .300 FOR 23 YEARS!

TY COBB

— BATTING CHAMP 12 TIMES!

TY FOUGHT FOR ALL HE GOT — FOUGHT THE PLAYERS, UMPS AND EVEN THE FANS!

NOW — HE TAKES LIFE EASY. HE WAS THE FIRST PLAYER TO BECOME A MILLIONAIRE!

— AND HE WAS SELECTED OVER BABE RUTH, CHRISTY MATHEWSON AND EVEN HANS WAGNER! HE HAD TO BE GOOD.

YOU DESERVES EVERY BIT OF IT TYRUS!

STOOKIE ALLEN

The culmination of Ty's professional life was his near-unanimous selection in 1936 for the Hall of Fame then being planned in Cooperstown, New York. Of 226 ballots cast by players and writers, Ty received 222. This was four short of a perfect score but seven more than Babe Ruth and Honus Wagner.

Ty Cobb Achieves Highest Niche In Modern Baseball Hall of Fame

Georgian Gets 222 Votes, 4 Short of Perfect Score and 7 More Than Ruth and Wagner—Mathewson and Johnson Only Others With Enough Ballots to Be Named in Nation-Wide Poll.

By The Associated Press.

CHICAGO, Feb. 2.—Tyrus Raymond Cobb, fiery genius of the diamond for twenty-four years, will be the No. 1 immortal in baseball's permanent hall of fame.

The famous Georgian, who shattered virtually all records known to baseball during his glorious era, won the distinction as the immortal of immortals today by outscoring even such diamond greats as Babe Ruth, Honus Wagner and Christy Mathewson in the nationwide poll to determine which ten players of the modern age should be represented in the game's memorial hall at Cooperstown, N. Y.

Margin of Seven Ballots.

Only Cobb, Ruth, Wagner, Mathewson and Walter Johnson, probably the speed ball king of them all, received the required majority to win places in the hall of fame, but Cobb had a margin of seven votes over his closest rivals, Ruth and Wagner.

Of 226 ballots cast by players and writers, the Georgia Peach received 222, or four less than a unanimous vote. Ruth and Wagner received 215 each. Mathewson was fourth with 205 and Johnson fifth with 189. Seventy-five per cent of the total votes, or 169, were needed.

Napoleon Lajoie, Tris Speaker, Cy Young, Rogers Hornsby and Mickey Cochrane ran in that order for the other five positions left for the moderns, players who starred from 1900 and on, but as none received 75 per cent of the total vote their cases will be submitted to the Cooperstown committee in charge of the memorial to be erected in time for baseball's centennial in 1939. Their names will be submitted in another poll next year with five or seven places open.

Young Honored in Two Polls.

Their votes were: Lajoie 146, Speaker 133, Young (who also received 32½ votes for the pre-1900 hall of fame) 111, Hornsby 105, and Cochrane 80.

The committee in charge of the vote tabulation, headed by Henry Edwards, secretary of the Baseball Writers Association, figured the struggle for ballots among the moderns would be a two-man battle between Cobb and Ruth. When the first 100 votes were counted, both Cobb and the home run king were unanimous.

Ruth was the first to fall out, losing a vote from a writer who had watched him hang up some of his greatest records. The committee was amazed. Vote counting stopped momentarily for a discussion on how any one could leave the great Ruth off the list of immortals.

The same happened when Cobb missed his first vote. Too, there was some surprise when the usual vote of Cobb, Ruth and Speaker was broken up with a series of ballots for other outfielders.

Times Wide World Photo.

TY COBB.

Sisler Ranked Eleventh.

George Sisler, whose great career with the St. Louis Browns was halted by impairment of vision, ranked eleventh, with 77 votes.

Fifty-one stars, past and present, were named, but few of the present ones received much support, for the reason that the voters figured they would get their chances later, as one or two will be added to the list of immortals each year.

Dizzy Dean, Charley Gehringer and Charles (Gabby) Hartnett, rated as three of the greatest stars of the game today, received only 1 vote apiece. There were many surprises of famous stars receiving only a handful of votes.

The others received votes as follows:

Eddie Collins, 60; Jimmy Collins (former Boston third baseman), 58; Grover Cleveland Alexander, 55; Lou Gehrig, 51; Roger Bresnahan, 47; Willie Keeler (he also received 33 in the old-timer poll), 40; Rube Waddell, 33; Jimmy Foxx, 21; Ed Walsh, 20; Ed Delehanty (also a leader in the old-timer poll), 17; Harold (Pie) Traynor, 16; Frank Frisch, 14; Robert Moses Grove, 12; Hal Chase, 11; Ross Young, 10; Bill Terry, 9; Johnny Kling, 8; Lew Criger, 7.

Johnny Evers, 6; Mordecai Brown, 6; Frank Chance, 5; Ray Schalk, John McGraw and Al Simmons, 4 each; Chief Bender, Eddie Roush and Joe Jackson, 2 each, and 1 vote each to the following: Rube Marquard, William Bradley, Nap Rucker, Jake Daubert, Sam Crawford, Connie Mack, Norm Elberfeld, Frank (Home Run) Baker, Fred Clarke, Dazzy Vance.

When the big day arrived three years later, Ty was late for the induction ceremonies. Still harboring a grudge over Judge Landis' mishandling of the Cobb-Speaker affair a dozen years earlier, Ty wanted to avoid the possibility of posing for photographs with the commissioner. Thus the official portrait of the charter class of Hall of Fame inductees was missing the game's number-one immortal. On hand were (seated, from left) Eddie Collins, Babe Ruth, Connie Mack, Cy Young, (standing, from left) Honus Wagner, Grover Alexander, Tris Speaker, Nap Lajoie, George Sisler, and Walter Johnson.

162

Ty was a great admirer of Bobby Jones, a fellow Georgian known as "The Emperor of Golf." The two are pictured at the Masters Invitational at Augusta in 1941.

skills. A little more than a year later, he participated in his first organized golf tournament, shooting an 83 over 18 holes to win a cup at the Augusta Country Club. In 1932 he moved his family from Augusta to a magnificent estate at 48 Spencer Lane in Atherton, California, about thirty-five miles south of San Francisco. The estate included a seven-bedroom house, servants' quarters, a guest house, and a swimming pool spread over several tree-filled acres.

The splendid trappings befitted Cobb's station in life. Because of his diversified investments in General Motors, Coca-Cola, and other stocks, he was already a millionaire. He was famous, a man of means and substance. He also was a man with whom it was impossible to live.

The Long Way Home

Charlie and the children had never found Ty easy to get along with, but it was worse now that baseball didn't take him away from the house for half of the year. Worn out by his sarcasm and afraid of his irrational rages, Charlie wanted out. Between 1931 and 1939, she filed for divorce on three occasions, only to change her mind each time—probably for the sake of the younger children. Her first suit charged Ty with "cruel treatment," a broad term that could include mental, physical, or emotional abuse. Based on the stories told by old Augustans today, and considering Ty's reputation, all three probably applied in Charlie's case.

Neither of Charlie's brothers, Alfred and Roz, could stand their famous brother-in-law. One day in the early 1920s, J. Marvin Wolfe, a print shop operator who also owned the Augusta ball club and park, was returning to his home, just a couple of houses away from the Cobbs' residence. A terrible argument between Cobb and one of the Lombard brothers attracted his attention. Asked what was going on, the enraged brother claimed, "This son of a bitch beat Charlie with a bat so bad she can hardly walk." Wolfe, whose brother was married to Charlie's sister, had little use for Cobb himself. But he intervened between the two, reportedly coaxing a pistol away from the enraged brother, who vowed, "I'm gonna kill him." He didn't, of course, but the effect was nearly the same. The Lombard family, important people in Augusta, froze Ty out of their immediate circle.

"It was no peaceful home from what I understand," Eugene "Woody" Wolfe, Marvin's son, said of Ty's Augusta residence. "The kids would just scatter when he came home. Dad wouldn't let us have anything to do with him."

If Ty did beat his wife, it would go a long way toward explaining his falling out with Ty Jr. Cobb's oldest child had already witnessed his father's propensity for violence. One infamous afternoon in 1921 he had watched as his father and umpire Billy Evans, both stripped to the waist, engaged in a bloody knock-down, drag-out fight under the stands in Washington. "Come on, Daddy," the then-11-year-old boy had pleaded, peeking through a forest of players' legs. One can only guess what ugly scenes he and his siblings saw at home as their parents argued and drifted farther apart.

With his own children, Ty was as demanding and spare in his praise as Professor Cobb had been with him. In fact, Ty's troubled relationship with his first-born, Ty Jr., mirrored his own adolescent difficulties. Sensitive and rebellious, young Ty grew up hating baseball. Such behavior shouldn't have surprised the elder Cobb. Two of his closest friends in the game, Mickey Cochrane and Christy Mathewson, also had oldest sons who felt burdened by their famous name. Both offspring ignored the diamond, looking to make their own

The modern game held little appeal for Cobb, who considered most of the new generation of players soft in dedication, guts, and brains. He even criticized Boston great Ted Williams, who many considered to be in the same class as Cobb as a hitter, for taking too many close pitches and for not punching singles to left. Conceding Ty was the greatest ballplayer of all time, Williams admitted the two were completely different hitters. "When he talked hitting," said Teddy Ballgame, "he talked Greek to me."

163

As a joke, a friend once gave Ty a putter in the shape of a bat.

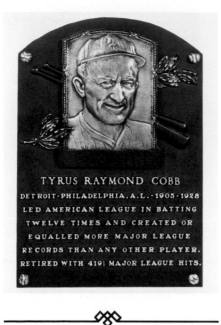

TYRUS RAYMOND COBB
DETROIT·PHILADELPHIA. A.L.·1905·1928
LED AMERICAN LEAGUE IN BATTING
TWELVE TIMES AND CREATED OR
EQUALLED MORE MAJOR LEAGUE
RECORDS THAN ANY OTHER PLAYER.
RETIRED WITH 4191 MAJOR LEAGUE HITS.

Ty's Hall of Fame plaque and exhibit today.

164

The Tiger in winter. Writer-artist S. J. Woolf sketched Ty in 1948 when he was sixty-one.

way. Christy Mathewson Jr. became an aviator, losing a leg and a young bride in a crash, while Gordon Stanley "Mickey" Cochrane Jr. would become an army paratrooper and die in the final weeks of World War II.

Ty Jr.'s rebellion consisted of driving fast cars, playing a lot of tennis, and flunking out of Princeton. By August 1939, when Charlie finally moved out for good into a house in Menlo Park, Ty Jr. and his father fell into an estrangement that would last through the war years.

At the same time his family life was unraveling, Ty was reconciling with men he had battled so long and so hard against. One was Babe Ruth, who scored points when he claimed a Georgia girl, Claire Merritt Hodgson, as his second wife in 1929. The new Mrs. Ruth, described by some as a gold digger, was the daughter of a prominent lawyer, James Merritt, who had at one time handled some of Cobb's legal affairs. "In Georgia," she recalled, "I had known Ty Cobb very well." According to Claire, she and Ty had occasionally dated after she moved to New York to pursue a modeling career in the early '20s, although the exact nature of their relationship can only be guessed at.

Ty, who had openly considered himself the better of the two feuding superstars, saw it made official in February 1936. That was when the first class of "immortals" was selected for the newly formed National Baseball Museum and Hall of Fame in Cooperstown, New York. Of ballots cast by 226 members of the Baseball Writers Association of America, Cobb was named on 222 of them. Honus Wagner and Ruth, who had retired just four months earlier, were next with 215. Of all the honors he accrued during his life, Ty was always proudest of the election that, in effect, named him the game's number-one immortal.

Three years later, on June 12, 1939, the museum was dedicated before 10,000 enthusiastic people and a national radio audience. Blaming missed train connections, Cobb arrived too late to participate in the induction ceremonies or to sit with Ruth, Wagner, Connie Mack, Cy Young, George Sisler, Eddie Collins, Willie Keeler, Tris Speaker, Nap Lajoie, and Grover Cleveland Alexander for the official portrait of the charter class of inductees. Years later, Ty confessed that he had been purposely late to avoid posing for photographs with Judge Landis. The commissioner would always rank near the top of Ty's "son-of-a-bitch list" for his mishandling of the Cobb-Speaker case in the winter of 1926–27.

Ty, always a sentimental man, enjoyed immensely the annual Cooperstown get-togethers. He could swap yarns with other balding, aging stars of his day and put down the modern game. A favorite target was Ted Williams, a pure hitter many considered nearly the equal of Cobb. Ty wasn't buying that—at least not until the stubborn Boston Red Sox slugger took his unsolicited advice and started dropping

He also corresponded freely with fans, players, and writers, devoting much of what he put on paper to discrediting what he considered his unjust legacy as a dirty ballplayer. "It has always hurt me deep," he wrote Harry Salsinger in 1953. "It happens to be the real weak spot in whatever armor I have."

165

Ty with the Tigers' first bonus baby, outfielder Dick Wakefield, at Briggs Stadium in 1941. Ironically, Ty's first steal of home had been against Dick's father, Cleveland catcher Howard Wakefield, thirty-four years earlier. The younger Wakefield's record $52,000 bonus could have met the combined payrolls of both World Series teams in 1907.

Before an exhibition game in Seattle in 1944, Ty showed that at fifty-seven he still could swing a bat with authority.

During the war years Ty traveled widely at home, appearing in exhibitions that benefitted the USO and other service organizations. He even reached a rapprochement with his old rival, Babe Ruth. They played a much-publicized series of golf matches in the summer of 1941, then four years later were honorary captains at the Esquire All-American All-Star game at the Polo Grounds.

third-base bunts against the so-called Williams Shift. "If they had tried that shift against Cobb," sniffed Nap Lajoie, defending his old adversary, "the Peach would have hit .800 every season."

During his first few years of retirement, Ty was twice a major investor in syndicates looking to buy a franchise: first the Cincinnati Reds (for $275,000 in 1929), then the Detroit club in the early '30s. Both bids were rejected, but Ty still managed to stay close to the game through old-timers' games, Cooperstown reunions, and golf matches.

The most memorable of the latter occurred in the summer of 1941, when Cobb and Ruth agreed to a best-of-three series to benefit the USO and other charities. The media dragged out the brain vs. brawn comparisons that had been at the heart of their diamond rivalry years earlier. Having lost none of his competitive zeal, Ty later admitted, "I went into the Ruth matches as determined to win as I ever was on the ball field."

After winning the first match in West Newton, Massachusetts, Ty lost the second match, played two days later at Fresh Meadows on Long Island, by a stroke. The rubber game was scheduled for Grosse Ile, Michigan, where Ty parlayed his passion for amateur psychology into another triumph. During a practice round in Cleveland, en route to the big match, Ty missed shots over and over again, moaning to everyone that he didn't stand a chance of beating the Babe. The gullible Ruth, his confidence boosted by Ty's supposed ineptitude, partied harder than he should have on that night's boat ride from Cleveland to Detroit. The following day arrived steamy and hot. As a gallery of 2,500 people followed the two competitors around, Ty easily beat his hot and hung-over opponent, claiming what he called "The Has Beens' Golf Championship of Nowhere in Particular."

After Pearl Harbor, Cobb and Ruth met several times during exhibition games designed to benefit war-related charities. Approaching sixty, nearly bald, and some forty pounds heavier than he had been in his prime, Ty nonetheless could still swing a bat with authority. He also continued to enjoy playing mind games with the opposition. To outwit someone—or to "slip him the oskafagus," as he liked to call it—remained a favorite hobby. During an old-timers' game at Yankee Stadium in 1947, Cobb approached the plate and offered an apology to catcher Wally Schang. He was afraid that the bat might slip out of his hands, Ty explained, so perhaps the catcher should back up several feet to lessen the possibility of injury. Schang obligingly moved back—whereupon Ty laid down a bunt, nearly beating it out for a base hit.

About this time Charlie Cobb was granted a divorce from Ty, whom she charged with "extreme cruelty from the date of marriage to the present time." Although the out-of-court settlement cost Ty a reported $500,000, he remained a millionaire several times over. And he soon found a new wife. On September 24, 1949, he married Frances Fairburn, the daughter of a Buffalo physician. Twenty-two years younger than Ty, she shared his interest in golfing, hunting, and traveling. They would remain married for nearly seven years.

During this period Ty lived the life of a country squire, playing golf, traveling widely, raising show dogs, entertaining guests at his

In his sixties, Ty lived the life of a country squire, playing golf, raising show dogs, entertaining guests, and watching his investments. He is seen here with one of his granddaughters at the Wayneboro field trials in about 1950.

167

On September 28, 1947, Ty joined Babe Ruth and Tris Speaker in an old-timers' contest at Yankee Stadium. Less than a year later, Ruth would be dead of cancer.

In 1943, Ty sat in on a game between the Great Lakes Naval Training Center, managed by Mickey Cochrane, and a group of Ford semipro players.

If the old ballplayer seemed contented, the reason was Frances Fairburn Cass, the outdoors-loving daughter of a Buffalo physician. They are pictured at her father's summer home in Point Abino, Ontario, shortly before their marriage on September 24, 1949. Cobb's second marriage would last fewer than seven years.

Atherton home, and carefully watching his investments. He also corresponded regularly with old players and sportswriters. Not surprisingly, much of what he wrote was in defense of his legacy, which others viewed as a dirty ballplayer. "It has always hurt me deep," he wrote Harry Salsinger in 1953. "It happens to be the real weak spot in whatever armor I have."

Actually, he had several weak spots. During the 1950s Cobb's campaigning helped get a pair of his former Detroit teammates, Harry Heilmann and Sam Crawford, selected for the Hall of Fame. In the case of Heilmann, who was a popular Detroit broadcaster at the time he was stricken with cancer, Ty visited his bedside to deliver the good news. Heilmann died on the eve of the 1951 All-Star Game in Detroit believing that he had been elected, although the vote hadn't even been taken.

Conversely, Ty hated modern baseball. "Baseball today is putrid," he complained, "and you can blame it on the lively ball and the home run. There are too many lopsided scores. What's happened to those grand old one-run, last-inning finishes?"

Many stories have been told about Ty's penny-pinching: How the tight-fisted millionaire would drive miles out of his way to frequent a gas station that offered green stamps, or create a nasty scene over a three-cent discrepancy in a dinner bill. While most of the stories are true, they overshadow his generosity. Cobb looked out after several down-on-their-luck ex-ballplayers, including Ray Schalk, Mickey Cochrane, and Lu Blue, sending money (often anonymously through a third party) or providing for medical care.

Cobb's largesse extended beyond the game and its performers. The projects that most occupied his time during the early 1950s were the Cobb Educational Fund and Cobb Memorial Hospital, good works that continue to flourish today.

Both filled a void in Ty's life. Although he had chosen baseball over college, he understood the benefits of higher education. In 1953 he announced the creation of a fund, named after his father, that would provide scholarships for needy college students in Georgia. One stipulation was that they have already completed their freshman year, thus demonstrating their drive to achieve. "We want stars," claimed Cobb, "stars in medicine, in law, in teaching and in life." After more than four decades, Cobb's original endowment of $100,000 has grown into assets exceeding $5 million. From that base administrators of the Cobb Educational Foundation annually dispense 100 or so grants ranging between $150 and $20,000 each.

Earlier, Ty had honored his parents by donating $100,000 to kick off a drive to build a modern hospital in his hometown of

Royston. A federal grant and contributions added another $110,000 to the building fund. The twenty-four bed hospital was dedicated in early 1950, Ty's new wife turning the ceremonial gold key. On hand was a buddy from Ty's Royston Reds days, Stewart Brown, who had grown up to become "one of Georgia's outstanding country doctors," pronounced Cobb. Cobb Memorial Hospital—"the hospital built with a bat"—has since doubled in size and added a convalescent center. The rest of his life Cobb donated all money from his writings and paid public appearances to his two pet projects. When he died, one-quarter of his estate was left to his educational foundation.

Cobb Memorial Hospital helped Ty reconcile his differences with his oldest son. In his early thirties, Ty Jr. had finally decided to get serious about a career, graduating from medical school and setting up practice in Dublin, Georgia. But soon after patching up their differences, tragedy struck. In 1952, Ty Jr. died of a malignant brain tumor. He was forty-two.

Ty Jr.'s death followed closely another blow. The previous year, Herschel Cobb, who Ty had helped set up as a Coca-Cola distributor, died suddenly of a heart attack. He was only thirty-four. His sons' unexpected deaths undoubtedly contributed to Cobb's frenzied search for place and meaning. Between bouts of high-stakes gambling and drinking, he brooded over missed opportunities with his children. "When you get older, you wish for companionship. I was just a loner; I couldn't have that with my children."

By 1956 Frances had had enough of Ty's erratic behavior. She confided to her friends that she was physically afraid of her husband. In this she joined half of America. Ty's affinity for headlines didn't end just because he was approaching seventy. In California, news items detailed how he punched out a heckler in a nightclub, shoved a prominent businessman into a fish pond, and went to jail for abusing a cop. Stories circulated around Arizona about how he pitched a salt shaker at a waiter and kicked a cab driver in the seat of his pants. His son-of-a-bitch list—actually a little black book containing the names of Dutch Leonard, Judge Landis, Eleanor Roosevelt, utility companies, and everyone who he felt he had a beef with—was growing by the day. Whenever someone threatened litigation, Ty would snarl, "Get in line, bub, there's a hundred ahead of you."

For much of the 1940s, Ty busied himself with his plans to build a modern hospital in Royston in memory of his parents. Groundbreaking for the twenty-five-bed facility took place in 1949, by which time Ty had donated $100,000 and helped raise tens of thousands of dollars more.

169

In early 1950, Cobb Memorial Hospital was dedicated before a crowd of 3,000. At Ty's side was Dr. Stewart Brown, who a half-century earlier had played with him on the Royston Reds. Ty described his boyhood friend as "one of Georgia's outstanding country doctors."

By 1951, death had claimed many of the stars Ty had competed with and against. Next to go was Harry Heilmann, a popular broadcaster on Detroit radio station WXYZ since 1934 and now dying of cancer. Heilmann passed away on the eve of that summer's All-Star game in Detroit, but not before Ty had whispered to his old outfield mate that he had been elected into the Hall of Fame. The following afternoon fans at Briggs Stadium observed a moment of silence for Heilmann, then exploded into applause as Ty threw out the first ball.

All this was too much for Frances. Charging Ty with "extreme mental cruelty," she was granted a divorce in Nevada, where they maintained a second residence in Lake Tahoe. The exact terms of the settlement weren't published, but Ty kept most of his money and both homes. Not that he found the sprawling, empty Atherton estate appealing. His three surviving children, all married and living in California, dreaded sharing the West Coast with their cantankerous father, much less a family room. "In this house," Ty sighed to a visitor, "I'm just a lonely old man."

By 1959, Ty was a lonely, *sick* old man. He had relocated to Cornelia, Georgia, near Royston, where he planned to live out his days in a mountaintop home that he hoped to build. He also had been diagnosed with prostate cancer—as well as diabetes, high blood pressure, and a weak heart. If that wasn't enough, he suffered from impacted bowels and his kidneys were failing him. Ignoring his prescribed medicine, Ty chose to kill the pain by drinking a quart of Jack Daniels bourbon, mixed with milk, each day. "This has an effect of dulling somewhat my senses and nerves," he explained.

Over the winter of 1959–60, Ty had most of his cancerous prostate removed. Radiation treatments followed. "I'm on the threshold of old age," he said, his skin hanging like crepe paper, "and believe me, it's quite an adventure."

Al Stump certainly believed him. A sportswriter from Santa Barbara, California, Stump had been assigned by Doubleday to assist Cobb in writing his autobiography. Despite his oft-expressed desire to "set the record straight," for years Ty had ignored repeated requests from publishers and movie producers for his life story. He once explained to Harry Salsinger that "those Jewish boys promise but pay no attention" to the truth. The book or movie would invariably portray him as "jumping down every man's throat with spikes and in general be a 'hell cat' . . . every boy who saw such a picture would think ill of me." For a time Salsinger, who Ty trusted, looked to have the inside track as Cobb's collaborator. But as it developed, neither Salsinger (who died in 1958) nor Cobb would live to see what Ty liked to call "my true record" between covers.

Following closely on the heels of the Cobb Memorial Hospital, Ty announced the creation of the Cobb Educational Fund, which provided college scholarships for needy Georgia students. He presented these medallions to the three trustees of the foundation. They would be responsible for administering Ty's original endowment of $100,000.

171

In 1957, Ty talked hitting with his granddaughter, Mary McLaren.

Ernie Harwell, voice of the Baltimore Orioles, introduced Ty to the crowd before a 1956 game in Baltimore.

Ty in his Atherton, California, home, shortly after his second marriage ended. "In this house," he told a visitor in the spring of 1957, "I'm just a lonesome old man."

172

Not long afterward he decided to sell the property and move back to his native Georgia.

Ty regularly accepted invitations to old-timers games, including one at Briggs Stadium in 1958, but he steadfastly refused to put on a uniform and play. "I wouldn't want to be remembered as a doddering old man," he said. Instead he signed autographs for fans who weren't even alive when he last played. He also chatted amiably with two Tiger batting champions of the 1950s, Harvey Kuenn (center) and Al Kaline.

The Long Way Home

Stump and Cobb worked on the book together in fits and starts throughout 1960 and into early 1961. During this period Stump watched in equal parts fascination and horror as Ty—half-crazed by booze, medication, and constant pain—battled terminal cancer and everyone who crossed his path as spiritedly as he had the Philadelphia Athletics 50 years earlier. Among Stump's adventures was a hair-raising ride down a mountain during a blizzard so Ty could hit the casinos in Reno, as well as an incident where Cobb fired several pistol shots into a motel parking lot to hush whoever had disturbed his nap. Upon moving to Cobb's Atherton house to continue work on the book, Stump was flabbergasted to discover that Ty's electricity had been shut off in a protracted dispute over a sixteen-dollar discrepancy in the bill. Stump wound up working under a single light bulb connected by extension cords to a neighbor's house 200 feet away.

Even Ty's periodic cobalt treatments involved a certain amount of adventure. He invariably quarreled with the staff, especially when they tried to take away his alcohol. "We'll have to slip them the oskafagus," he told Stump. Ty managed to fool the nurses by placing his false teeth in a glass of scotch.

Stump worked heroically, enduring Cobb's foul moods while shaping Ty's candid and insightful reminiscences into one of the finest sports autobiographies ever. The book, published in August 1961, was followed a few months later by Stump's engrossing magazine article, "Ty Cobb's Wild Ten-Month Fight to Live," which has since become a staple of baseball anthologies. Taken together, they reveal both sides of what Stump called a "badly disturbed personality."

The most lucid moment of Stump's time with Cobb came on Christmas Eve, 1960. That snowy evening he took Stump to the Royston cemetery, to a stone burial vault that he had just had built to accommodate his parents and sister. Ty's mother had died in 1936, shortly after he had been voted into the Hall of Fame. Florence had died eight years later. Ty had had all three disinterred.

"My father was the greatest man I ever knew," Ty said, weak with pain and emotion. "He was a scholar, state senator, editor, and philosopher. I worshipped him. So did all the people around here. He was the only man who ever made me do his bidding."

Ty, his eyes welling with tears, continued slowly, "My father had his head blown off with a shotgun when I was eighteen years old—*by a member of my own family.* I didn't get over that. I've never gotten over it."

The past weighed heavily on Cobb. When an old friend, comedian Joe E. Brown, visited him in Atherton the following spring, Ty was full of self-recrimination. Maybe he'd been too aggressive, he told Brown, went a little too far. "I always had to be right in any argument I was in," he confessed, "and wanted to be first in everything." Later Ty

The bloom was off Ty's second marriage by 1955, when both partners filed for divorce. Each charged the other with "mental cruelty." On May 12, 1956, Judge Frank Gregory awarded Ty the divorce in a Minden, Nevada, district court.

On the Detroit Tigers' forty-man roster in the spring of 1959 was a career minor leaguer named Maury Wills, who was released but then caught on with the Los Angeles Dodgers. In 1962, a year after Ty's death, the shortstop shattered Cobb's seemingly invincible single-season base-stealing record by swiping 104 bases. Wills' success—he led the National League in thefts 6 straight seasons—ushered in a new age of base stealers, most notably Lou Brock and Rickey Henderson, both of whom would pass Cobb in career steals.

Fifty years earlier, the outfield of Davy Jones, Ty Cobb, and Sam Crawford had hawked fly balls and sped around the bases like young colts. Now, at a 1957 banquet honoring Crawford's (center) induction into the Hall of Fame, the three were old warhorses, swapping stories and doing their best to keep their ties out of the gravy.

174

Ty was diagnosed with cancer in December 1959, just as he was turning seventy-three. "I'm on the threshold of old age," he said at the time, "and believe me, it's quite an adventure."

added, "Joe, I do indeed think I would have done things different. And if I had, I would have had more friends."

In April 1961, tests showed that Ty's cancer had spread into his brain. He flew back to Cornelia, where on May 22 he drew up his will. An inventory of his estate, the bulk of which was left to his three children and a trust fund for his 15 grandchildren, was never filed. But contemporary estimates of his wealth ranged between $6 million and $11.8 million. Whatever it was, it was of little use where he was headed. When Ty entered Emory Hospital on June 5, he knew that he would only leave it feet first. From his hospital bed he mailed a photograph of his mausoleum to Stump. "Any day now," was written across it. No longer able to endure the pain of the cancer coursing through his back and skull, he finally surrendered to a variety of drugs. He slipped in and out of consciousness, regularly praying with a local Baptist minister when he was lucid. "He loved to talk about how much Christ meant to him during his suffering and as he faced the future," said Rev. John Richardson of Atlanta. But Ty remained in character up to the end. On the table next to his bed was a paper bag containing one million dollars in negotiable securities, weighed down by his favorite Luger pistol.

Who can say what thoughts danced through his drug-addled mind at this stage? Did the faces of those he abused throughout his long life emerge Marley-like from the shadows, goading him with scenes of what might have been? Or did a greater fear—that of being forgotten—creep over him? As Robert Wilkins has observed, "Fear of being forgotten after death is one of man's most deep-rooted anxieties. It is uncomfortable to think that we will not be alive 100 years from now; it is even more disturbing to think that hardly anyone then alive will remember that we existed at all." Forced to face his own mortality, Ty had in his final years embraced those old standbys—religion, good

The adventure that had been Ty Cobb's life ended nineteen months later. Ty died July 17, 1961, in Atlanta's Emory Hospital. Two days later, a couple of sandlot players stood at attention, caps in hand, as his body was carried from a Cornelia funeral home to a waiting hearse.

175

The chamber of commerce had erected a sign honoring Royston's most famous native a year or so before his death. On his last two visits to Royston, Ty doffed his cap for a local fan . . . and then rode silently through town on his way to eternity.

works, and autobiography—in an attempt to validate his existence. Whether it was all enough to save his soul or his reputation remains open to conjecture.

"More than anything else, Ty Cobb wanted to be remembered," said his hospital nurse Betty Jo Parsons. The planned Cobb memorial in Royston—a building eventually turned into city hall because of a lack of funds, artifacts, and visitors—would have pleased him, even if he never would have admitted it, she added. "He acted as if he didn't care whether the world remembered Ty Cobb for a minute. But he cared. He cared so much."

Baseball's greatest performer, his body wracked by cancer, diabetes, and cardiac problems, finally passed away at 1:18 on the afternoon of Monday, July 17, 1961. He was seventy-four.

"For the last dozen years he had been trying to go home again," Ralph McGill, publisher of the *Atlanta Constitution*, wrote the following day. "He could never quite make it, and it angered him that here was

The Cobb burial vault, here receiving a memorial wreath from Royston officials. Inside are several family members, including a demanding school-teacher and his tempestuous but loving son.

This tribute by Hillerich & Bradsby appeared in the July 19, 1961, editions of the Louisville Courier Journal, Louisville Times, North East Georgian (Cornelia, Georgia), Recorder & Gazette (Menlo Park, California), Detroit News, and Detroit Free Press. It also was published nationally in The Sporting News.

something with which he could not come to grips and have it out. Try as he would, Ty Cobb could not find the old dream in the hills of north Georgia where he was born. But he made it at last. He went to sleep for the last time on the sunny afternoon of July 17 just about the time the players of his day would have been taking the field for batting practice. He died in a coma-like sleep. He went home as quietly as if his father had come and taken him in his arms and carried him away."

A light rain fell as Ty was placed in the Cobb family vault two days later. "Ty—old Ty—is at rest for the first time in his life," cried one lady. The melodrama was lost on the uniformed Little Leaguers in attendance, a few of whom offended the solemnity of the moment by flashing self-conscious grins or whispering to one another. Stern looks from sober-faced parents stopped the fidgeting. Some in the crowd of 400 or so watched the disciplinary tug-of-war in silent amusement. Fathers and sons, they knew, can sometimes be that way.

Royston's ambitious Ty Cobb Memorial, located just down the road from Cobb Memorial Hospital, died a slow death from a lack of funds, artifacts, and visitors and was eventually converted into a new city hall. Today, citizens stopping in to pay their water bill stroll past some of the inadvertent but telling symbols of Ty Cobb's life—a Coke machine, a Confederate flag—and scratch their heads over the stone tablet that portrays him as a right-handed batter.

STROKES OF GENIUS

When a man hits .367 over a 24-year major-league career, his advice on batting is naturally sought. In retirement, Ty jotted down his thoughts on the subject for Hillerich & Bradsby. The bat company first published them in the 1944 edition of its *Famous Sluggers Year Book*. What some consider the best treatise on hitting is reprinted here in its entirety.

THE SCIENCE OF BATTING

By Ty Cobb

Foreword

I gladly submit my ideas on the subject of batting, and consider your asking for them a compliment to me. There are so many different angles to cover that I jotted down these bits of advice as they came to mind; therefore, I ask each reader to forgive whatever the article lacks in the way of order.

Selection of Bat and Where to Grip

First of all is selection of bat. For a swing hitter (one who starts his bat from as far back as he can reach and completes his swing with a full follow-through), I suggest using a bat with the feel on the light side; for one who is not a swing hitter, the bat should feel slightly heavy. The "swinger" should catch the bat down near the knob, but the hand should not be up against it. Other types, with shorter and more compact swings, such as the "choke" hitter, grip up farther—nearer the barrel end of the handle. However, the individual, regardless of which type of hitter, should find the place on the handle most comfortable to him.

My personal Louisville Slugger model, as they will verify at Hillerich & Bradsby, was never revised in any way throughout my career, except in weight. It is $34^1/2$ inches—a length easy to handle—has a medium small barrel with slight taper to medium large handle, then flares out slightly to a medium shallow knob. My bats were 40 ounces right down to the last few seasons, during which I went to 35 and 36 ounces.

As for type, mine was somewhere between the swinger and choke hitter, but definitely nearer the choke.

Position of Body

Next comes position. Never copy another batter's position if it should be some exaggerated form of crouch. Take all your best hitters—*they stand up and have the look of a hitter.* You may find it frequently the case that, having made ready for the pitch, your position becomes uncomfortable. Breaking of the knees—a slight dipping or squatting—will relieve this, but of course you must *always come back to the position first assumed.*

Most important at the plate, however, is position of the feet and arms. I hesitate to say which should come first, but will start with the feet.

Position of Feet—Balance—Adjusting Stance for Hitting to All Fields

The space between the feet should be measured by how well-balanced you feel. Using a yardstick, this space will measure close to fourteen inches for players of average height. But I would advise against thinking of a thing of this kind in terms of inches. Just stand so that you feel balanced on both feet and can step in or out.

If you are able to put a little extra weight on the front foot (the one nearest the pitcher) and still feel well enough balanced to step either way, so much the better. The ability to do this will *insure proper stride,* and, when swinging, brings the body and arms up to the ball more automatically. I emphasize the value of proper stride for the sake of safeguarding against over-striding, which is fatal. The over-stride lowers one's body from the position he assumes as stance, causing upper-cutting and fly balls. It also upsets coordination, but most costly is the loss of freedom to step in or out.

I strongly favor the hitting to all fields, and therefore shall get down to some detail concerning the position of the feet for hitting into each field. The ability to send the ball into one field or another by design can be developed by practice and the use of the "closed" or "open" or "square" stance.

For example, a right-handed hitter, when attempting to hit to right field (or the opposite field, as I term it) should use the closed stance. Closed stance means the right-handed hitter's left foot is closer—about four inches—to the line of the plate than his right.

The same batter should revert to the open stance when trying to pull the ball—that is, hit to left. His right foot will be about four inches nearer than his left to the plate line. For hitting straight away, the square stance is the thing, meaning both feet are at an equal distance from the plate line.

179

Keep in mind that when I speak of assuming these various stances in order to hit to different fields, it does not mean you can expect to hit to certain points or narrow zones. These adjustments of stance help you to unleash power more easily in the direction you are aiming and to hit into that general direction. Taken in proper relation to the plate, any of the three different stances will permit free body action and better precision swinging, in addition to the use of power.

Where to Stand

What might next be asked is, "Where should I stand in the box, and how far from the plate?" In handling this I shall divide the question and take "Where should I stand in the box?" first.

Always keep behind the plate to protect yourself from curve balls. I had trouble with left-handed pitching, and especially against left-handers with good curves, until I went all the way to the back line of the box. The right-handed hitter will benefit by doing the same against a right-hander with a good curve.

As a final word on this point, I wish to impress you with one thing a batter should never forget—*the pitcher must get the ball up to and over the plate, regardless of where the batter stands.* By standing back of the plate you are taking advantage of those few more inches from the pitcher to which the batter is entitled, and the fraction of a second it takes the ball to travel them. This little advantage often enables you to see whether the ball will be "over" and how the curve is breaking.

In answering the second part of the question, ". . . how far from the plate?" I feel it necessary to go into more detail, assuming that the average reader has not yet gotten around to where he does the right thing automatically.

The one definite remark that can be made on this subject is: *do not crowd the plate.* Otherwise, the amount of distance from the plate depends entirely on the individual and to what field he is trying to hit.

If you are a right-handed batter and have taken a closed stance trying for the opposite (right) field, you must stand at just that distance from the plate where you feel able to get power into a possible inside pitch. In that position you are automatically placed for also hitting a ball over the outside of the plate.

On the other hand, should you plan to pull the ball, your distance from the plate, using an open stance, should be so that you can get power into the ball if it is over the outside of the plate. Then you will be right where you can really pull the ball should it come over the inside. For hitting straight away, with stance squared, you of course should stand where you can properly connect with any ball that comes within the strike zone.

Position of Arms

Position of arms comes next. *Keep your arms, and particularly your elbows, away from your body.* This insures freedom of swing regardless of where the ball comes over. Also, I recommend that the elbow nearest the pitcher be raised and exaggerated, and the slight bending of the body from the waist up. This really gives you better body balance, insures automatically hitting out in front, and *brings your eyes in a better focusing position.*

Other Suggestions

Do all your "fixing" as to grip, arms, and stance before the pitcher delivers, *and then forget about your swing,* about hitting the top of the ball, or what-not. Just keep your mind concentrated on hitting the ball. *Watch the pitcher's every move and never let your eye leave the ball.* It means only disaster to divide mind or attention.

Many batters are thrown out by a split second. So when you hit the ball, run it out with all the speed you have, no matter where or how you hit it. This I claim will earn you many hits during the season that you would not get otherwise.

Practice what you are called upon to do in the game, and you are bound to improve. If you are ambitious enough, you can improve your speed and arrival at first by practicing time after time the quickest break. Go your very hardest for, say, ten steps. Try never to let a defensive thought enter your mind. *Make yourself believe and think you are better than the opposition.*

Never try to guess and get set for a certain kind of ball, for more often than not the pitcher will outguess and catch you flatfooted with what you're not looking for. In time, you will develop the ability to *sort of know* what is coming in most cases.

Another important thing to remember—don't overswing for a long hit. This weakness causes slumps. After hitting a long and hard ball the thought will come to mind that you did not swing hard. *Actually, it was timing.* And the next time up, you will be tempted to take an unnatural cut trying for a still longer ball. Watch that, for as a rule the results are not good.

When getting into the ball, never pull speed. Hit with the curve of the ball or with the rotation. When you see how the ball is breaking, strike as if to drive it back into the direction from which it is coming.

181

Better results can be obtained also by following the system of *not* attempting to "pull" the offerings of a good speed-ball pitcher. The same rule applies when facing a good curve-ball tosser. Against either of these types, try to hit to right if you're a right-handed batter, and to left if you hit from the same side of the plate as I did.

Summary

As a starter in summing up this article on batting, let me repeat that the plate is the one and final objective the pitcher must come to. In my case, I had the freedom of body movement and therefore ability to apply snap or power, and yet *the plate was always guarded*. The pitcher will try to make you hit at ones just a little bad—but you can make him come across. And when he does come to the plate, you are fortified by good stance and position to hit properly.

Always be watchful and observing. You will be surprised at how much you can learn that will be helpful. As the subject is hitting, the observations I suggest are to center on the pitcher, mainly, then the catcher and fielders. I have warned elsewhere in this article about guessing at what the pitcher is going to throw and against getting set for a certain kind of ball. But guessing and knowing, as they say, are two different things.

Close and constant observation will enable you to know in frequent cases what is coming. Through some fault or other many pitchers give cue to what they are going to try on you. Others, whether conscious of it or not, are so consistent in doing the same things in certain situations that it really amounts to a system. The catcher, being the other half of the battery, should be watched, and of course always note to see if infielders and outfielders are playing out of position and leaving an opening to hit for. Through observation you learn these things, and *making use of facts is not guessing*.

I have kept for last the following advice to leave with you: your chances of becoming a good hitter depend on your learning well the proper fundamentals of hitting and continued practice of them. Otherwise, your chances are limited. If your stance and position are correct, the action that follows should be automatically more or less right.

When a thing can be done right automatically—and this comes only through constant practice—the mental hazard of thinking of this and that at the moment of execution is eliminated.

Now my final word is—*get the proper fundamentals, practice and practice them, and take care of yourself physically.*

TY COBB'S PLAYING RECORD

Regular Season

Year	Club	G	AB	R	H	BA	2B	3B	HR	RBI	BB	SO	TB	SA	SB	CS	HP	SH
1904	Augusta	37	135	14	32	.237	6	0	1	—	—	—	41	.304	—	—	—	—
1904	Anniston	32	128	22	40	.313	4	**8**	0	—	—	—	60	.469	10	—	—	—
1905	Augusta	103	411	60	134	**.326**	13	4	1	—	—	—	158	.384	41	—	—	—
1905	Detroit	41	150	19	36	.240	6	0	1	15	10	—	45	.300	2	—	0	4
1906	Detroit	98	350	45	112	.320	13	7	1	41	19	—	143	.406	23	—	2	14
1907	Detroit	150	605	97	**212**	**.350**	29	15	5	**116**	24	—	**286**	**.473**	49	—	3	12
1908	Detroit	150	581	88	**188**	**.324**	**36**	**20**	4	**108**	34	—	**276**	**.475**	39	—	7	14
1909	Detroit	156	573	**116**	**216**	**.377**	33	10	**9**	**107**	48	—	**296**	**.517**	**76**	—	6	24
1910	Detroit	140	509	**106**	196	**.385**	36	13	8	91	64	—	279	**.554**	65	—	4	17
1911	Detroit	146	591	**147**	**248**	**.420**	**47**	**24**	8	**144**	44	—	**367**	**.621**	**83**	—	8	11
1912	Detroit	140	553	119	**227**	**.410**	30	23	7	90	43	—	324	**.586**	61	34	5	8
1913	Detroit	122	428	70	167	**.390**	18	16	4	67	58	31	229	**.535**	52	—	4	11
1914	Detroit	97	345	69	127	**.368**	22	11	2	57	57	22	177	**.513**	35	17	6	6
1915	Detroit	156	563	**144**	**208**	**.369**	31	13	3	99	118	43	**274**	.487	**96**	**38**	10	9
1916	Detroit	145	542	**113**	201	.371	31	10	5	68	78	39	267	.493	**68**	24	2	14
1917	Detroit	152	**588**	107	**225**	**.383**	**44**	**23**	7	102	61	34	**336**	**.571**	**55**	—	4	16
1918	Detroit	111	421	83	161	**.382**	19	**14**	3	64	41	21	217	.515	34	—	2	9
1919	Detroit	124	497	92	**191**	**.384**	36	13	1	70	38	22	256	.515	28	—	1	9
1920	Detroit	112	428	86	143	.334	28	8	2	63	58	28	193	.451	14	10	2	7
1921	Detroit	128	507	124	197	.389	37	16	12	101	56	19	302	.596	22	15	3	15
1922	Detroit	137	526	99	211	.401	42	16	4	99	55	24	297	.565	9	13	4	27
1923	Detroit	145	556	103	189	.340	40	7	6	88	66	14	261	.469	9	10	3	22
1924	Detroit	155	625	115	211	.338	38	10	4	74	85	18	281	.450	23	14	1	15
1925	Detroit	121	415	97	157	.378	31	12	12	102	65	12	248	.598	13	9	5	5
1926	Detroit	79	233	48	79	.339	18	5	4	62	26	2	119	.511	9	4	1	13
1927	Philadelphia	134	490	104	175	.357	32	7	5	93	67	12	236	.482	22	—	5	12
1928	Philadelphia	95	353	54	114	.323	27	4	1	40	34	16	152	.431	5	8	4	2
Major League Totals		3034	11429	2245	4191	.367	724	297	118	1961	1249	357	5861	.513	892	196	92	296

Bold indicates led league

World Series

Year	Club	G	AB	R	H	BA	2B	3B	HR	RBI	BB	SO	TB	SA	SB	CS	HP	SH
1907	Detroit	5	20	1	4	.200	0	**1**	0	0	0	3	6	.300	0	1	1	0
1908	Detroit	5	19	3	7	.368	1	0	0	**4**	1	2	8	.421	2	1	0	1
1909	Detroit	7	26	3	6	.231	3	0	0	5	2	2	9	.346	2	1	1	0
Totals		17	65	7	17	.262	4	1	0	9	3	7	23	.354	4	3	2	1

Bold indicates led Series

Bibliography

Charles C. Alexander. *Ty Cobb* (New York: Oxford University Press, 1984).

Lee Allen. *The American League Story* (New York: Hill and Wang, 1962).

Mark Alvarez. "An Interview with Smokey Joe Wood." *Baseball Research Journal* (1987).

Steve Babson. *Working Detroit* (New York: Adama Books, 1984).

Richard Bak. *Cobb Would Have Caught It: The Golden Age of Baseball in Detroit* (Detroit: Wayne State University Press, 1991)

———. *Turkey Stearnes and the Detroit Stars: The Negro Leagues in Detroit, 1919–1933* (Detroit: Wayne State University Press, 1994).

Edward Grant Barrow. *My 50 Years in Baseball* (New York: Coward-McCann, 1951).

"Baseball's Badass." *Detroit Monthly* (September 1991).

"Baseball in the Dead Ball Era." *The National Pastime* (Spring 1986).

E. A. Batchelor. "Cobb, Great Player and Great Showman, a Tiger for 20 Years." *Detroit Saturday Night* (August 29, 1925).

Norman Beasley and George W. Stark. *Made in Detroit* (New York: G. P. Putnam's Sons, 1957).

Michael Betzold and Ethan Casey. *Queen of Diamonds: The Tiger Stadium Story* (West Bloomfield: A & M Publishing, 1992).

Malcolm W. Bingay. *Detroit Is My Own Home Town* (New York: Bobbs-Merrill, 1946).

Furman Bisher. "A Visit with Ty Cobb." *Saturday Evening Post* (June 14, 1958).

Christy Borth. "The First 50 Years." *D.A.C. News* (April 1965).

Jack Cannon and Tom Cannon (eds.). *Nobody Asked Me, But . . . The World of Jimmy Cannon* (New York: Holt Rinehart Winston, 1978).

Mel Chipp. "Inside-the-Park Home Runs." *Baseball Research Journal* (1980).

Ty Cobb. *Busting 'Em and Other Stories* (New York: Edward J. Clode, 1914).

_____. "They Don't Play Baseball Any More." *Life* (March 17, 1952).

_____. "Tricks That Won Me Ball Games." *Life* (March 24, 1952).

Ty Cobb (with Al Stump). *My Life in Baseball: The True Record* (New York: Doubleday, 1961).

Richard M. Cohen, et al. *The World Series* (New York: Dial Press, 1976).

Robert W. Creamer. *Babe: The Legend Comes to Life* (New York: Simon and Schuster, 1974).

Jack Francis Cremer. "Detroit's Baseball Players As They Really Are." *Detroit Saturday Night* (October 16, 1909).

William Curran. *Big Sticks: The Phenomenal Decade of Ruth, Gehrig, Cobb and Hornsby* (New York: William Morrow & Co., 1990).

"The D.A.C. Heritage." *D.A.C. News* (April 1965).

Frank Donovan. *Wheels For a Nation* (New York: Thomas Y. Crowell Co., 1965).

Lawrence Engelmann. *Intemperance: The Lost War Against Liquor* (New York: Free Press, 1979).

Joe Falls. *Detroit Tigers* (New York: Collier, 1975).

Steve Fiffer. *Speed* (Alexandria: Redefinition, 1990).

Margaret Walker Freel. *Our Heritage: The People of Cherokee County, North Carolina, 1540–1955* (Asheville: Miller Printing Co., 1956).

David Fulk and Dan Riley (eds.). *The Cubs Reader* (Boston: Houghton Mifflin Co., 1991).

Eddie Gold. "Baseball Movies." *Baseball Research Journal* (1983).

Rod Gragg. *The Illustrated Confederate Reader* (New York: Harper & Row, 1989).

Tom Granahan. "The Day the Tigers Walked Out, But the Game Went On." *Detroit Free Press Magazine* (April 15, 1984).

Harry Grayson. "Ty Cobb Wanted to Pitch." *Baseball Digest* (May 1943).

Hank Greenberg (with Ira Berkow). *Hank Greenberg: The Story of My Life* (New York: Times Books, 1989).

Donald Gropman. *Say It Ain't So, Joe! The True Story of Shoeless Joe Jackson* (New York: Citadel Press, 1992).

Fred Haney. "My Most Unforgettable Character." *Reader's Digest* (June 1964).

Ernie Harwell. *Tuned to Baseball* (South Bend: Diamond Communications, 1985).

David Holland. "The One and Only Cobb." *American Mercury* (September 1956).

Jerome Holtzman. *No Cheering in the Press Box* (New York: Holt Rinehart Winston, 1973).

Bibliography

John B. Holway. *Blackball Stars: Negro League Pioneers* (Westport: Meckler Books, 1988).

_____. *The Sluggers* (Alexandria: Redefinition, 1989).

Donald Honig. *Baseball When the Grass Was Real* (New York: Coward, McCann and Geoghagan, 1975).

_____. *The Man in the Dugout* (Chicago: Follett, 1977).

Bill James. *The Bill James Historical Baseball Abstract* (New York: Villard Books, 1986).

Alex Jaramillo. *Cracker Jack Prizes* (New York: Abbeville Press, 1989).

John Kuenster (ed.). *From Cobb to "Catfish"* (Chicago: Rand McNally & Co., 1975).

Walter M. Langford. *Legends of Baseball: An Oral History of The Game's Golden Age* (South Bend: Diamond Communications, 1987).

Ring W. Lardner. "Tyrus, the Greatest of 'Em All." *American Magazine* (June 1915).

"Last Inning of an Angry Man." *Sports Illustrated* (August 21, 1961).

Fred Lieb. *Baseball As I Have Known It* (New York: Coward, McCann & Geoghagen, 1977).

_____. *The Detroit Tigers* (New York: G. P. Putnam's Sons, 1946).

Ron Liebman. "George Sisler the Pitcher." *Baseball Research Journal* (1977).

_____. "Consecutive-Game Hitting Streaks," *Baseball Research Journal* (1979).

Don Lochbiler. *Detroit's Coming of Age, 1873–1973* (Detroit: Wayne State University Press, 1973).

John C. Lodge. *I Remember Detroit* (Detroit: Wayne State University Press, 1949).

William W. Lutz. *The News of Detroit* (Boston: Little, Brown & Co., 1973).

Paul MacFarlane (ed.). *Hall of Fame Fact Book* (St. Louis: Sporting News Publishing Co., 1983).

Connie Mack. *My 66 Years in the Big Leagues* (New York: Winston, 1950).

John D. McCallum. *Ty Cobb* (New York: Praeger, 1975).

James A. Michener. *Sports in America* (New York: Random House, 1976).

Jessie Julia Mize. *The History of Banks County, Georgia, 1958–1976* (Homer: Banks County Chamber of Commerce, 1977).

Leigh Montville. "Last Remains of a Legend." *Sports Illustrated Classic* (Fall 1992).

J M Murphy. "Napoleon Lajoie." *The National Pastime* (Spring 1987).

Jack Newcombe. "Black Mike of the Tigers." *Sport* (April 1960).

Anthony Papalas. "Lil' Rastus Cobb's Good Luck Charm." *Baseball Research Journal* (1984).

Robert Peterson. *Only the Ball Was White* (Englewood Cliffs: Prentice-Hall, 1970).

Joseph L. Reichler (ed.). *The Baseball Encyclopedia* (8th ed., New York: Macmillan, 1990).

Steven Riess. *Touching Base: Professional Baseball and American Culture in the Progressive Era* (Westport: Greenwood Press, 1980).

Rae Elizabeth Rips (ed.). *Detroit In Its World Setting* (Detroit: Detroit Public Library, 1953).

Lawrence Ritter. *The Glory of Their Times* (New York: Macmillan, 1966).

Francis Russell. *The American Heritage History of the Confident Years, 1865–1916* (New York: American Heritage/Bonanza Books,1987).

H. G. Salsinger. "The Detroit Tigers." *Sport* (November 1950).

Gene Schoor. *The Story of Ty Cobb* (New York: Julian Messner, 1952).

Harold Seymour. *Baseball: The Early Years* (New York: Oxford University Press, 1960).

_____. *Baseball: The Golden Age* (New York: Oxford University Press, 1971).

Ken Sobol. *Babe Ruth and the American Dream* (New York: Ballantine Books, 1974).

J. G. Taylor Spink. *Judge Landis and 25 Years of Baseball* (St. Louis: Sporting News Publishing Co., 1974).

Harry Stein. *Hoopla* (New York: St. Martin's Press, 1983).

Al Stump. "Ty Cobb's Wild Ten-Month Fight to Live." *True* (December 1961).

George Sullivan and David Cataneo. *Detroit Tigers: The Complete Record of Detroit Tigers Baseball* (New York: Macmillan, 1985).

John Thorn and Pete Palmer (eds.). *Total Baseball* (New York: Warner Books, 1989).

Vic Tomlinson. "Vic Tomlinson Anylizes [sic] Ty Cobb." *D.A.C. News* (September 1916).

David Quentin Voigt. *American Baseball: From the Gentleman's Sport to the Commissioner's System* (Norman: University of Oklahoma Press, 1966).

_____. *American Baseball: From the Commissioners to Continental Expansion* (Norman: University of Oklahoma Press, 1970).

"Why Ty Cobb Is Tired—and Retired." *Literary Digest* (November 20, 1926).

Ted Williams (with John Underwood). *My Turn At Bat: The Story of My Life* (New York: Simon and Schuster, 1969).

Charles Reagan Wilson. *Baptized in Blood: The Religion of the Lost Cause, 1865–1920* (Athens. University of Georgia Press, 1980).

Frank B. Woodford and Arthur M. Woodford. *All Our Yesterdays: A Brief History of Detroit* (Detroit: Wayne State University Press, 1969).

C. Vann Woodward. *The Strange Career of Jim Crow* (3rd. rev. ed., New York: Oxford University Press, 1974).

S. J. Woolf. "Tyrus Cobb, Then and Now." *New York Times Magazine* (September 19, 1946).

Bertram Wyatt-Brown. *Southern Honor: Ethics and Behavior in the Old South* (New York: Oxford University Press, 1982).

Jonathan Yardley. *Ring: A Biography of Ring Lardner* (New York: Random House, 1977).

Acknowledgments

This book is a mosaic of many contributions, both large and small, from a number of people and institutions. First and foremost are the good folks of Taylor Publishing, who thought the subject worthy of another book-length biography. My research was facilitated by Robert Giles, editor and publisher of the *Detroit News,* who allowed me to use the newspaper's Catlin Library. Director Pat Zacharias produced scrapbooks of clippings and several envelopes of photographs, including a long-forgotten syndicated biography of Cobb that *News* sports editor Harry Salsinger wrote for the North American Newspaper Alliance in 1924. Salsinger, who died in 1958, kept up a regular correspondence with Cobb after the ballplayer's retirement. Recently, many of these letters surfaced at DuMouchelle's Art Gallery in Detroit. Auctioneer Ernie DuMouchelle allowed me to read them before they were sold and to extrapolate certain passages from them.

Many people from outside of Detroit were of immeasurable help. Kathie Johnson went through the Hillerich & Bradsby archives at the University of Louisville, producing much useful information on Cobb's batting philosophy and several advertisements and photographs. In Philadelphia, John Goodman took valuable time away from his own work to research the infamous 1912 game between the Athletics and Detroit's strikebreakers. Phil Mooney, head archivist at Coca-Cola headquarters in Atlanta, sent along material from the company's files, including old advertisements. Larry Amman of Washington, D.C., the foremost Cobb expert in terms of statistics, generously allowed me to use information on Cobb's steals of home and lifetime batting performance, broken down by individual pitcher. This book would be much poorer without these figures.

Also lending assistance and advice at various times were writers Bill Plott, Donald Honig, and James Riley; Charles C. Alexander, a professor of history at Ohio University and the author of a well-received scholarly biography of Cobb; and the staffs of the Cobb Memorial Hospital in Royston, Georgia, and the National Baseball Library in Cooperstown, New York. Perhaps my biggest debt is to Lucy Copas of Royston, who hunted down several rare photographs of the Cobb family and turn-of-the-century Royston and arranged for their reproduction. John Evans provided similar assistance in Murphy, North Carolina.

Few of Cobb's contemporaries are still alive; however, those that I have spoken to over the years added significantly to the final product, contributing anecdotes, insights, and background information. They include Eddie Batchelor Jr., John Bogart, Herman "Flea" Clifton, Ray Fisher, Eddie Forester, Milt Gaston, Charlie Gehringer, Ernie Harwell, Edgar Hayes, Ray Hayworth, Harry Heilmann Jr., Willis "Ace" Hudlin, Bill Kennedy, Jasper Miner, Kirk Miner, Bill Moore, Robert "Gunner" Reeves, Billy Rogell, Stanley Roginski, George Sanders, George Uhle, Eddie Wells, Eugene "Woody" Wolfe, and Archie Yelle.

This book includes nearly 300 photographs, easily the largest collection of Cobb images published at one time. Of the scores of individuals and institutions I consulted, Jeannette Bartz of the *Detroit News* and David Poremba of the Burton Historical Collection of the Detroit Public Library were especially helpful. Mike Opipari in Detroit and Jason Machem in Georgia expertly reproduced many of the images found on these pages. My sincere thanks to them and to everyone else who contributed to this project. Without their help this volume would have been impossible.

Index

Adams, Babe, 58, 59*
Adams, Franklin P., 38, 42
Alexander, Grover Cleveland, 162*, 165
All-Star Games, (1911) 71*, (1951) 170*
Anniston Noblemen, 14–15, 16*
Armour, Bill, 20, 21*, 23*, 29
Atlanta Constitution, 176
Atlanta Journal, 7, 14–15
Augusta, Georgia, 11, 14*, 87, 143*
Augusta Tourists, 11–12, 14, 15*
Austin, Jimmy, 50*
Automobile industry, 60*, 61, 62*, 63–64, 65*,
    66–67, 68–69*, 72–74*
Automobile racing, 72–74*

Baer, Bugs, 48, 82
Bagby, Jim, 138
Baker, Frank, 46–48, 49*, 55, 71*, 75, 77*, 83
Baltimore Orioles (International League), 107
Baltimore Orioles (National League), 29–30
Baltimore Sun, 114
Barrett, Jimmy, 22, 23*
Barrow, Ed, 22*
Barry, Jack, 35*, 48, 77*, 83
Baseball Hall of Fame, 161–162*,164*, 165, 168,
    174*
Baseball Magazine, 97, 108*, 121*
Bassler, Johnny, 105*
Batchelor, Eddie, 101, 123, 124*, 139, 141
Battle of Atlanta, 5, 34
Battle of the Narrows, 1
Battle of Vicksburg, 2
Beckendorf, Heinie, 46
Belle Isle, 69*
Bender, Chief, 55*, 67
Benjamin Confectionary Co. (Ty Cobb Candy
    Bar), 119*
Bennett Park, 21, 26, 34–35*, 38, 40, 44–45*, 47,
    58, 62, 68, 74, 76–77*
Bingay, Malcolm, 126
Blankenship, Ted, 80*
Blue, Lu, 105*, 128*, 148*, 168
Bogart, John, 105*
Boston Red Sox, 68, 101, 103
Bowerman, Frank, 27
Bradley, Bill, 10*, 29
Bressler, Rube, 45
Briggs Manufacturing Co., 65
Briggs Stadium, 66, 165*, 170*, 172*
Briggs, Walter O., 65*, 66, 123
Brock, Lou, 55, 85, 173
Brooklyn Dodgers, 110
Broun, Heywood, 76
Brown, Joe E., 173
Brown, Stewart, 169*
Brown, "Three-Finger", 38, 43, 47*
Browning, Pete, 96
Buick, David, 64
Bulger, Bozeman, 78
Burman, "Wild Bob", 72*
Burns, George, 144*
Bush, Donie, 37*, 41, 82–83, 88*, 105*
Byron, Bill, 20

Candler, Asa G., 111
Candler, John, 111
Carey, Max, 84

Carpenter, William L., 95
Carr, Charles D., 19
Carrigan, Bill, 68
Chalmers Award, 66*, 67–72, 75–76
Chalmers, Hugh, 65*, 67, 72
Chance, Frank, 38, 42*
Charleston, Oscar, 127*
Chase, Hal, 34, 71*
Chesbro, Jack, 21*
Chevrolet, Louis, 64
Chicago American Giants, 127
Chicago Cubs, 38, 41, 42*, 43, 74
Chicago White Sox, 40–41, 95*, 104*, 145–146
Chitwood, Caleb, 1–2
Cicotte, Eddie, 19–20
Cincinnati Reds, 166
Civil War, 1–2, 4–5, 7, 131
Clark, B. N., 121
Clarke, Fred, 59
Clarke, Nig, 85*
Cleveland Indians, 10, 30–31, 41, 69–71, 110,
    142–143, 151, 153*, 154, 156
Cobb, Amanda (Chitwood), 2, 11, 15–16, 17*,
    71*, 173
Cobb, Beverly, 89
Cobb, Charlie (Charlotte Lombard), 39*, 40, 71*,
    89, 92, 94*, 124*, 141, 150*, 163–164, 167
Cobb Educational Fund, 168, 171*
Cobb, Florence Leslie, 2, 7*, 124*, 173
Cobb, Frances (Fairburn Cass), 167, 168*, 169–170
Cobb, Herschel, 89, 113, 124*, 169
Cobb, Sen. Howell, 4*, 5
Cobb, Jimmy, 89, 113, 124*
Cobb, John ("Granddad Johnny"), 3–4, 8–9, 87
Cobb, John Paul, 2, 7*, 149*
Cobb Memorial Hospital, 168, 169*
Cobb, Shirley Marion, 71*, 87*, 94*, 124*
Cobb, Gen. Thomas Reade Rootes, 5*
Cobb, Ty (Tyrus Raymond)
    acting career, 89, 93*
    appears on magazine covers, 120–121*
    appears on gum and tobacco premium cards,
        115–118*
    awards and ballpark ceremonies, 20, 38, 41,
        66*, 72, 75–76, 80*, 137*, 138, 148*, 150
    base running tactics, 27–28, 33–35, 45–46,
        50–51, 92–94
    base running style, 25, 27–28, 35*, 46, 49*,
        83*, 106*, 153*, 154, 156
    base stealing tactics, 50–51
    base stealing style, 26, 46–48
    bats used by, 96–99, 100*, 152
    gives batting instruction, 125, 149, 151
    batting performance vs. American League
        pitchers, 52–54
    batting performance vs. World Series
        pitchers, 57
    batting strategy, 20, 25, 28, 35–36, 43–44,
        100, 178–182, 106–107
    batting records, 101, 183
    batting stance, 25, 28, 43–44
    batting swing, 39*, 100*
    batting titles, 38–39, 45, 70–72, 75, 84, 100–
        101, 105–106
    birthplace of, 1–2, 5*
    breaks into major leagues, 19, 20–21*, 22,
        23–24*

bunting techniques and strategy, 20, 48, 50,
    70*
    wins Chalmers Awards, 66*, 67–72, 75–76
    childhood, 2–6, 7*, 8, 9*, 10–13
    Cobb-Speaker scandal, 141, 142–144*,
        145–147
    commercial endorsements, 38, 74*, 86*, 87,
        89, 97–98, 99*, 111, 112*, 113, 114*,
        116*, 119*
    death and funeral of, 174–177*
    divorces Charlie Lombard, 163, 167
    divorces Frances Fairburn Cass, 169–170, 173*
    with dogs, 123–124*, 159–160, 165*
    domestic life, 87*, 89, 92, 94–95, 108*,
        123–124*, 160*, 162–164
    elected to Hall of Fame, 161*, 164, 165
    fielding, 44*, 51, 150, 155
    fights, 6, 28, 30–31, 39–40, 80–82, 94–95,
        103–106, 128, 132, 160
    golf outings, 162–163*, 166*, 167
    harassment by fans, 23–29, 51, 79, 92, 101
    hitting streaks, 44
    home runs, 35, 37, 134*, 136–137
    hunting trips, 4, 109*, 124*, 150*, 155,
        159–160
    injuries and illnesses, 25–26, 110, 132, 134,
        138*
    interviewed for Movietone News, 159–160
    investments, 64–67, 99*, 106, 162
    joins Philadelphia Athletics, 146*, 147–148
    managerial career, 105*, 123, 125–132, 133*,
        134–137, 138*, 139–142
    marries Charlie Lombard, 39*, 40
    marries Frances Fairburn, 167, 168*
    military service, 101*, 106
    minor league career, 11–12, 14, 15–16*,
        19–21
    nickname acquired, 24, 28
    philanthropy, 125*, 168, 169*, 171*
    as pitcher, 53
    plays exhibition series in Cuba, 127
    photography as hobby, 10*, 36*, 149*
    racial attitudes, 6–7, 80–81, 123*, 127
    racial confrontations, 30–31, 39–40, 51
    racing, 72–73*, 74
    retires from Tigers, 141–142
    retires from Athletics, 157
    rivalry with Babe Ruth, 107–110, 129–132,
        133*, 137–139, 152, 156*, 166–167*
    salary, 11, 22, 39, 86–87, 106, 123, 137–138,
        147, 154–155
    spikings by, 46–48, 49*, 50–51
    spring training, 22, 23–24*, 25, 28–31, 64*,
        103–105, 147–148, 149*
    steals of home, 31, 58, 74, 84*, 85–86, 90–91,
        150, 152, 156
    suspensions, 80–82, 84, 150
    World Series performances, 38, 43, 56*, 57–
        59, 121*
Cobb, Ty Jr., 67*, 71*, 87*, 94*, 124*, 160*,
    163–164, 168
Cobb, William Herschel, 2*, 3, 9–11, 12*, 13–17,
    35, 173–175
Coca-Cola, 38, 111–114*
Cochrane, Mickey, 147*, 148–149, 160 *, 163–
    164, 168*
Cochrane, Mickey Jr., 164

Cole, Bert, 105*, 132
Colgan's Chips, 116*
Collins, Eddie, 71*, 75, 77*, 148, 152*, 156, 162*, 165
Collins, Fred, 39–40
Columbia Park, 35, 37
Comiskey Park, 70
Conkwright, Allen, 105*
Conlon, Charles, 50
Connally, George, 156
Coombs, Jack, 67
Corn States Serum Co. (calendar), 122*
Corriden, Red, 70–71
Coughlin, Bill, 21*, 23*
Couzens, James, 65
Coveleski, Harry, 101
Cracker Jack, 118*
Cramer, Doc, 147–148
Crawford, Wahoo Sam, 5, 8, 21–22, 23*, 24–25, 26*, 29, 36–38, 50, 71*, 72, 74, 75*, 80, 82, 88*, 92–93, 101, 168, 174*
Criger, Lou, 47*
Crowder, General, 152
Cullen, Jim, 92
Cunningham, Joe, 6, 17, 97

Dauss, George, 101, 126
Davis, Harry, 37, 97
Delahanty, Frank, 31
Detroit, 25, 59, 60*, 61–62, 63*, 64–65, 69*, 71*, 73, 126, 133*, 167
Detroit Athletic Club, 27*, 65–66, 105
Detroit Free Press, 20*, 21, 24, 28, 33, 176
Detroit News, 124, 176
Detroit Saturday Night, 48*
Detroit Stars, 127*
Detroit Tigers,
    strike game of 1912, 79–81, 82*, 83–84
    World Series games, 38–39, 42–43*, 55, 56*, 57, 58–59*, 121*
Detroits (National League team), 38
Disch, George, 23*
Dodge Brothers, 64
Donovan, Bill, 20, 23*, 25, 28, 34*, 36*, 37–38
Doran, Tom, 23*
Drill, Lew, 23*
Dugan, Joe, 153
Dykes, Jimmie, 149, 157

Elberfeld, Kid, 20*, 21, 46*
Engel, George, 12
Engle, Clyde, 19–21
Esquire All-American All-Star Game, 166*
Eubank, John, 23*
Evans, Billy, 47*, 128*, 163
Evans, George ("Honey Boy"), 82*
Everitt, Barney, 65
Evers, Johnny, 38, 42*

Famous Sluggers Year Book, 178
Faulkner-Blanchard "Gunboat Six", 72
Federal League, 87, 93*
Fenway Park, 92*
Fisher, Ray, 51
Fletcher, Art, 103–105
Flick, Elmer, 30*, 31
Foley, Thomas, 79
Ford, Henry, 61–62, 65, 68*, 153
Ford, Russ, 71*
Fothergill, Bob, 29, 105*, 132*, 138
Fullerton, Hugh S., 81–82

Gandil, Chick, 142*, 146
Gehrig, Lou, 150, 152*, 156
Gehringer, Charlie, 114, 127, 134, 135*
Gibson, Sam, 150
Gilmore, James, 87
Glidden Tour, 64
Grabowsky "Power Wagon", 72
Grand Circus Park, 69*
Grantham, George, 138
Gray, Dolly, 59
Gregory, Judge Frank, 173
Gregg, Vean, 84
Griffith, Clark, 31, 94
Guiney, Ben, 27*

Haney, Fred, 107*, 125
Harding, Harold, 95
Harper, Jameson, 23
Harrison, Ulysses (Lil' Rastus), 58*, 123*
Hartley, Grover, 150
Harwell, Ernie, 171*
Hawthorn, Hope, 137*
Hayes, Thad, 14
Heilmann, Harry, 123, 125, 129, 130*, 132, 133*, 135, 168, 170*
Henderson, Rickey, 85, 173
Herzog, Buck, 95, 103–104
Heydler, John, 59
Hillerich, J. Frederick, 96
Hillerich, John A. ("Bud"), 96
Hillerich & Bradsby Co., 96–99, 176
Hilltop Park, 79–80, 81*, 84
Hodapp, Johnny, 153*
Hoff, Red, 84
Hooper, Harry, 88*, 107, 109
Hornsby, Rogers, 109*, 126
Hotel Vanderbilt, 123
House of the Good Shepherd, 132
Howard, Del, 38
Howell, Harry, 71
Hoyt, Schoolboy, 138*, 149
Hubbell, Carl, 128, 135*
Hudlin, Willis, 151

Indianapolis Speedway, 72–73
Ingram, Frances, 94*
Irvin, Ed, 83

Jackson, Joe S., 24, 28*, 49
Jackson, Shoeless Joe, 23*, 75*
Jennings, Hughie, 29–31, 43, 46*, 58–59, 74, 80–81, 84, 101, 104*, 106, 123, 142
Johnson, Ban, 47, 58, 70–72, 129, 131*, 142–147
Johnson, Hank, 153*, 157
Johnson, Jack, 31
Johnson, Walter, 37*, 43–44, 71*, 162*, 165
Jones, Bobby, 162*
Jones, Davy, 22*, 24, 174*
Jones, Tom, 59*
Joss, Addie, 41, 43*, 71

Kaline, Al, 39, 172*
Kauff, Benny, 93*
Keeler, Willie, 165
Keener, Sid, 136
Kelsey, John, 65*, 66, 123
Kelsey Wheel Co., 27, 65–66
Kennedy, Bill, 130–131
Kerr, Dickie, 145
Kettering, Charles, 72–73
Killian, Ed, 23*

King, Charles Brady, 61
"King of Clubs" (sheet music), 119*
Kitson, Frank, 23*
Koenig, Mark, 153, 157
Krause, Harry, 74
Kreisler, Fritz, 152
Krichell, Paul, 84*
Ku Klux Klan, 126*
Kuenn, Harvey, 170*
Kuhn, Bowie, 71

Lajoie, Nap, 66*, 67–72, 97, 162*, 165–166
Landis, Judge Kenesaw Mountain, 131*, 142*, 144*, 145–147, 169
Lardner, Ring, 25, 28, 139
Leach, Tommy, 56

Leidy, George 19–20
Leinhauser, Bill, 84
Leonard, Dutch, 48, 50, 142*, 143–146, 169
Lewis, Duffy, 88*
Lieb, Fred, 126, 129, 132, 141
Lindbergh, Charles, 153
Livingston, Paddy, 71
Lodge, John C., 27
Lombard, Alfred, 163
Lombard, Roz, 163
Louisville Courier Journal, 176
Louisville Slugger bats, 96–99, 100*, 121
Louisville Times, 176
Lowe, Bobby, 23*
Lucker, Claude, 79–80, 81*, 94

Mack, Connie, 35, 37, 47, 51*, 146*, 147, 155, 157, 162*, 164
Magee, Sherry, 67
Manush, Heinie, 133*, 135, 138
Masonic Order, 125*
Mathewson, Christy, 27, 41, 47, 106, 163
Mathewson, Christy Jr., 164
Mays, Carl, 48, 50, 92*, 101
Mays, Willie, 57
McAleer, Jimmy, 71*
McClure, George, 27
McCreary, Bob, 9–10
McCreary, H. F., 17
McFarlane, Paul, 71
McGill, Ralph, 176–177
McGraw, John, 29, 93, 95*, 103–105
McGuire, Deacon, 82–83
McInnis, Stuffy, 77*
McIntyre, Matty, 21–22, 23*, 25*, 28–29, 35, 45*
McLaren, Mary, 171*
McNey, Bob, 72, 74
Mendez, Jose, 127*
Merkle, Fred, 41
Merritt, James, 164
Meusel, Bob, 105*, 132, 141
Michener, James, 157
Milan, Clyde, 71*, 75, 88*
Miner, Jack, 92, 110*
Miner, Jasper, 92
Model T Ford, 61–62, 68–69*, 153
Moore, Bill, 135–136, 137*
Morehouse, Ward, 93*
Moriarty, George, 34, 56, 68, 74, 148*, 151
Morrow, Henry, 98
Movietone News, 159
Mullin, George, 23–24*, 29, 45, 82
Murphy, North Carolina, 3–4, 7–8*, 13
Musial, Stan, 57

Narrows, The (Georgia), 1–2
Navin Field, 66, 80*, 84, 101*, 109, 123*, 130*, 134, 137–138, 143, 148*, 150–151, 160*
Navin, Frank, 20, 31, 37, 38*, 51, 68, 73, 82, 84, 86, 87*, 106, 123, 128, 130*, 134, 137–138, 142–143
Negro Leagues, 127*
Neun, Johnny, 134
New York Giants, 41, 95*, 103–105, 128, 132
New York Highlanders, 21, 31, 34, 79–81
New York Yankees, 102*, 105*, 108–110, 126, 129–134, 138–139, 141,149–150, 152*, 153–155, 156*
New York World, 33
North East Georgian, 176
Northern, Hub, 70

O' Conner, Jack, 70–71
O' Doul, Lefty, 151*
O' Leary, Charlie, 23*
Oldfield, Barney, 74
Ormsby, Red, 150
Overall, Orvie, 38, 43
Owen (automobile), 62*
Owens, Brick, 73*

Parsons, Betty Jo, 176
Payne, Fred, 29, 38
Peckinpaugh, Roger, 105*
Pennock, Herb, 84
Petrella, Franceso, 69*
Petway, Bruce, 127*
Pfiester, Jack, 38
Philadelphia Athletics, 34–35, 37–38, 45–47, 48–49*, 51–52, 67–68, 74–75, 77*, 82–84, 147, 148*, 149, 150–153*, 154–157
Philadelphia Carmel Co. (premium card), 115*
Piedmont Park, 10
Pipp, Wally, 105*, 152
Pittsburgh Pirates, 43, 55, 56*, 57, 58, 59*
Plank, Eddie, 54*
Polo Grounds, 123, 166*
Pontchartrain Hotel, 61*, 63*, 64, 66
Progressive Meat Market, 95
Prohibition, 110, 126, 133*
Pruett, Hub, 136

Radcliffe, Ted, 127
Rawlings, Johnny, 132
Recorder & Gazette, 176
Reulbach, Ed, 38
Rhem, Flint, 138
Rice, Grantland, 11*, 13–14, 33, 93
Richardson, Rev. John, 175
Rickey, Branch, 93
Risberg, Swede, 142*, 146
Rogell, Billy, 156
Rogers, Will, 143*
Roosevelt, Eleanor, 169
Rose, Pete, 1
Rossman, Claude, 28
Rowland, Pants, 123
Royston, Georgia, 3*, 15–17, 170, 173, 176–177*
Royston Record, 9–10

Royston Reds, 9*, 10
Rucker, Nap, 19, 64*, 73
Ruppert, Jacob, 107*, 108
Ruth, Babe, 56–57, 94*, 102*, 105*, 106, 107*, 108–110, 129–132, 133*,134–138, 139*, 150, 152–153, 156*, 162*, 164–165, 166–167*
Ruth, Claire (Merritt Hodgson), 164

Salsinger, Harry, 58, 109, 124*, 136, 165, 168, 171
San Francisco Seals, 138
Santop, Louis, 127
Sargent, Joe, 105*
Schaefer, Germany, 19, 23–24*, 25–26, 29*, 71*
Schalk, Ray, 168
Schang, Wally, 167
Schmidt, Charlie, 30, 31*, 34*, 38
Sewell, Joe, 99
Sharpe, Sir Isaac, 160
Sherman, Gen. William T., 5, 34
Shibe Park, 82–83, 146*, 150–151*, 157
Siever, Ed, 28
Simmons, Al, 145, 155
Sinclair, Harry, 87
Sisler, George, 53*, 108*, 129, 152, 162*, 164
Smith, Hoke, 7, 86
Smith, Ken, 46
Smith, Red, 127
Somewhere in Georgia, 89, 93*
South Side Park, 41
Speaker, Tris, 71*, 88–89*, 109*, 126, 142–147, 152*, 155–157, 162*, 165, 167*
Sport Kings Chewing Gum, 118*
The Sporting Goods Dealer, 98, 100*
Sporting Life, 22
The Sporting News, 49, 71–72, 114, 176
Sportsman's Park, 134*, 136–137
Stanage, Oscar, 104
Stansfield, George, 51
Steinfeldt, Harry, 38
St. Louis Browns, 28, 30*, 41, 70–71, 93–94, 134*, 136–137, 154
St. Louis Cardinals, 141
Stone, George, 28, 30*
Street, Gabby, 71*, 126
Strouthers, Con, 11–12, 14–15
Stump, Al, 171, 173, 175
Sullivan, Billy, 38
Summers, Eddie, 24*

"Take Me Out to the Ball Game," 118
Tammany Hall, 79, 94
Temple Theatre, 62
Tenge, Alfred, 133
Tinker, Joe, 38
Tomlinson, Vic, 105
Travers, Aloysius, 82–83
Tuthill, Harry, 24*, 58, 104
Ty Cobb Candy Bar, 119*
Ty Cobb Day, 148*, 150
Ty Cobb Memorial, 176, 177*
"Ty Cobb' s Wild Ten-Month Fight to Live," 173
Tyre (Phoenician city), 2, 5
Tyson, Edwin ("Ty"), 150

Uncle Ezra (field hand), 10
Uhle, George, 151

Veach, Bobby, 86, 88*, 101, 125

Waddell, Rube, 35–36
Wagner, Honus, 55, 56*, 58, 72, 96–97, 101,162*, 164–165
Wakefield, Dick, 165*
Wakefield, Howard, 165
Wallace, Bobby, 71*
Walsh, Ed, 41, 43*, 74–75
Waner, Paul, 138
Warner, Jack, 23*
Warren Park, 12, 20, 23*, 30
Washington Senators, 37, 43–44, 126, 128*
Weaver, Buck, 104*
Weilman, Zeke, 154*
Weisman, Lefty, 130–131
Wells, Eddie, 128
Welzer, Tony, 150
West, Fred, 143–144
West Side Park, 121*
Western League, 131
Wheat, Zack, 147
White, Doc, 28*, 43
Whitehill, Earl, 130*
Wilkins, Robert, 175
Who's Who in Baseball, 120*
Wiggs, Jimmy, 23*
Willett, Edgar, 25*
Williams, Joe, 153
Willams, Ted, 57, 163*, 165
Wills, Maury, 173*
Wilson, Hack, 155*
Wolfe, J. Martin, 163
Wolfe, Woody, 163
Wood, Smokey Joe, 71*, 89*, 101, 143–145
Woodruff, Ernest, 111
Woodruff, Robert, 111, 113*
Woolf, S. J., 164
World Series
    1906, 38
    1907, 38,121*
    1908, 42*,43
    1909, 55, 56*, 57, 58, 59*
    1910, 67–68
    1911, 75, 77
    1919, 145–146
    1920, 110
    1922, 132
    1923, 107*
    1926, 141
    1927, 150
    1928, 156*
    1929, 155
    1932, 56
World War I, 101*, 103–105, 106, 110
WWJ (radio station), 150
WXYZ (radio station), 170

Yankee Stadium, 107*, 126, 129, 149, 157, 167
Young, Cy, 45*, 162*, 165

Zimmerman, Heinie, 104

193

Photo Credits

Augusta History Center: 14, 64
Eddie Batchelor Jr.: 124 left
Bettman Archive: 162 bottom
John Bogart: 105 both top
George Brace: 10, 15, 21 top, 23, 30 bottom, 47 bottom left, 85 right, 86 top, 151 top, 153 top, 154
Sylvia Brown: 3
Brown Brothers: 32, 78
Ed Budnick: 86 bottom
Buick Public Relations: 72 left
Burton Historical Collection: 20 bottom, 21 bottom, 25 both, 31, 34 top, 36 top, 39 both bottom, 42 both top, 44, 45 top, 59 top, 63, 66 left, 77 bottom, 83 top, 84 top, 85 left, 88 both top, 89 top, 94 top left, 95 both bottom, 107 bottom right, 130 top, 133 bottom left, 135 top, 137 bottom 3, 140, 148 both bottom, 149, 152 bottom, 165 top, 171 top, 172 top, 173 top
Dick Clark: 127 top, 171 bottom left
Cobb Memorial Hospital: 2
Cobb Hospital Association: 87 top
Coca-Cola Archives: color 1, 2, 3, 4 all
John Cole: 133 top right
Bill Curry: 69 both bottom
Detroit Athletic Club: 27 both, 65 top, 133 bottom right
The Detroit News: 36 bottom, 40, 42 bottom, 47 bottom right, 59 bottom, 80 top, 83 bottom, 94 top center/right, 107 top, 108 bottom, 123 bottom, 124 top, 125, 129, 138 top, 148 top, 170 top, 171 bottom left
DuMouchelle Galleries: 124 bottom
Alan Feldman Collection: 20 top, 39 top, 101 top
Georgia Department of Archives: 12, 17
Georgia State Archives: 167 top
Greg Hall: 175 bottom left
Ernie Harwell: 171 bottom right
Henry Ford Museum: 68 both, 168 top
Hillerich & Bradsby Archives, University of Louisville: ii, viii, 49 top, 150 bottom, 176 bottom
Kashmanian Collection: color 6 top
Library of Congress: 4, 5 bottom
Kirk Miner: 110 all, 160 both bottom, 184
Bill Moore: 137 top
Margie Bond Moore: 9, 169 bottom
Motor Vehicle Manufacturers Assn.: 62, 73 both
National Baseball Library: vi, xiv, 11, 18, 24 bottom, 30 top, 34 bottom, 35, 41, 49 bottom, 50, 56 both, 66 right, 70, 71 top, 75, 77 top, 82 top, 93 top, 104 both top, 107 bottom left, 109 top, 128 bottom left, 130 bottom left, 132, 136, 143 top, 144 top, 145, 150 top, 152, 153 bottom, 156 bottom, 158, 162 top/center, 163 both, 164 both top, 168 bottom, 172 both right, 174 all, 175 bottom right, 177
National Portrait Gallery: 164 bottom
Ron Petrella: 69 top
Picture Perfect: 7 bottom, 8
Public Library of Anniston Calhoun County: 16 both
Royston News-Leader: 176 top
Royston News-Leader: 7 top, 71 bottom
Selek Collection: 45 bottom, 84 bottom, 95 top, 106, 109 bottom, 131 both, 142 bottom, color 8 top, color 9 all, color 12
Jeanne Terge-Shook: 133 top left
Transcendental Graphics: color 7, color 11 top
Western Reserve Library: 49 center